Writing India
1757 – 1990

This volume provides an analytic survey of the literature produced as a consequence of the long history of Britain's rule in India, from the establishment of British hegemony in the 1750s to the achievement of Indian independence in the post colonial era almost two centuries later.

Each chapter combines contemporary literary and cultural theories with close readings of individual texts. Not only do contributors utilise the ideological critique of colonial representation initiated by Said's *Orientalism* (1978), but more recent work informed by attention to questions of gender, sexuality and psychic affect in colonial relations.

As well as 'canonical' figures such as Kipling, Forster and Scott, the volume tackles, for example, material from the eighteenth century, the Romantic period and the writing of British women on India. *Writing India* concludes with a chapter on Salman Rushdie in order to suggest the complex relation of continuity as well as conflict between colonial and postcolonial constructions of India.

Bart Moore-Gilbert is Lecturer in English at Goldsmith's College, University of London.

Writing India
1757–1990
The literature of British India

EDITED BY BART MOORE-GILBERT

MANCHESTER UNIVERSITY PRESS
Manchester and New York

distributed exclusively in the USA and Canada by St. Martin's Press

Published by Manchester University Press
Oxford Road, Manchester M13 9NR, UK
and Room 400, 175 Fifth Avenue,
New York, NY 10010, USA

Distributed exclusively in the USA and Canada
by St. Martin's Press, Inc.,
175 Fifth Avenue, New York, NY 10010, USA

British Library Cataloguing-in-Publication Data

A catalogue record for this book is available from the British Library

Library of Congress Cataloging-in-Publication Data

Writing India, 1757–1990 : the literature of British India / edited by Bart Moore-Gilbert.
    p.   cm.
  ISBN 0-7190-4265-8. — ISBN 0-7190-4266-6 (pbk.)
    1. Indic literature (English) – History and criticism. 2. Anglo-Indian literature – History and criticism. 3. Literature and society – India – History – 18th century. 4. India – Intellectual life – 18th century. 5. English language – India – Rhetoric. 6. Discourse analysis. I. Moore-Gilbert, B. J., 1952–
PR9489.4.W75   1996
820.9'954 – dc20   95-31538 CIP

ISBN 0 7190 4265 8 *hardback*
ISBN 0 7190 4266 6 *paperback*

First published in 1996

99 98 97 96   10 9 8 7 6 5 4 3 2 1

Printed in Great Britain
by Bell & Bain Ltd, Glasgow

197-50

Contents

Acknowledgements

I would like to thank Anita Roy at Manchester University Press for enthusiastically supporting this project from inception and the contributors for making my life as editor relatively painless. I owe a particular debt to the students on the 'Empire, Literature and Afterwards' course at Goldsmiths College, who have done much to sharpen my understanding of the complexities of colonial discourse. Finally this one is for Chib.

The illustrations are reproduced by permission of the India Office Library, London.

Contributors

DANNY COLWELL lectures part-time at Goldsmiths' College, University of London. He completed his doctorate at Oxford on the postcolonial novel in Africa and has written a number of articles and reviews on postcolonial literature.

CHRISTOPHER LANE is Associate Professor of English and Comparative Literature at the University of Wisconsin, Milwaukee. He is the author of *The Ruling Passion: British Colonial Allegory and the Paradox of Homosexual Desire* (Duke University Press, 1995) and of essays in such journals as *Raritan*, *ELH*, *Differences*, *Cultural Critique*, *Discourse*, *LIT*, *Contemporary Literature*, *Prose Studies*, *Literature & Psychology*, and *The New Statesman & Society*. He has also contributed to several forthcoming collections on psychoanalysis, postcolonialism and homosexuality, and, in 1995–96, is a Mellon fellow at the University of Pennsylvania.

NIGEL LEASK is Fellow and Director of Studies in English at Queens' College, Cambridge, and a lecturer in the Faculty of English. He is the author of *The Politics of Imagination in Coleridge's Critical Thought* (1988) and *British Romantic Writers and the East* (1992), as well as numerous articles on Romantic literature. He is currently writing a book on the relations between Romantic literature and archaeology and ethnography.

JAVED MAJEED lectures in the Department of the Languages and Cultures of South Asia at the School of Oriental and African Studies, University of London. He is the author of *Ungoverned Imaginings: James Mill's 'The History of British India' and Orientalism* (Oxford: Clarendon, 1992). He is currently working on aspects of the politics of language in British India, with special reference to changing conceptions of rhetoric in English and Urdu.

BART MOORE-GILBERT lectures in the English Department at Goldsmiths College, University of London. He is the author of *Kipling and 'Orientalism'* (1986) and has edited *Literature and Imperialism* (1984), *'Cultural Revolution': The Challenge of the Arts in the 1960s* (1992) and *The Arts in the 1970s: Cultural Closure?* (1994). He is currently writing a book on postcolonial theory for Verso.

TIM PARNELL lectures in English at Goldsmiths College, University of London. He is the British editor of *The Scriblerian* and author of a number of articles on both eighteenth-century experimental writing and postmodernism.

NANCY PAXTON is Associate Professor of English at Northern Arizona University. She is the author of *George Eliot and Herbert Spencer: Feminism, Evolutionism and the Reconstruction of Gender* (Princeton: 1991) and is completing a book entitled *Writing Under the Raj: Gender, Race, and Rape in the British Colonial Imagination: 1830–1930.*

ALISON SAINSBURY is Assistant Professor of English at Illinois Western University. She is the author of a number of articles on postcolonial writing and is currently working on a book which examines the intersection of patriarchy and imperialism, focusing on the English woman as imperial citizen from the 1880s to the 1930s.

KATE TELTSCHER lectures in English at the Roehampton Institute of Higher Education. She is the author of *India Inscribed: European and British Writing on India, 1600–1800* (Oxford University Press: 1995). She has reviewed exhibitions and books on India for the *Times Literary Supplement* and *International History Review*, and researched a BBC Radio 4 feature on the popular mythology of the Black Hole of Calcutta.

INTRODUCTION
Writing India, reorienting colonial discourse analysis

BART MOORE-GILBERT

This volume may be read in a number of different ways. Firstly, considered as a collection of discrete individual essays, it is designed for those wishing for concise introductions to a range of authors, genres and periods within the literary discourse of British India – and for those seeking fresh perspectives on material with which they may already be familiar. As well as 'canonical' figures such as Kipling, Forster and Scott (whose work is at times approached from what may seem quite unfamiliar angles), then, the volume provides chapters on less well-known aspects of this tradition of representation. Thus it includes analysis of material from the eighteenth century, the Romantic period and the writing of British women in India. The volume concludes with a chapter on Rushdie in order to suggest the complex relation of continuity as well as conflict between colonial and postcolonial constructions of India.

Secondly, the volume provides an analytic, chronologically-organised survey which investigates the discursive consistency of the literature produced as a consequence of the long history of Britain's rule in India. A particular aim is to correct the still common belief that there were no significant representations of India prior to Kipling. Thus while D.C.R.A. Goonetilleke's *Images of the Raj* (1988) and Ralph Crane's *Imagining India* (1992) begin their analysis of the literature of British India with Kipling, we argue that it is worth looking much further back. As Kate Teltscher's chapter suggests, from at least the moment when Britain became the dominant power in the subcontinent, the project of representing India – in the double sense identified by Gayatri Spivak in her important essay 'Can the Subaltern Speak?' (1988) – assumed particular urgency. The scope of this volume, then, is the historical period which runs from the establishment of British hegemony in the 1750s to the achievement of Indian independence in the postcolonial era almost two centuries later. Arranging this material in terms of its historical development is designed to illuminate both the consistencies and the changes in the way that the British conquerors of India viewed both themselves and the cultures they assumed control of.

Thirdly, the volume seeks to apply to this substantial case study of the literature of empire some of the theory and methodologies elaborated in contemporary colonial discourse analysis, a reading practice which has emerged as one of the most radical and exciting of the various new ways in which questions of cultural production and authority have been rethought in the West since the 1970s. Thus it brings to bear not simply the kind of ideological critique of colonial representation initiated by Said's *Orientalism* (1978), but more recent work informed by attention to questions of form, gender, sexuality and psychic affect in colonial relations. Finally, by rereading some of this critical work through the literature in question, rather than simply reading the texts through the theory, we suggest some of the problems evident in colonial discourse analysis as currently practised. It is to be hoped that the volume is written in such a way that further comment on the first way of using this text is unnecessary. Rather than summarising the arguments and conclusions of each individual chapter, then, this introduction will concentrate on contextualisation of the other aims outlined above, since such perspectives are of necessity beyond the brief of any individual chapter to describe.

Opening up colonial discourse analysis

Contemporary colonial discourse analysis (in the West if not elsewhere) may be said to emerge with Said's *Orientalism* (1978), which the author described as generated by dissatisfaction with established 'humanist' approaches to the study of the relationship between western culture on the one hand and the material history of imperialism on the other. Said's particular contribution was to emphasise the relations of power which structure western regimes of knowledge and representation, particularly as these are brought to bear upon 'the Orient' and, by implication, the rest of a world increasingly subject, in the period since the Enlightenment, to western domination. Said concludes that the principal effect of the western will to power through knowledge is the production of an 'absolute demarcation between East and West', in which the latter term is always dominant and privileged, discursively, morally and politically.[1]

While Said does not address literature as such in any detailed or consistent way in *Orientalism* – reserving it for sustained analysis in *Culture and Imperialism* (1993) – literary critics in the West were quick to seize on the implications of his analysis of discourses such as anthropology, political economy and travel writing for their own field. The common thread running through much recent literary criticism informed by the politics and methodology of *Orientalism* is suspicion of any attempt to exempt the 'aesthetic' sphere from complicity in the West's historical will to power through representation. At times, indeed, it has suggested that deployment of categories like 'literature' to describe such work is an obfuscating manoeuvre designed to recuperate what is in reality a body of texts with often deep structures of involvement in the processes of imperial domination. Thus Aijaz Ahmad vigorously condemns all forms of literary analysis 'governed by the ideology of the literary text as a discrete, aesthetic object – partly canonical in the New-Critical way, partly spiritual in the iconographic mould – and of literature as a treasure-chest, virtually a temple, of such objects'.[2]

Literary critics influenced by *Orientalism* generally repeat Said's gesture of sharply distinguishing their work from earlier analysis of the relations between literature and empire, which they see as grounded in the values Ahmad condemns. Abdul JanMohamed's biting comments on Molly Mahood's *The Colonial Encounter* (1977) are typical in this respect. Noting that Mahood's choice of authors is informed by their supposed 'distance' from the politics of domination, JanMohamed suggests that Mahood's approach 'restricts itself by severely bracketing the political context of culture and history'.[3] Benita Parry is equally harsh about the cultural politics of Alan Sandison's *The Wheel of Empire* (1967). In her view, Sandison reconstructs the literature of empire as a body of existential allegories in which 'Man' faces and attempts to overcome the threatening 'otherness' of a hostile universe. To Parry, such a conceptual structure is 'calculated to drain the writings of historical specificity'; this 'naturalizes the principles of the master culture as universal forms of thought and projects its authorized representations as truth'.[4]

While these examples suggest the establishment of Saidian critique as an accepted part of modern literary studies, colonial discourse analysis as constituted in *Orientalism* has not been without its critics. Aijaz Ahmad has summarised in polemical fashion many current objections in a series of essays collected together as *In Theory* (1992). For example, he questions the positioning of colonial discourse analysis at the centre of the broader postcolonial critical project; in Ahmad's eyes, this constitutes a reinscription of the authority of colonial culture which is analogous in its cultural/political implications to the reconstruction of imperialism (in the guise of neo-colonialism) in the period since formal decolonisation. For Ahmad this implies not just an unhealthy privileging of the western canon over 'Third World' culture, but a dangerous shift of attention from current forms of economic and cultural imperialism to the less contentious area of fictions produced in an era of formal imperialism now safely in the past. Perhaps most radically, Ahmad complains that Said's model of colonial discourse analysis is a domestication of the real, material struggles in which the 'Third World' has engaged in its attempt to free itself from western domination. Said is thus accused of 'greatly extending the centrality of *reading* as the appropriate form of politics' with which to challenge contemporary forms of western domination.[5]

In attempting to deflect such charges, proponents of *Orientalism*'s model of colonial discourse analysis have come up with a number of arguments. Benita Parry, for instance, has defended it as necessary in view of the left's historical (and continuing) neglect of the interrelationship between culture and imperialism. She concludes that until such time as the left produces a coherent theorisation of this relationship, the right-wing explanation of imperialism as an essentially benevolent historical process of modernisation, emancipation and enlightenment in the non-western world, cannot be seriously challenged.[6]

Laura Chrisman provides a different answer to the kind of objections raised by Ahmad. While welcoming the focus of texts such as *The Empire Writes Back* (1987) on postcolonial literature and theory, Chrisman expresses the anxiety that this emphasis 'risks being premature and misleading, if it suggests that the present can be analysed in isolation from the imperialism which formally produced it'.[7] The danger is first of all that imperialism will remain unchallenged by virtue of its apparently safely historical character (thus disguising its continuation in contemporary neo-colonialism); secondly, that the dialectical relation between (neo-)colonial and postcolonial culture will be obscured. This may well lead, in Chrisman's view, to a vision of the latter which both essentialises it and deprives it of any politically committed, counter-discursive identity.

While Ahmad's argument suggests his desire to abandon altogether colonial discourse analysis as conceived in *Orientalism*, Said's own sympathisers have increasingly expressed the necessity of reformulating and broadening the parameters established in this landmark text. What unites such critics is a perception that Said unifies and homogenises the identity and operationality of colonial discourse to an unwarranted degree. This problem has been approached from a number of perspectives which variously inform some of the chapters in the current volume.

For example, Homi Bhabha's essays, recently collected in *The Location of Culture* (1994), constitute a major rethinking of the approach handed down by *Orientalism* (1978). Bhabha's earlier work, in particular, shifts the focus of colonial discourse analysis from how western will and intention construct a public sphere (whether patterns of representation and formations of scholarship on the one hand, or institutions of state repression on the other), which mediates colonial power. Instead Bhabha emphasises the unconscious sphere of colonial relations, and suggests that this is structured by complicitous kinds of psychic affect circulating between coloniser and colonised. This troubles the absolute binary division which colonial power – and *Orientalism* itself – constructs between the two sides of the colonial relationship. Central to the argument of 'The Other Question', Bhabha's celebrated essay of 1983, is the following proposition which, crucially, makes no clear distinction between coloniser and colonised:

> A repertoire of conflictual positions constitutes the subject in colonial discourse. The taking up of any one position, within a specific discursive form, in a particular historical conjuncture, is thus always problematic – the site of both fixity and fantasy. It provides a colonial 'identity' that is played out – like all fantasies of originality and origination – in the face and space of the disruption and threat from the heterogeneity of other positions.[8]

For Bhabha, ambivalence in the psychic economy of colonialism is largely the product of an unresolved conflict between recognition and disavowal of the Other on both sides of the colonial relationship. On the coloniser's side, its effects are registered principally in varieties of discursive disturbance which, according to Bhabha, haunt colonial narrative of all kinds – legal, literary, political, evangelical; these constitute contradictions and irresolutions which prevent colonial discourse from ever attaining the unity and authority to which it aspires. Perhaps the most important implication this argument has for colonial discourse analysis is the way Bhabha opens up the possibility of reconfiguring colonial relations in terms other than the master/ slave model invoked by *Orientalism*. In particular, Bhabha's scheme allows for the possibility of subaltern resistance to what in *Orientalism* often seems a monolithically powerful and unchallengeable system of domination.

Bhabha's perception of affective ambivalence and discursive disturbance in the operation of colonial discourse – and the challenge these imply for colonial authority – is amply confirmed by several chapters in this volume. Danny Colwell's chapter, for instance, argues that the all-important relationship between the policeman Merrick and his Indian victim Hari Kumar in Paul Scott's *Raj Quartet* is structured largely round a complicitous process of mutual identification, in which Merrick's persecution of his victim is complicated by desire on the part of the colonial official. Desire for the Other – whether in its predominantly heterosexual form, or as expressed in what Sara Suleri describes as the trope of 'the effeminate groom'[9] – is a major and consistent preoccupation of the literature of British India, running from the poetry of Thomas Medwin in the Romantic period to the novels of Scott himself. Beneath the apparently prurient and politically coercive surface of this concern lies a deeper and more interesting structure of at times disabling anxiety about the dividing line between colonial power and identity on the one hand, and its subjects on the other.

The contradictory structure of psychic affect which Bhabha describes can also be identified in the equally common theme of spying and cultural infiltration – activities more often than not inscribed in the trope of cultural 'cross-dressing'. Again apparent as early as Medwin, as Nigel Leask's chapter suggests, it is taken up in Meadows Taylor's fictional account of the suppression of *thagi* in *Confessions of a Thug*, and recurs in Kipling, most notably in *Kim*, but also in tales such as 'Beyond the Pale' and the various stories involving the policeman Strickland. While then treated parodically in E. M. Forster's *A Passage to India* – with its ludicrous figure of another policeman, MacBryde, patrolling

Chandrapore disguised as a Holy Man – it returns once again for tragic treatment in *The Raj Quartet*. Here, Merrick assumes Pathan guise – in part, like MacBryde, to further official investigations – in part, like Kipling's Trejago, in pursuit of forbidden cross-cultural sexual pleasures.

This volume suggests that such thematic tropes point, not as Gail Ching-Liang Low has argued, to simple affirmations of colonial dominance,[10] but to both political insecurity (otherwise why would such kinds of surveillance of the subject culture be necessary?) and the progressively problematic nature of cultural identification for Anglo-India, caught as it was between the more assured and rooted cultures of both Britain and India. As the nineteenth century progresses, the problem of self-identification becomes almost obsessive in the literature of British India, and perhaps constitutes the central theme of the discourse. Kim's agonised question ' "Who is Kim?" ', a question which remains unanswered at the end of the text, takes on increasing urgency; it culminates in Susan Layton's despair as colonial hegemony finally fragments in Paul Scott's *The Day of the Scorpion*: ' "But what am I? What am I? Why – there's nothing to me at all. Nothing. Nothing at all!" '[11] The thematic frequency of such psychic breakdown is astonishing in the literature of British India – and, indeed, in 'imperial' literature as a whole.[12] Moreover, as comparison of Danny Colwell's chapter on Scott with Tim Parnell's discussion of cultural dislocation in Salman Rushdie's work suggests, there is a radical and perhaps surprising thematic continuity between colonial and postcolonial discourse in this respect.

If Bhabha's critique of Said emphasises the potential of psychoanalytic methodology to enrich colonial discourse analysis, so other forms of contemporary theory, based on a variety of discourses of identity, have pointed to different lacunae in *Orientalism*, further loosening its binarist methodology. The question of gender is a case in point. *Orientalism* does recognise to some degree the gendered nature of Orientalist discourse; thus Said argues that it 'encouraged a peculiarly (not to say individiously) male conception of the world', for three principal reasons. It isolated the Oriental male for study; it persistently feminised the Orient on the basis of a patriarchal understanding of the feminine; and it was a specifically male institutional practice.[13]

Nonetheless, such arguments remain largely undeveloped in *Orientalism* and the sketchiness of Said's treatment of issues of gender has elicited some hostile responses from feminist critics. A good example is Jane Miller's claim in *Seductions* (1990) that the audience assumed by Said is male and that a female reader must efface, or suspend, her gender in order to enter his discourse. Miller points not just to a consistent suppression of female experience and testimony at the level of content but equally serious problems in Said's methodology. In so insistently figuring the West as the male voice which enunciates 'Orientalism', and the East as the silent, passive and feminised recipient of the discourse, for instance, Miller contends that Said reinscribes the authority of a patriarchal economy of representation at the very moment that he is deconstructing a discourse of racial oppression.

Miller sees the distortions of counter-discourse as practised by Said (and Fanon) as symptomatic of the 'seductiveness' of 'high' theory itself. In order to attain academic status, according to Miller, a critical theory needs to have a high level of both consistency and generalisability. There is thus a temptation to ignore contradictory material; in the case of colonial discourse analysis, as in some other contemporary theory, this involves suppressing the experience of women (on both sides of the imperial relationship): 'Such an omission simultaneously separates, subsumes and subordinates the category of women. It also takes women for granted ... as undifferentiated elements of a collective humanity, a view which would be easy to accept were that collective humanity not itself, within such theories, under perpetual scrutiny for its splits and conflicts especially'.[14]

Lisa Lowe's *Critical Terrains* (1991) fleshes out this strategic critique of *Orientalism* with detailed empirical reference to Orientalist textuality. Her analysis of the writing of Lady Mary Wortley Montagu, for example, concludes that the Orientalist elements of women's travel writing operate differently to those in male travel writers – as regards eighteenth-century Turkey at least. In certain respects Montagu thus pointedly contradicts the account of Turkey given by figures like Robert Withers and Jean Dumont. Most indicative of these differences is the way that Montagu's writing attests to 'an emergent feminist discourse that speaks of common experiences among women of different societies'.[15] This 'rhetoric of identification' complicates the clear divide assumed by *Orientalism* to operate within western representations of the East, and also points to a struggle for authority *within* Orientalist discourse which Said does not sufficiently recognise. Lowe's text insists throughout on the variety and heterogeneity of Orientalist discourse and argues – perhaps contentiously – that the theory best equipped to register its contradictions and tensions is one drawn from feminism. For Lowe this is because, more than any other kind of cultural theory, feminism is sensitive to the idea of the subject as multiply inscribed and positioned – an argument echoed in Alison Sainsbury's chapter on Anglo-Indian women's novels.

Conflict and heterogeneity within Orientalist discourse is also registered in the homo-eroticism which Lowe detects in Montagu's writing on Turkish women. This particular form of identification raises further problems in the methodology of *Orientalism*; from the perspective of 'queer theory', certainly, it may be seen to reinforce the heterosexist vision of colonial discourse – in which the Orient is typically figured as female, and to be possessed or 'protected' by the western male. *Orientalism* fails to register adequately the strong elements of homo-eroticism which run throughout the history of colonial representation. Joseph Bristow's *Empire Boys* (1991), which focuses on the construction of masculinity in the popular literature of empire, Sara Suleri's *The Rhetoric of English India* (1992), which traces the trope of 'the effeminate groom' through the discourse of British India, and Tony Davies and Nigel Wood's collection of essays, *A Passage to India* (1994), are notable examples of how 'queer theory' is increasingly coming to inflect colonial discourse analysis.

Several of the chapters in this volume suggest the usefulness of these new approaches. What is particularly striking about the application of such theory is how 'canonical' figures within the field of the literature of empire, like Kipling and Forster, are reinterpreted. Thus the Kipling who emerges from Nancy Paxton's chapter is one who allows at least a partial counter-vision to the patriarchal and heterosexist norms of imperial culture to emerge. By contrast, the Forster who emerges from Christopher Lane's attention to the sexual politics of Forster's minor colonial fiction differs radically from the figure whose apparently liberal views in *A Passage to India* have long been understood to provide a biting critique of the ethnocentrism of mainstream Anglo-Indian culture.

Colonial discourse analysis and literary criticism

While discourses of psychoanalysis, sexuality and gender have done much to reorient the analytic models of *Orientalism*, Said's methodology can also be reconfigured from the perspective of the formal analysis traditionally associated with literary criticism. One of the earliest critiques of *Orientalism* came in Dennis Porter's investigation of the place of travel writing within colonial representation. Porter shows how attention to the local material properties of textuality produces a more differentiated model of the operation of colonial discourse than Said allows. In particular, Porter suggests that it encourages recognition of conflict and struggle *within* colonial discourse. While *Orientalism* has been much criticised for its failure to attend to both material and discursive resistance on the part of subject peoples, Porter argues – like Lowe and Bhabha – that such resistance can also be detected *inside* the dominant itself.

In '*Orientalism* and its Problems' (1983), Porter examines one particular manifestation of counter-hegemony within colonial textuality which, following Althusser, he ascribes to the relative autonomy of the aesthetic work. This relative autonomy is manifested in its internal distantiation of dominant ideologies at the moment that it stages them. Focusing on Marco Polo and T. E. Lawrence as travel writers, Porter proceeds to demonstrate how the characteristic 'heterogeneity and fragmentation'[16] of their texts derives in part from each author's mixing of different genres, a tactic which produces contradictory perspectives *vis-à-vis* both white narrator and the subject peoples. Equally interestingly, Porter sees contradiction and inner tension in such work as the product of the writers' use of language in particularly self-conscious or literary ways. Thus Porter analyses passages from *The Seven Pillars of Wisdom* to argue that the excess of the signifier over the signified at these moments produces a heterogeneity of meanings which cannot be stabilised or unified. Such writing cannot, therefore, be understood as unproblematically mediating a confident or unified will to power over the Orient and its peoples.

Said's discrimination, at the end of *Orientalism*, between what he calls 'vision' and 'narrative' in Orientalist discourse, might at first reading be taken to imply at least some recognition of the kind of conflict which Porter identifies:

Against this static system of 'synchronic essentialism' I have called vision because it presumes that the whole Orient can be seen panoptically, there is a constant pressure. The source of pressure is narrative, in that if any Oriental detail can be shown to move, or to develop, diachrony is introduced into the system. What seemed stable – and the Orient is synonymous with stability and unchanging eternality – now appears unstable ... Narrative, in short, introduces an opposing point of view, perspective, consciousness to the unitary web of vision; it violates the serene Apollonian fictions asserted by vision.[17]

However it soon becomes clear that by 'narrative', Said means *history*, and he shows little interest, at least in *Orientalism*, in showing how literary narrative might similarly problematise Orientalist 'vision'.[18] Early on, Said does ask the following question: 'How did ... novel-writing, and lyric poetry come to the service of Orientalism's broadly imperialist view of the world?'[19] However, the very terms within which this question is framed, of course, exclude the possibility that western literature might at times have a critical function *vis-à-vis* the juridical or political elements of Orientalist discourse or the material practices of imperialism. In effect, Said treats literature as simply one more manifestation of the western will to power. Thus the Anglo-Indian poet Alfred Lyall is considered only in terms of his useful-ness in helping to authorise Lord Cromer's executive policy, and Kipling, too, is seen solely as an ideologue and never as an artist. While the principle behind Said's approach to such writers is the laudable one of reminding us that literary texts act in and on the world, it is obviously highly problematic to collapse a novel like Kipling's *Kim*, written in 1901, together with legal edicts pro-scribing the immolation of Hindu windows in the 1820s, or Dr Thievenot's seventeenth-century Indian travelogues.

Porter is, of course, treating texts which are only ambiguously 'literary', determined as they are by large amounts of reportage, ethnography, history and autobiography. (Said himself consigns travel writing to the realm of 'vision' and describes Lawrence's work as defeated in the end by the pressure of 'vision'.)[20] But what Porter's analysis clearly implies about the kind of 'ideologi-cal' critique developed in *Orientalism* is that it is primarily thematically-oriented and generally oblivious to the complica-tions and instabilities of textuality, a problem exacerbated by the status of certain kinds of colonial discourse as 'literature'.

This is by no means to imply the desirability of returning to a bankrupt 'humanist' notion of the 'literary' which fetishises the 'aesthetic' as a category of representation which is wholly undetermined by historical and political affiliations. Clearly, the literature of empire needs to be situated within the material contexts of its production and consumption, with full recognition of the politics it implies – as is generally the case with the chapters in this volume. Equally it must be contextualised with non-'literary' forms to understand how it operates within the larger frameworks of colonial discourse. This is a model followed by Alison Sainsbury's chapter, which reads Maud Diver against the anthropological theory of Radcliffe Brown and vice versa. But to place the work of writers like Kipling or Scott alongside its non-literary equivalents also involves the responsibility of recognising not just similarities but differences between the various forms of knowledge and kinds of signifying practice which constructed and mediated imperial power. This is perhaps the weakness of texts such as Peter Hulme's *Colonial Encounters* (1984); by putting the 'literary' status of works like *Robinson Crusoe* and *The Tempest* into suspension, he is able to demonstrate their continuity in important respects with other kinds of colonial discourse. The problem remains, however, of what happens when that 'literary' status is returned once more to such texts. To suggest that in the end the difference between, say, *The Tempest* and the documents of Spanish bureaucracy in the Caribbean is 'superficial' is disingenuous.[21]

The results of the failure to accept this responsibility are widely apparent in the literary criticism influenced by *Orientalism* in the 1980s. In order to concretely illustrate its disfiguring and simplifying effects I have chosen to focus briefly on some Kipling criticism from this period. Kipling is chosen because he is such a representative example of 'literary' colonial representation. (He is given as much attention – minimal though this is – as any comparable figure in *Orientalism*, for example.) Moreover, he provides a recurrent reference point for recent literary-critical versions of colonial discourse analysis.

Many contemporary critics deny Kipling the status of 'great writer' on the grounds that he subscribed enthusiastically to Victorian theories of the 'racially'-grounded fitness of British culture to dominate its subject peoples. In such work, the classic instance of Kipling's allegedly unambiguous racial supremacism – and related assumptions about the transparent and monologic nature of his narrative technique – is the opening paragraph of 'Beyond the Pale' (1888), which reads as follows: 'A man should, whatever happens, keep to his own caste, race and breed. Let the White go to the White and the Black to the Black. Then, whatever trouble falls is in the ordinary course of things – neither sudden, alien nor unexpected'.[22]

Taking such lines at face value, out of context, lends apparent credibility to influential recent interpretations of Kipling's work such as John McClure's, whose *Kipling and Conrad* (1981) sees them unproblematically as 'racist'.[23] Subsequent commentators like Mark Paffard and Patrick Williams follow this lead. The former rehearses McClure's argument without demur while Williams, in an essay which is notably reductive in its treatment of Kipling's politics, insists once again that 'the overt racism with which "Beyond the Pale" opens' is typical of Kipling's vision of colonial relations.[24] Meanwhile Parry concludes that the tale is one 'where native subordination and Oriental passion, those staples of colonial discourse, come together in the ecstatic and ceremonial yielding of the native as female to the dominating presence of a masculine West'.[25]

The meaning of the tale is in fact much more complex, as is evident even if one confines oneself to a primarily thematic reading of the story. First of all the narrator explicitly seeks to modify staple ideas about 'Oriental passion': 'Much that is written about Oriental passion and impulsiveness is exaggerated and compiled at second hand, but a little of it is true' (*Plain Tales*: 166). Secondly, 'the native' in this story cannot in any simple way be considered subordinate; despite her disadvantaged status in terms of race, gender and age *vis-à-vis* Trejago, it is Bisesa who both initiates and ends (in no uncertain terms) the relationship which becomes (and remains) so precious to Trejago. Moreover, the idea that 'the masculine West' is presented as uncomplicatedly dominant in its dealings with the Orient is contradicted by the violent response of Durga Charan on discovering the affair. Trejago is stabbed in the groin by Charan's spear and left with a permanent limp, which is hardly evidence of imperial masculinity triumphant. This symbolic castration implies quite the opposite in fact – and in this respect it is significant that Trejago appears to remain a bachelor. Certainly one hears no more of the Englishwoman whom Bisesa identifies as her rival for Trejago's affections, thus precipitating the tragedy which follows.

The major problem with these treatments of 'Beyond the Pale' is, of course, that there is no attention to the formal properties which make it a 'literary' work. McClure at least is honest enough to admit ignoring the 'aesthetic dimensions' of Kipling's work – which perhaps explains his acceptance of received wisdom about 'its aggressively confident style'; in the context of 'Beyond the Pale', more specifically, McClure assumes that 'Kipling's voice and the narrator's are one', thus reducing it to a propagandist imperial tract.[26] Williams isolates the opening paragraph not just from Kipling's Indian stories as a whole but from the volume of which it forms part. To read it alongside 'Lispeth', the first story of *Plain Tales from the Hills*, for instance, is to see immediately the distorting effect this manoeuvre has. In 'Lispeth', both the missionary's wife and the Englishman subscribe to the truth of the opening statements in 'Beyond the Pale'; and both are the object of unambiguous satire for doing so. Even more mutilating to the integrity of 'Beyond the Pale' is that Williams fails to consider the opening lines even in relation to the rest of the tale. Considered in this context, as will be demonstrated, they may be understood as an introduction which is as complex and ironic as the famous beginning of *Pride and Prejudice*. Indeed, the opening lines of Kipling's tales are often traps for the unwary. In the same volume, 'The Phantom Rickshaw', for example, starts with an unambiguous statement about the great 'knowability' of India, before launching into an extraordinary dramatisation of its alienness.

In order to appreciate the real complexity, formal and ideological, of 'Beyond the Pale', one might begin by returning to Louis Cornell's 'superseded' reading of the story in *Kipling in India* (1967), an interpretation which both McClure and Paffard explicitly rebut. The virtue of Cornell's analysis is its recognition of, and attention to, the distinction between frame and embedded narratives in the story. ('Beyond the Pale' is formally typical of a number of Kipling's Indian stories in being mediated by a first-person narrator, who introduces and sometimes interprets a record of events in which he is not, characteristically, directly involved.) After identifying and exploring some elements of the fraught relations between the frame and embedded narratives, Cornell concludes that 'Kipling sees round his narrator and lets us know that the reporter is wrong, that we are not to accept his cautious warnings, that Bisesa and the world she represents are worth the terrible risks Trejago has run'.[27]

But there is more to add to Cornell's account, enabling as its method and implications are. The first point to note, perhaps, is that the epigraph to the tale (a feature which none of the more recent critics cited above mention) works to contradict the bluff and certain judgement of the narrator's opening remarks. The Hindu proverb reads: 'Love heeds not caste nor sleep a broken bed. I went in search of love and lost myself' (*Plain Tales*: 162). The epigraph constitutes a 'native perspective' that provides a further, and crucial, framing of the narrator's own contextualisation of Trejago's misadventure. This reflects ironically on his apparently authoritative analysis, one which the reader has been encouraged to identify with the 'official' voice and values of colonial power.

More importantly, perhaps, the apparently considered detachment of the narrator from the events described – on which the authority of his initial judgements rests – is progressively undermined as he mediates Trejago's experience. Relations between narrator and protagonist are destabilised by an increasing suspicion of the former's complicity in Trejago's attitudes, a complicity which may derive from having had a parallel experience of forbidden interracial love. Thus the narrator is not only curiously knowledgeable about the topography of the native city, but himself knows 'The Love Song of Hyar Dyal', which is instrumental in initiating contact between the lovers, to the extent that he can claim the song 'is really pretty in the vernacular' (*Plain Tales*: 164). Crucially, perhaps, he is able to provide a translation of the object-letter which Bisesa sends to Trejago. The narrator prefaces this translation with the comment: 'No Englishman should be able to translate object-letters' (p. 163), thus begging the question of how he himself came to such knowledge. While the obvious answer is through Trejago, this is not conclusively the case, as is suggested by the narrator's dismissal of 'second-hand' accounts of Oriental passion (p. 166). And to argue that Trejago is the conduit of the narrator's information raises the question of why Trejago should confide in someone who genuinely represents the 'official' position on interracial liaisons. The narrator's complicity is further revealed in perhaps what remains the greatest irony of the tale: that in telling it, the narrator is himself now circulating the glamorous knowledge which he declares should be suppressed.

That the narrator's sympathies are with Trejago, despite his implied condemnation of such behaviour, is apparent in a number of ways. While disclaiming the myth of Oriental passion as exaggerated, the narrator presents the relationship between Trejago and Bisesa in a positive light. He finds no reason to contradict

Trejago's claim 'that he loved her more than any one else in the world' (*Plain Tales*: 165), especially since his acquaintance faces ruin and disgrace if his affair is discovered. The genuineness of the attachment is also indicated by Trejago's guilt and grief once the liaison ends. In contrast to such strength of feeling, the narrative suggests how mundane and constrained are the relationships available within the white community. Trejago's attachment to the English woman is described in terms of routine, formality and compulsion. Its apparent joylessness and conventionality further justify Cornell's interpretation of the story as an endorsement of the risks Trejago takes.

Such a reading suggests not only that Kipling's relation to imperial ideology is more conflictual than generally perceived, but that his narrative technique is a good deal more sophisticated than suggested in much recent criticism of his work which derives from *Orientalism*. Indeed, it suggests the degree to which such criticism relies for its operation on precisely the kind of fixed and simple binary oppositions of which it complains not only in Kipling, but colonial discourse more generally. Such problems are likely to persist given Said's continuing authority and only partial modification of his earlier methodology. His recent work, such as *Culture and Imperialism* (1993), recognises some of the dangers of the essentially thematic, ideological approach to colonial discourse elaborated in *Orientalism* – at least where 'aesthetic' forms of textuality are concerned. But the admirable wish to retain a conception of literature – and especially of the literature of empire – as having political effects still leads at times to crudely reductive readings. While Conrad may be complicit in Orientalist-style discourse by virtue, for example, of his failure to imagine and represent resistance to empire, there can be no doubt of his opposition to what he saw of Belgian rule in the Congo, whether in his fiction or personal journal. Thus for Said to claim that *Heart of Darkness* is ideologically a 'short step away from King Leopold's account of his International Congo Association, "rendering lasting and disinterested services to the cause of progress" ',[28] seems well wide of the mark.

At the same time, paradoxically, Said recuperates Conrad precisely because he *is* engaged in a 'worldly' project, even if a highly dubious one. Moreover, Said argues that because of the 'complex affiliations [of texts like *Heart of Darkness*] with their real setting, they are *more* interesting and more valuable as works of art'.[29] This emphasis on 'complexity' suggests Said's desire to keep straightforward propaganda – either for or against imperialism – out of the canon. Yet Kipling, who according to Said wears his propaganda on his sleeve, is admitted to the canon as a 'great artist'. While there are 'few more imperialist and reactionary than he', Said suggests that Kipling nonetheless bears comparison *as an artist* with major figures like Proust, James and George Eliot.[30]

Such comments imply that Conrad and Kipling transcend their potentially damaging affiliation to imperial discourse because, as 'great writers', their work also belongs to an *aesthetic* sphere which enjoys 'relative autonomy from the economic, social and political worlds'.[31] This traditional 'liberal humanist' argument is motivated by Said's suspicion of interpretations which will reduce literature to subsidiary forms of ideology, or class interest. There is thus a certain degree of justice in Ahmad's accusation that Said reinscribes some of the values and categories he ostensibly deplores in the western academy, even that 'humanism-as-ideality is invoked precisely at the time when humanism-as-history has been rejected so unequivocally'.[32] Certainly this seems corroborated in the course of an interview with Michael Sprinker, where Said states: 'I have this strange attachment ... to what I consider in a kind of dumb way "great art"'. Pressed by Sprinker to define what he means by this, Said somewhat limply replies: 'There is a kind of intrinsic interest in them, a kind of richness in them'.[33]

Said's difficulties in *Culture and Imperialism* suggest that literary material poses an acute problem for contemporary colonial discourse analysis. While Said's greater attention and sensitivity to the specific modes of signification of the literature of empire is to be applauded, uneven as it is, it also threatens to deprive such texts – and their analyses – of political effectivity. There is certainly a danger of readmitting reprehensible politics under the guise of 'great art', against which possibility only a scrupulous reading practice can guard; there seems little point, however, in claiming that all forms of colonial textuality can be reduced to one model of operation, or that the literature of empire simply sugars the will to power of the non-literary discourses of imperialism. To fail to understand this is to promote a reprehensible politics in the practice of colonial discourse analysis itself. First of all it can lead to a reinscription of the epistemology of which it complains in colonial discourse; the essentialist binaries by which such discourse is held to operate are only reversed – not displaced – by seeing the whole western cultural canon as what Aijaz Ahmad calls an archive of bad faith and orientalist deformation.[34] Secondly, it encourages the assumption that resistance from within the colonial formation to the practices of imperialism is impossible, even at a textual level. Finally it promotes the idea that only certain privileged kinds of *critical* consciousness can escape (in a way which is never satisfactorily explained) the constraints of a supposedly totalising system to provide a counter-vision which mere *artists* like Kipling and Conrad, as more or less conscious stooges of imperialism, are incapable of entertaining.

The literature of British India: reorienting *Orientalism*

If this is the most important way in which a literary-critical perspective opens up the critique inaugurated by Said, the analysis of the literature of British India which this volume undertakes points to other significant difficulties in *Orientalism*. Said's argument rests to a large degree on the assumption that western representations of the Orient were based overwhelmingly upon a 'textual attitude'. 'At most', Said comments, 'the "real" Orient provoked a writer to his vision; it very rarely guided it'.[35] Said provides ample evidence to support this claim, and more recent criticism, such as John Drew's *India and the Romantic Imagination* (1987), has seemed to confirm his argument. For instance, Drew demonstrates how Sydney Owenson's influential novel *The Missionary* (1811) was generated by her readings of translations in Sir Charles Ormsby's great oriental library; in turn her novel became an important source for some of the great 'Oriental' poetry of both Byron and Shelley.[36]

In contrast to the tradition of 'wholly bookish Orientalism', however, Said admits that 'there is another tradition that claimed its legitimacy from the peculiarly compelling fact of residence in, actual existential contact with, the Orient'.[37] But Said's attention is not directed consistently enough to this body of work, partly, perhaps, because of the fracture it would necessarily open up between his conceptions of 'truth' (or the 'real' Orient) as the product of discourse and 'truth' as prior to discourse and – potentially at least – accessible through textuality. Whatever the reason, the effect of this neglect is to reinforce Said's conception of orientalist discourse as essentially unified. Moreover, insofar as he does direct attention to the latter kind of work, his examples are drawn almost exclusively from travel writing, a form which implies only fleeting kinds of existential contact with the cultures being traversed. It is this, precisely, which provides recurrent cause for complaint about globe-trotters and their travelogues in British India from the 1860s onwards.

This emphasis on the overwhelmingly 'textual' attitude of colonial discourse has been followed in more recent criticism, even amongst those who challenge other aspects of Said's *Orientalism*. For example, Sara Suleri, who has provided the most substantial and interesting recent discussion of some of the figures and genres addressed in the present volume in *The Rhetoric of English India*, allows no distinction between those with lived experience of India, such as Kipling, and those without, such as Edmund Burke. Similarly, Jenny Sharpe's excellent account of the role of women in colonial discourse, *Allegories of Empire* (1993), makes no discrimination between white women writers in the metropolis who deal with questions of empire and their counterparts based abroad, whose experience 'in the field' might be presumed to induce significant inflections in colonial discourse. As Lisa Lowe's account of Lady Mary Wortley Montagu's writing on Turkey suggests, the 'rhetoric of identification' between the English aristocrat and her female Turkish friends is a direct consequence of Montagu's residence in Turkey and virtually impossible to imagine in a contemporary writer based in Britain.

This volume, then, explores the degree to which literary texts generated by those with significant 'lived experience' of the Indian empire produced variations in, or even challenges to, the discourses of imperialism as described in *Orientalism*. This question is necessarily linked to the larger issue of the specificity of the cultural identity of the British in India, and the degree to which their sense of Britishness was modified by exile and contact with the cultures which they controlled politically. While Sara Suleri perhaps exaggerates in arguing that British India came to identify itself as in some senses equivalent to a separate nation,[38] significant differences between metropolitan British and Anglo-Indian cultural identity were, from an early stage, quite apparent to both constituencies. Thackeray's satire of returned Anglo-Indians like Jos Sedley in *Vanity Fair* suggests the outlandish oddity of such figures to their metropolitan contemporaries; by contrast the recurrent theme of the inability on the part of Anglo-Indians to adjust or readjust to life in Britain is already a theme of Thomas Medwin at the beginning of the nineteenth century, and continues through Kipling (in tales such as 'Baa Baa, Blacksheep') to Paul Scott, particularly in such work as *Staying On*.

This insistence on differences between the two cultures may seem paradoxical given the rapidity with which, in certain respects, they were apparently being brought closer together from the middle of the nineteenth century onwards. Thus to some observers, the incorporation of Indian government within the jurisdiction of Westminster as a consequence of the uprisings of 1857, promised to bring the two cultures into alignment. As William Ireland suggested in 1863:

> I have not been in India since the spring of 1860. Meanwhile a series of sweeping changes have been brought about. The extinction of the old Company's army, and the breach in the exclusive privileges of the covenanted Civil Service, must have done much to modify the tone and manners of society.
>
> The reader ought, then, to bear in mind that the India of 1857 and 1858 is not altogether the India of 1862, and will soon be much less so. The features which distinguish the Anglo-Indian from the Englishman in India will become fainter.[39]

Advances in the field of communications, especially in the decades after the 1857 uprising, might have been expected to quickly realise Ireland's prediction, especially as these mitigated the alienating effects of physical distance between the two cultures. Such developments included the opening of the Suez Canal, a greatly extended Indian railway network and the telegraph – all of which brought Britain in important ways closer to Anglo-India. However, despite the ever-expanding number of visitors from the metropolis, increases in the amount and frequency of home leave for those working in India and, perhaps above all, greater numbers of English women settling in the subcontinent after 1857, the evidence suggests that, if anything, the divergence between British India and metropolitan culture was exacerbated.

One simple but striking index of this process was Anglo-India's increasingly extensive inflection of Standard British English into a distinctive dialect. Already a significant marker of Anglo-Indian cultural difference by the early nineteenth century, as Nigel

Leask's analysis of Thomas Medwin's poetry suggests, by Kipling's time the argot was sufficiently complex to merit its own lexica. G. C. Whitworth's *Anglo-Indian Dictionary*, a volume of 370 pages, appeared in 1885, to be followed the next year by *Hobson-Jobson: A Glossary of Colloquial Anglo-Indian Words and Phrases*. This ran to nearly 1000 pages in double columns. The editors described their project as the explication of words and expressions which 'recur constantly in the daily intercourse of the English in India, either as expressing ideas not really provided for by our mother-tongue, or supposed by the speakers ... to express something not capable of just denotation by any English term'.[40]

It is arguable that the literary convention of British India becomes similarly distinct from its metropolitan parent, particularly in terms of its representations of India. As one might expect, the earlier part of this literary 'tradition' is more closely tied to metropolitan convention than the later. As Kate Teltscher's chapter suggests, early narrativisation of the experience of the Black Hole of Calcutta depended heavily on the tropes of eighteenth-century British sentimental literature; and Nigel Leask demonstrates a large debt amongst the poets he considers to the stylistic qualities and tropes of the British Romantics. Nor does the literature of British India ever become entirely independent of metropolitan influences. As Alison Sainsbury's chapter argues, Anglo-Indian women's writing at the turn of this century draws as much on the model of popular metropolitan romance as on earlier Anglo-Indian texts in the 'adventure' mode.

However, as early as the 1830s, according to Javed Majeed's chapter, one can begin to discern a distinctively Anglo-Indian literary discourse, a claim corroborated by the *Calcutta Review*, which in 1846 drew a sharp distinction between metropolitan writers and 'our Indian novelists'.[41] Certainly by the 1880s, there is a widespread conviction, at least within Anglo-Indian quarters,[42] of radical differences between metropolitan and local representations of India. Thus Kipling's 'On the City Wall' (a text which is subjected to extended analysis in Chapter 4) satirises the sloppy and stereotypical Orientalist conventions of British-based writers. The narrator's strong sense of speaking from a distinct subcultural location, defined in the last analysis by its existential position *within* India, is indicated in the comments which attend his description of Wali Dad:

He possessed a head that English artists at home would rave over and paint amid impossible surroundings – a face that female novelists would use with delight through nine hundred pages. In reality he was only a clean-bred young Mohammedan, with pencilled eyebrows, small-cut nostrils, little hands and feet, and a very tired look in his eyes.[43]

The discursive consistency of the literature of British India – and the community's increasingly strong sense of its separate cultural identity – are partly registered in the degree to which thematic tropes identified in the first three chapters of this volume recur in subsequent writing. Thus the trauma of the Black Hole of Calcutta has its analogues in later texts, most notably in the 'Mutiny' narratives, with their stress on the confinement and deprivation of the besieged colonialists. In Kipling the trope returns in claustrophobic tales such as 'City of Dreadful Night' or 'The Strange Ride of Morrowbie Jukes', as well as in his recurrent figuring of Anglo-Indian existence as a kind of imprisonment, for instance in stories such as 'With the Main Guard' or 'A Wayside Comedy'. In Forster's *A Passage to India*, Adela's confinement in the cell-like Marabar caves is perhaps the key event in the novel, producing catastrophic repercussions for both herself, the Anglo-Indian community and Dr Aziz. And as Danny Colwell's chapter argues, the motif returns in Paul Scott's *Raj Quartet*, which turns obsessively on the confrontation in the interrogation cell between the policeman Merrick and his victim Hari Kumar. As has already been observed, the tropes of cultural infiltration, interracial liaison and psychic breakdown are equally entrenched and persistent in the literary discourse of British India.

The recurrence of these tropes might seem to confirm the suggestion of *Orientalism* that western knowledge of the Orient is expressed in a 'textual attitude' based on an unchanging regime of representations, which is intended to fix and typify subject cultures in order to classify and dominate them. Said does ask the question: 'What changes, modulations, refinements, even revolutions take place within Orientalism?'[44] But while implying a change of episteme in the latter part of the eighteenth century, and again in the 1920s, the principal thrust of his argument is to insist on an essentially invariant process of repetition of tropes and styles in western representation of the East. This allows Said to discuss Aeschylus's *The Persians* in much the same terms as the work of an Anglo-Indian poet like Alfred Lyall, two millennia later, as part of a consistent western will to power over the Orient which is equally apparent today.

However, the literature which this volume analyses suggests that orientalist discourse, at least in its literary manifestations, as these are produced by those with existential experience of India, is not so much a static archive but a process of cultural negotiation in constant conflict and evolution. The thematic tropes in the literature of British India in fact respond to changes in the nature and circumstances of its relationship with its subjects. Thus the motif of 'riot' is barely apparent in the first half of the nineteenth century when confidence in the security of control over India is relatively high; in post-'Mutiny' narrative, as one would expect, the theme is strongly marked and remains important in the work of Kipling and his contemporaries. It then becomes central in Forster, Orwell and Scott, corresponding to the increasing threat of organised political opposition to British rule as the twentieth century advanced. Similarly, as Jenny Sharpe has argued in *Allegories of Empire*, the related motif of the sexual threat to the white woman is not to be found prior to 1857 and must be understood as a discursive mobilisation generated by the uprising and its aftermath.

Equally, well-established tropes may disappear as the political realities of the Indian empire change. Thus the preoccupation with *sati*, officially abolished in 1829, is far less a feature of the later work of this corpus of writers than the earlier, where it is recurrently used as a means to justify British rule in India by emphasising the relative enlightenment and humaneness of its cultural values. Similarly, the motif of the 'mild Hindoo', which is so widespread in late eighteenth-century representations of India, is radically revised in the aftermath of 1857 and by the time of the emergence of organised political opposition to British rule in the 1880s, is barely available to Anglo-Indian writers. By this time, the parallel eighteenth-century vision of the blood-thirsty Muslim is being replaced by a vision in which Islam is a potential counterweight to the wily Bengali 'babu'.

The meaning of other tropes is modified, or even reversed, as historical circumstances are transformed, especially as the security of British rule comes into question. By the time of *Kim*, for example, the figure of the disguised agent of imperial power is no longer even exclusively English. Hurree Chunder assumes an exaggerated persona of Anglicised 'babudom' in order to defeat not the native conspirators who are the real danger in Meadows

Taylor's *Confessions of a Thug*, for example, but European spies, who represent Britain's Continental rivals. Meanwhile, in 'Beyond the Pale', the wound which Trejago receives during his night-time visit to the native city, while robed in his *boorka*, attests not so much to Kipling's sense of the security with which such disguises may be assumed, but the dangers as well as glamour of cultural hybridisation.

Paul Scott's *Raj Quartet* represents one of the clearest examples of the reinscription of earlier thematic tropes. The motif of cross-dressing is radically redefined to suggest the amenability of colonial power to subversion – or, indeed, seen in the terms in which the text itself presents Merrick's sexual preferences, perversion. Equally, the affective charge of the 'Black Hole' narrative is redirected in Scott's novels, as the relationship of barbarous Indian torturer to suffering English victim in eight-eenth-century accounts is reversed in order to stress Merrick's persecution of the innocent Hari Kumar. Here, haunted by his hybrid double, Merrick ironically demonstrates his own imprisonment within an ideology of racial superiority rendered hollow by historical processes outside the cell; indeed, events such as the Japanese victory at Singapore were leading, imminent-ly, to Indian independence. Perhaps most dramatically, the trope of rape, which becomes so marked in Anglo-Indian literature in the wake of the 1857 rebellions as a signifier of native 'incivility', is similarly reversed, so that Merrick's sexual assault on Kumar, rather than the sentimental idea of *man-bap* espoused by figures like Bingham, comes to figure the true nature of British India's long relationship with its subjects.

This is not to suggest that writers with existential experience of India were necessarily any less concerned with helping to secure Britain's position in India than their metropolitan counter-parts working within the 'textual' regime of representation, or, indeed, that they were themselves wholly impervious to its constraints. Nor does it suggest that their vision of India was necessarily 'truer' than metropolitan constructions of the sub-continent. But it does imply the necessity for several important modifications to Said's general thesis in *Orientalism*. In par-ticular, if the 'local' tradition of representation differed signifi-cantly from metropolitan constructions of India as a consequence of the historical and social situatedness *in* the empire of the subculture producing it, this again implies a greater variation and struggle *within* imperial discourse than Said allows. While

one must not homogenise the attitudes and politics of the discourse of British India, it recurrently and most ostentatiously
differentiates itself from its metropolitan equivalent on the
question of 'the textual attitude'. Thus in his 1848 preface to a
revised edition of James Mill's *History of British India* (1817),
the Anglo-Indian scholar H. H. Wilson savaged Mill's argument
that his never having visited India constituted an important
qualification for writing its history. Wilson repeatedly finds
instances of 'the operation of preconceived opinions', for example
in Mill's habit of representing native subjects in such a way as
to 'outrage humanity'.[45] Indeed, Wilson charges Mill with substantial responsibility for the creeping illiberalism of the Anglicist
party in India, whose policies were to provoke rebellion in the
following decade.

Even if it is true, as Said implies, that the 'textual attitude'
of the metropolis produces an unvarying range of tropes and styles
which constructs the Orient as static, female, passive, irrational
and 'backward' – itself a debatable proposition – the case of
British Indian cultural production suggests a vision of India which
is much more nuanced, contradictory, and subject to changing
historical and political circumstances. Most importantly, perhaps, this volume suggests that this existential situatedness
generated conflictual modes of cultural (self-) identification
which often militated against unthinking reliance on fixed,
hierarchical models of the relationship between colonial power
and native subject. For too long now, colonial discourse analysis,
as derived from *Orientalism*, has assumed that identical regimes
of power and knowledge organised both the political management
of empire and all the varied literature which represented it.

Notes

1 Edward Said, *Orientalism* (1978; London: Penguin, 1991), p. 39.

2 Aijaz Ahmad, *In Theory: Classes, Nations, Literatures* (London: Verso, 1992), p. 256.

3 Abdul JanMohamed, 'The Economy of Manichean Allegory: The Function of Racial
Difference in Colonialist Literature' in H. L. Gates (ed.), *'Race', Writing and Difference*
(1985; London: Chicago University Press, 1986), p. 78.

4 Benita Parry, 'The Content and Discontents of Kipling's Imperialism', *New Formations*,
6 (Winter 1988), p. 50.

5 Aijaz Ahmad, *In Theory*, p. 3. See Bart Moore-Gilbert, 'Which Way Postcolonial Theory?:
Current Problems and Future Prospects' in *History of European Ideas*, 18, 4 (1994) for
a more detailed account of Ahmad's controversy with Said.

6 Parry, 'The Content and Discontents of Kipling's Imperialism', pp. 51–62.

7 Laura Chrisman, 'The Imperial Unconscious? Representations of Imperial Discourse', *Critical Quarterly*, 32, 3 (1990), p. 38.

8 Homi Bhabha, *The Location of Culture* (London: Routledge, 1994), p. 77.

9 Sara Suleri, *The Rhetoric of English India* (Chicago: University of Chicago Press, 1992), p. 16.

10 Gail Ching-Liang Low, 'White Skins/Black Masks: the Pleasures and Politics of Imperialism', *New Formations*, 9 (Winter 1989), p. 93.

11 Rudyard Kipling, *Kim*, ed. Edward Said (1901; Harmondsworth: Penguin, 1987), p. 166; Paul Scott, *The Day of the Scorpion* (London: Granada, 1977), p. 342.

12 For further discussion see Bart Moore-Gilbert, *Kipling and 'Orientalism'* (London: Croom Helm, 1986), pp. 140ff.

13 Said, *Orientalism*, p. 207.

14 Jane Miller, *Seductions: Studies in Reading and Culture* (London: Virago, 1990), p. 133.

15 Lisa Lowe, *Critical Terrains: French and British Orientalisms* (Ithaca: Cornell University Press, 1991), p. 32. For further feminist critiques of *Orientalism*, see Sara Mills, *Discourses of Difference: An Analysis of Women's Travel Writing and Colonialism* (London: Routledge, 1993) and Zakia Pathak *et al.*, 'The Prisonhouse of Orientalism', *Textual Practice*, 5, 2 (Summer 1991), pp. 195–218.

16 Dennis Porter, '*Orientalism* and its Problems', reprinted in Patrick Williams and Laura Chrisman (eds.), *Colonial Discourse and Postcolonial Theory* (1983; Hemel Hempstead: Harvester Wheatsheaf, 1993).

17 Said, *Orientalism*, p. 240.

18 Said's attempt to exempt historical writing from the project of essentialising and fixing the identity of the East is, in any case, dubious, as a glance at the list of demeaning stereotypes under the index entry 'Hindus' in James Mill's *History of British India* (1817), for example, attests.

19 Said, *Orientalism*, p. 15.

20 Said, *Orientalism*, pp. 161–2 and 239.

21 Peter Hulme, *Colonial Encounters: Europe and the Native Caribbean 1492–1797* (London: Methuen, 1984), pp. 5–9.

22 Rudyard Kipling, 'Beyond the Pale' in *Plain Tales from the Hills*, ed. H. R. Woudhuysen (Harmondsworth: Penguin, 1987), p. 162. This will hereafter be cited as *Plain Tales* with page references given in the text.

23 John McClure, *Kipling and Conrad: The Colonial Fiction* (London: Harvard University Press, 1981), p. 47.

24 Mark Paffard, *Kipling's Indian Fiction* (London: Macmillan, 1989), p. 37; Patrick Williams, '*Kim* and Orientalism' in Williams and Chrisman (eds.), *Colonial Discourse and Postcolonial Theory*, p. 482.

25 Parry, 'Content and Discontents of Kipling's Imperialism', p. 56.

26 McClure, *Kipling and Conrad*, pp. 7 and 139.

27 Louis Cornell, *Kipling in India* (London: Macmillan, 1967), p. 139.

28 Edward Said, *Culture and Imperialism* (London: Chatto and Windus, 1993), p. 200.

29 Said, *Culture and Imperialism*, p. 13.

30 *Ibid.*, pp. xiii and 188.

31 *Ibid.*, p. xii.

32 Ahmad, *In Theory*, p. 164.

33 Michael Sprinker (ed.), *Edward Said: A Critical Reader* (Oxford: Blackwell, 1992), pp. 250–2.

34 Ahmad, *In Theory*, p. 178. Said's comments on the ontological incapacity of westerners to represent the Orient truthfully come on p. 204 of *Orientalism*. (They are contradicted on p. 322.) For a very different reading of Orientalism, see David Kopf, *British Orientalism and the Bengal Renaissance: The Dynamics of Indian Modernization, 1773–1835* (Berkeley: University of California Press, 1969).

35 Said, *Orientalism*, p. 22.

36 John Drew, *India and the Romantic Imagination* (Delhi: Oxford University Press, 1987), pp. 254–65.

37 Said, *Orientalism*, p. 156.

38 Suleri, *The Rhetoric of English India*, p. 10.

39 William Ireland, *Randolph Methyl: A Story of Anglo-Indian Life*, 2 vols. (London: Ward Lock, 1863), I, p. vi.

40 Henry Yule and A. C. Burnell (eds.), *Hobson-Jobson: A Glossary of Colloquial Anglo-Indian Words and Phrases* (1886; London: Routledge, 1985), pp. xv–xvi.

41 *Calcutta Review*, 5, Jan.–June 1846, p. 206. The establishment of the *Calcutta Review* in 1844 testifies to Anglo-India's need for a further cultural review responsive to local interests. For discussion of the material base of Anglo-Indian culture, see Bart Moore-Gilbert, *Kipling and 'Orientalism'*, chapter 1.

42 While the *OED* traces the term 'Anglo-India' to the 1840s, it was certainly already being used in the 1820s. In 1911 Lord Hardinge decreed that it be used to describe those of mixed race. I've tended to use the term British India, since a number of writers analysed in this volume are outside this period.

43 Rudyard Kipling, 'On the City Wall' in *The Man who Would Be King and Other Tales*, ed. Louis Cornell (Oxford: Oxford University Press, 1987), p. 222; see also the biting comments on the representation of India by temporary visitors on p. 223.

44 Said, *Orientalism*, p. 15.

45 H. H. Wilson, Preface to James Mill's *History of British India*, 4th edn. (1817; reprinted London, 1848), vol. 1, pp. vii–viii.

Bibliography

Ahmad, Aijaz, *In Theory: Classes, Nations, Literatures* (London: Verso, 1992).

Ashcroft, Bill, Gareth Griffiths and Helen Tiffin, *The Empire Writes Back: Theory and Practice in Post-colonial Literatures* (London: Routledge, 1989).

Bhabha, Homi, *The Location of Culture* (London: Routledge, 1994).

Bristow, Joseph, *Empire Boys: Adventures in a Man's World* (London: Routledge, 1991).

Calcutta Review, 5, Jan.–June 1846.

Chrisman, Laura, 'The Imperial Unconscious? Representations of Imperial Discourse', *Critical Quarterly*, 32, 3 (1990), pp. 38–58.

Cornell, Louis, *Kipling in India* (London: Macmillan, 1967).

Crane, Ralph, *Inventing India: A History of India in English-Language Fiction* (Basingstoke: Macmillan, 1992).

Davies, Tony and Nigel Woods (eds.), *A Passage to India* (Buckingham: Open University Press, 1994).

Drew, John, *India and the Romantic Imagination* (Delhi: Oxford University Press, 1987).

Goonetilleke, D. C. R. A., *Images of the Raj: South Asia in the Literature of Empire* (Basingstoke: Macmillan, 1988).

Hulme, Peter, *Colonial Encounters: Europe and the Native Caribbean 1492–1797* (London: Methuen, 1984).

Ireland, William, *Randolph Methyl: A Story of Anglo-Indian Life*, 2 vols. (London: Ward Lock, 1863).

JanMohamed, Abdul, 'The Economy of Manichean Allegory: The Function of Racial Difference in Colonialist Literature', in H. L. Gates (ed.), *'Race', Writing and Difference* (1985; London: Chicago University Press, 1986), pp. 78–106.

Kipling, Rudyard, *Kim*, ed. Edward Said (1901; Harmondsworth: Penguin, 1987).

Kipling, Rudyard, *Letters of Marque*, reprinted in Rudyard Kipling, *From Sea to Sea and Other Sketches: Letters of Travel*, vol. I (1891; London: Macmillan, 1913).

Kipling, Rudyard, *The Man who Would Be King and Other Tales*, ed. Louis Cornell (Oxford: Oxford University Press, 1987).

Kipling, Rudyard, *Plain Tales from the Hills*, ed. H. R. Woudhuysen (Harmondsworth: Penguin, 1987).

Kopf, David, *British Orientalism and the Bengal Renaissance: The Dynamics of Indian Modernization, 1773–1835* (Berkeley: University of California Press, 1969).

Low, Gail Ching-Liang, 'White Skins/Black Masks: the Pleasures and Politics of Imperialism', *New Formations*, 9 (Winter 1989), pp. 83–104.

Lowe, Lisa, *Critical Terrains: French and British Orientalisms* (Ithaca: Cornell University Press, 1991).

McClure, John, *Kipling and Conrad: The Colonial Fiction* (London: Harvard University Press, 1981).

Meadows Taylor, Philip, *Confessions of a Thug* (London: Bentley, 1839).

Miller, Jane, *Seductions: Studies in Reading and Culture* (London: Virago, 1990).

Mill, James, *History of British India*, 4th edn. ed. H. H. Wilson (1817; reprinted London, 1848).

Mills, Sara, *Discourses of Difference: An Analysis of Women's Travel Writing and Colonialism* (London: Routledge, 1993).

Moore-Gilbert, Bart, *Kipling and 'Orientalism'* (London: Croom Helm, 1986).

Moore-Gilbert, Bart, 'Which Way Postcolonial Theory?: Current Problems and Future Prospects' in *History of European Ideas*, 18, 4 (1994), pp. 553–71.

Owenson, Sydney, *The Missionary: An Indian Tale* (London: Stockdale, 1811).

Paffard, Mark, *Kipling's Indian Fiction* (London: Macmillan, 1989).

Parry, Benita, 'The Content and Discontents of Kipling's Imperialism', *New Formations* 6 (Winter 1988), pp. 49–64.

Pathak, Zakia *et al.*, 'The Prisonhouse of Orientalism', *Textual Practice*, 5, 2 (Summer 1991), pp. 195–218.

Porter, Dennis, 'Orientalism and its Problems', reprinted in Patrick Williams and Laura Chrisman (eds.), *Colonial Discourse and Postcolonial Theory* (1983; Hemel Hempstead: Harvester Wheatsheaf, 1993), pp. 150–62.

Said, Edward, *Culture and Imperialism* (London: Chatto and Windus, 1993).

Said, Edward, *Orientalism* (1978; London: Penguin, 1991).

Scott, Paul, *The Day of the Scorpion* (London: Granada, 1977).

Scott, Paul, *Staying On* (London: Heinemann, 1978).

Sharpe, Jenny, *Allegories of Empire: The Figure of Woman in the Colonial Text* (London: University of Minneapolis Press, 1993).

Spivak, Gayatri C., 'Can the Subaltern Speak?' in Cary Nelson and Lawrence Grossberg (eds.), *Marxism and the Interpretation of Culture* (Basingstoke: Macmillan, 1988), pp. 271–313.

Sprinker, Michael (ed.), *Edward Said: A Critical Reader* (Oxford: Blackwell, 1992).

Suleri, Sara, *The Rhetoric of English India* (Chicago: University of Chicago Press, 1992).

Whitworth, G.C., *Anglo-Indian Dictionary: A Glossary of Indian Terms Used in English* (London: Kegan Paul, 1885).

Williams, Patrick, '*Kim* and Orientalism' in Patrick Williams and Laura Chrisman (eds.), *Colonial Discourse and Postcolonial Theory* (Hemel Hempstead: Harvester Wheat-sheaf, 1993), pp. 480–97.

Yule, Henry and A. C. Burnell (eds.), *Hobson-Jobson: A Glossary of Colloquial Anglo-Indian Words and Phrases* (1886; London: Routledge, 1985).

1

'The fearful name of the Black Hole': fashioning an imperial myth

KATE TELTSCHER

> From my very early years few things had filled my mind with more
> horror than the very name of the Black Hole of Calcutta, although
> the exact history of its tragic celebrity was unknown to me.[1]

The name of the Black Hole of Calcutta echoes through the
narratives of British India, a resonant metonym for colonial
horror. Acquiring proverbial status, the name even now signifies
a place to be avoided, somewhere overcrowded and overheated,
a site of discomfort and pain. Why should the name live on as a
proverb, part of that common pool of axioms, sayings and stereotypes that contribute to a sense of national identity? What role
does the Black Hole play in the construction of colonial histories,
British and Indian? This essay aims to reconnect the myth with
its original circumstances of production, and then to explore
some of the numerous subsequent versions of the story. For the
story of the Black Hole of Calcutta is one that has been com-
pulsively told and retold, challenged and contested throughout
two centuries of colonial rule. The narrative of this trauma,
symptomatic of the wider insecurities of eighteenth-century
British involvement in India, was refashioned into one of the
founding myths of empire.

Howell's *Narrative*

On June 16 1756 Siraj-ud-Daulah, the Mughal Nawab of Bengal,
attacked the British town of Calcutta. Relations between the
British East India Company and the local Mughal authorities had
been deteriorating for some time. Calcutta was one of the three
British 'Presidencies' which, with Bombay in the west and
Madras in the south, functioned as the East India Company's

main trading bases in India. The town was ruled by a British governor and council, and defended by a garrison of soldiers. The British had become increasingly involved in Bengal's trade over the preceding decades, and the Nawab was concerned both to limit Calcutta's growing power and independence, and to raise more substantial revenues from Company trade. When the British refused to accept the new conditions, Siraj-ud-Daulah resorted to force. The Nawab's army greatly outnumbered the Company's garrison, and after a short siege, Calcutta was taken. In the course of the siege, many of the British residents fled, including the city's governor. The remaining members of the council appointed the *zamindar* or magistrate of Calcutta, John Zephaniah Holwell, as substitute governor. Holwell was among the 146 captives rounded up by the Nawab's troops and placed in the Black Hole, an 18 feet square punishment cell in the fort. After a night spent in the terrible conditions of the Black Hole, only 23 of the 146 prisoners incarcerated remained alive.

Or so Holwell tells it. Holwell's account of the events of the night of June 20 1756, *A Genuine Narrative of the Deplorable Deaths of the English Gentlemen, and Others, who were suffocated in the Black-Hole in Fort-william, at Calcutta*, published as a short book in 1758, and reprinted the same year in *The Annual Register*, lays the foundations of the Black Hole mythology. The accuracy of the *Genuine Narrative* has been questioned by twentieth-century historians; Holwell has been accused of self-justificatory exaggeration and fabrication. The figures and measurements have been intoned, scrutinised and revised. (A modern study has calculated that there could only have been a total of 64 captives in the prison, with 21 survivors.[2]) My concern in this essay, however, is not that of traditional historians who, to quote Natalie Zemon Davis, aim to 'peel away the fictive elements' in texts to 'get at the real facts', but rather to 'let the "fictional" aspects of these documents be the center of analysis'.[3] For we must look at the narrative technique, rather than the numbers and dimensions, to begin to understand the hold that this story exerted over the British imagination.

Holwell frames his account with a Latin epigraph from Book II of *The Aeneid*. He chooses the moment when the Trojan prince Aeneas begins his narrative of the fall of Troy to the Greeks, the implied parallel conferring epic authority on Holwell's account of the fall of Calcutta, and heroic status on Holwell himself. The epigraph reads:

> – Quaeque ipse miserrima vidi,
> Et quorum pars magna fui. Quis talia fando,
> Myrmidonum, Dolopumve, aut duri miles Ulyssei
> Temperet a lachrymis?[4]

In translation, Aeneas's words are: 'I witnessed that tragedy my-self, and I took a great part in those events. No one could tell the tale and refrain from tears, not even if he were a Myrmidon or a Dolopian [members of Greek tribes] or some soldier of the un-pitying Ulysses'.[5] Holwell claims with Aeneas the authority of chief protagonist and eyewitness (or ' "I"-witness', to borrow Clifford Geertz's pun), and so carves out a central role in the narrative for himself. But while the story is told by the voice of experience, the tragedy exceeds personal suffering; the tale itself would elicit tears from an enemy soldier. With classical precedent for the idea of manly weeping, Holwell appeals to the reader for sympathy.

His account takes the form of a letter to a friend written on the voyage home, and at times the narrative is interrupted by apostrophes to the recipient ('Oh! my dear Sir') which establish an intimate relation between the author and the (male) reader. The focus is on the suffering narrator's feelings and bodily sen-sations; on his composure, despair and pain. The reader is invited to identify with the protagonist, to shed tears of compassion for him and his fellow victims. Holwell is here drawing on the techniques of sentimental literature, the genre which dominated European fiction from the 1740s to 1770s. This literary fashion took as its central tenet the idea of the natural goodness of humanity. Sentimental literature characteristically focuses on helpless and unfortunate victims to provoke a compassionate response in the reader, such humanitarian concern itself pro-viding evidence of innate benevolence. The sentimental elements in Holwell's *Genuine Narrative* are, however, grafted onto an older form, the tradition that Mary Louise Pratt has termed 'sur-vival literature – first-person stories of shipwrecks, castaways, mutinies, abandonments, and ... captivities'; popular, sensational tales of overseas adventure which originated in the first phase of European expansion, during the late fifteenth century.[6] The fusion of these two literary forms results in a hero who combines manly fortitude in the face of extreme horror with a feminised helplessness and sensibility.

From the start Holwell represents himself as stoically enduring the ordeal while evincing concern for his fellow captives:

Death, attended with the most cruel train of circumstances, I plainly
perceived must prove our inevitable destiny. I had seen this common
migration in too many shapes, and accustomed myself to think on
the subject with too much propriety to be alarmed at the prospect,
and indeed felt much more for my wretched companions than myself.

(India Tracts: 393)

Holwell shows restraint, and (to paraphrase Kipling, that later
colonial mythographer) keeps his head while all around are losing
theirs. As conditions deteriorate, the inmates begin 'to grow
outragious [sic] and many delirious', and demand water from
the guards. The officer in charge, an 'old Jemmautdaar', a kindly
if misguided figure who is notably absent from later versions of
the story, takes pity on the captives and complies, 'little dreaming', Holwell warns the reader, 'of its fatal effects' *(India Tracts*:
395). The skins of water arrive:

Until the water came, I had myself not suffered much from thirst,
which instantly grew excessive. We had no means of conveying it
into the prison, but by hats forced through the bars; and thus myself
and Messrs. Coles and Scot ... supplied them as fast as possible. ...
Though we brought full hats within the bars, there ensued such
violent struggles, and frequent contests, to get at it, that before it
reached the lips of any one, there would be scarcely a small tea-cup
full left in them. These supplies, like sprinkling water on fire, only
served to feed and raise the flame.

Oh! my dear Sir, how shall I give you a conception of what I felt
at the cries and ravings of those in the remoter parts of the prison,
who could not entertain a probable hope of obtaining a drop, yet
could not divert themselves of expectation, however unavailing!
And others calling on me by the tender considerations of friendship
and affection, and who knew they were really dear to me. Think, if
possible, what my heart must have suffered at seeing and hearing
their distress, without having it in my power to relieve them; for
the confusion now became general and horrid ... many forcing their
passage from the further part of the room, pressed down those in
their way, who had less strength, and trampled them to death.

Can it gain belief, that this scene of misery proved entertainment
to the brutal wretches without? But so it was; and they took care to
keep us supplied with water, that they might have the satisfaction of
seeing us fight for it, as they phrased it, and held up light to the bars,
that they might lose no part of that inhuman diversion.

(India Tracts: 395–7)

The narrator is removed from the general atmosphere of hysteria
and panic, paying little regard to his own needs. Stressing his
emotional response to the plight of those around him, he calls

on the reader to identify through empathy not so much with him, but with his feelings for others: 'Think, if possible, what my heart must have suffered at seeing and hearing their distress, without having it in my power to relieve them'. The 'seeing', 'hearing' narrator is powerless to intervene in the scene that he represents. But there are other, less feeling, observers: the guards. These 'brutal wretches' break every rule in the sentimental book. Cast as sadistic voyeurs, their 'inhuman diversion' contravenes all accepted tenets of human behaviour, relegating them, so to speak, from the species.

Why are the guards demonised? They are, after all, only complying with the prisoners' demands by supplying them with water. But the desperate captives, when represented as victims of Indian torture, are absolved from responsibility for their actions. An ugly fight for survival is transformed into a less disturbing image – that of savage Indians delighting in suffering. Indeed Holwell attributes the idea that the captives are fighting each other to the guards themselves: 'they took care to keep us supplied with water, that they might have the satisfaction of seeing us fight for it, *as they phrased it'* (my emphasis). But is it only the guards who derive satisfaction from this scene? It could be said that the author who stages the display of suffering is, at some level, gratifying the voyeuristic impulses of his readers. Such forbidden pleasures are here displaced onto the guards; these then become Indian Others who seem to function as demonised versions of European Selves. Holwell's account effectively inverts the respective roles constructed for westerners and Indians by centuries of European writing about India. For throughout the earlier literature, European travellers have invariably been represented as onlookers at displays of Indian suffering. Accounts of the extreme physical penances of Hindu and Muslim holy men and devotees, and of *sati*, the Hindu rite of widow-burning, become established Indian *topoi*, reproduced in every book of travels. In the standard version of the *sati* scene, the male European stares with horrified but unwavering attention, as the beautiful young widow is burnt alive on her husband's funeral pyre. By way of contrast, in the *Genuine Narrative*, the habitual observers find the subjects of their gaze staring back. The voyeuristic fascination with others' suffering, never directly acknowledged by European travel writers but easily discernible in their detailed descriptions, is written all over the faces of the guards.[7]

The reversal of the conventional relationship encapsulates the larger shift in power. For the true horror of the account resides in the sense of British helplessness. The prisoners are deprived of the ability to take decisions, to determine their own course of action. Unreasonable, hysterical, responding only to the demands of their bodies, the captives are reduced to a state of feminised powerlessness. They are also amoral, anarchic, uncivilised. All sense of community and co-operation is destroyed as the precious water is spilt and they trample one another to death. Yet in the midst of this frantic mêlée, the composed narrator makes a curious gesture at more civilised modes of behaviour. The hats, emblems of European identity, have been transformed to water vessels, but the quantity remaining in the bottom is described as 'a small tea-cup full'. This reference to the genteel rituals of the tea table must, I think, be read as a grim antithesis to the struggles for refreshment in the Black Hole. The image of the teacup also inevitably recalls the wider context of the Nawab's dispute with the East India Company. For the Company's trading activities in Bengal were linked to the most profitable of its concerns: the trade in Chinese tea. The implication, perhaps, is that the captives are losing their lives in the service of trade.[8]

At moments like this, the narrator's wry detachment from the scene of misery is strangely at odds with his much-vaunted sensibility. The narrative tone switches registers throughout the account, ranging in mood from suicidal despair to black humour. After the struggle for water subsides, the narrator explains how he sustained himself through part of the night:

[I] kept my mouth moist from time to time by sucking the perspiration out of my shirt-sleeves, and catching the drops as they fell, like heavy rain from my head and face: you can hardly imagine how unhappy I was if any of them escaped my mouth. ... I was observed by one of my miserable companions on the right of me, in the expedient of allaying my thirst by sucking my shirt-sleeve. He took the hint, and robbed me from time to time of a considerable part of my store; though after I detected him, I had ever the address to begin on that sleeve first, when I thought my reservoirs were sufficiently replenished; and our mouths and noses often met in the contest. ... Before I hit upon this happy expedient, I had, in an ungovernable fit of thirst, attempted drinking my urine; but it was so intensely bitter there was no enduring a second taste, whereas no Bristol water could be more soft or pleasant than what arose from perspiration.

(India Tracts: 399–400)

The earlier fight for water is replayed in parodic form in the sweat-sucking contest. Holwell again introduces notions of gentility in the incongruous pairing of sweat and spa water. The 'Bristol water' represents British fashion and health (Bristol Hotwell was a resort frequented by the leisured classes) in the midst of squalor and degradation. The narrator may be reduced to drinking his own body fluids but, the analogy implies, he retains his original cultural identity.[9] Such signs of civility, combined with the self-mocking tone and wry perspectival distance, indicate that the narrator will emerge unscathed and uncontaminated from his ordeal. The humour is clearly predicated on survival. Holwell informs the reader of the identity of his fellow sleeve-sucker: 'This plunderer, I found afterwards, was a worthy young gentleman in the service, Mr Lushington, one of the few who escaped from death, and since paid me the compliment of assuring me, he believed he owed his life to the many comfortable draughts he had from my sleeves' (*India Tracts*: 399–400).

The anticipation of a return to civility is, Pratt argues, the basic premise of 'survival literature' which

> furnished a 'safe' context for staging alternate, relativizing, and taboo configurations of intercultural contact ... The context of survival literature was 'safe' for transgressive plots, since the very existence of a text presupposed the imperially correct outcome: the survivor survived, and sought reintegration into the home society.[10]

But the 'taboo configuration' of the Black Hole narrative – the Nawab's imprisonment of the British – is not made wholly safe for the simple reason that most of the British prisoners do perish. The deaths of the 123 captives remain to be avenged. The 'imperially correct outcome' or happy ending of the Black Hole story is only supplied later, as we all shall see. Pratt's model does however help to explain the striking changes in register of Holwell's account. The gruesome tragedy is also a record of survival. Holwell writes from on board the *Syren Sloop* on the voyage home; the transgressive plot is righted.

The horrors of the *Genuine Narrative* are also, in a sense, predictable. The account confirms the reading public's expectations of Islamic cruelty, a European stereotype dating back at least as far as the Crusades. While Siraj-ud-Daulah is not held personally responsible for the loss of life, he is represented as completely unmoved by it – like any oriental despot. The Nawab is fixed in the role of eastern tyrant, defined most famously a decade earlier in Montesquieu's *De l'esprit des Lois*, which contains an elaborate and hugely influential theory of oriental despotism based on ideas of climatic determinism. To cast the Nawab as oriental despot is an attempt to establish a structure of absolute difference between East and West; a barrier of difference which is reinforced by complimentary self-representations. Contemporary readers of Holwell would have read other narratives which typically stress the benign behaviour of the British. They might have read, for instance, the account of the kindly treatment of Indian captives taken in the British attack on the fort of Gheria a year earlier.

Situated on India's western coast, Gheria was the base of the Maratha chief, Tulaji Angria, who disrupted Company trade by attacking British shipping. In 1756 an expedition led by Charles Watson and Robert Clive captured the fort. An anonymous account of the operation appeared in the November issue of *The London Magazine* of 1757, and was reprinted in Edward Ives' *Voyage from England to India* of 1773, with a footnote identifying Ives as the author of the earlier account in 'one of the monthly magazines'.[11] Ives, described as a former 'Surgeon of Admiral Watson's Ship' on the title page, writes that Watson is remembered with affection at his death: 'His *integrity, humanity, generosity*, and *disinterestedness* of heart were such, as to become almost proverbial among the natives, as well as the *Europeans* residing in the East Indies'.[12] The episode which constructs Watson as the epitome of benevolence occurs at the end of the siege of Gheria, when the victorious Watson visits his captives, the family of Tulaji Angria, who had himself already fled. The Maratha chief, described as 'an arbitrary, cruel tyrant', provides a marked contrast to Watson, who displays every possible virtue in his dealings with the prisoners:

Admiral Watson, soon after the reduction of the place, took an opportunity of visiting these unfortunate captives; and the interview between them was beyond measure affecting. Upon his entering their house, the whole family made a grand salaam, or reverential bending of their bodies, touching the very ground with their faces, and shedding floods of tears. The admiral desired them to be comforted; adding, 'that they were now under his protection; and that no kind of injury should be done them.' They then again made the salaam. The mother of Angria, though strongly affected with these testimonies of goodness and humanity, yet could not help crying out, 'that the people had no king, she no son, her daughters no husband, the children no father!' The admiral replied, 'that from henceforward they must look on him as their father and their friend.' Upon which the youngest child, a boy of about six years old, sobbing said, 'Then you shall be my father;' and immediately took the admiral by the hand, and called him 'father'. This action of the child's was so very affecting, it quite overpowered that brave, that good man's heart, and he found himself under a necessity of turning from the innocent youth for a while, to prevent the falling of those tears, which stood ready to gush from his eyes.[13]

This tableau incorporates many of the characteristic elements of the literature of sensibility: the feeling man moved to tears with benevolent concern at the sight of the vulnerable female victim and children. The scene also functions as a dramatic realisation of ideas of benign paternalism: the infant prince calls the admiral father, and takes him by the hand. The narrative is so 'affecting' not only because of the thick layers of pathos and sentiment, but also because it enacts the British ideal of colonial relations: the childlike Indian spontaneously entrusts his fate to the kindly British adult.

It is difficult to imagine a more striking contrast to the Black Hole story of captivity: the surrogate family opposed to the chamber of death. While Watson supplies a happy ending, taking the place of the absent father/chief, the 123 corpses in the Black Hole call out for vengeance, a revenge to be achieved only through blood-letting. When news of the fall of Calcutta reached Madras, Clive and Watson again combined forces to recapture the city. Calcutta was quickly taken in January 1757, and Siraj-ud-Daulah forced to restore British trading privileges. But the peace was short-lived. Clive started to intrigue with a discontented faction of nobles, merchants and bankers against Siraj-ud-Daulah. A new treaty was negotiated whereby British forces would back the claims of the Nawab's uncle and rival, Mir Jafar, in return for substantial trade concessions, financial restitution for the Company, and massive payments to individuals. In June 1757 Siraj-ud-Daulah's army was defeated at Plassey, and the Nawab was later captured and killed.

These two events – the battle of Plassey and the death of Siraj-ud-Daulah – were represented by Holwell as retribution, not so much for the capture of Calcutta, as directly for the Black Hole deaths. Although, as we have seen, the *Genuine Narrative* exempts Siraj-ud-Daulah from personal responsibility for the massacre, in 1760 Holwell erected a monument in Calcutta to commemorate the incident and vilify the dead Nawab. A plan of

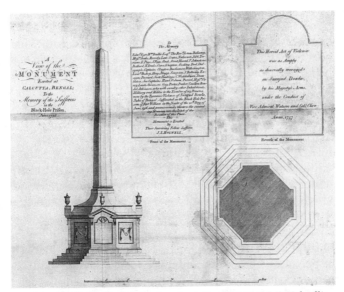

1] Plan of Holwell's Black Hole monument. Frontispiece to J. Z. Holwell's *India Tracts* (3rd edn., 1774). India Office Library and Records.

2] John Zephaniah Holwell. Unknown artist, 1760. Platinotype print, India Office Library and Records (P 587).

the monument was included as the frontispiece to Holwell's collected writings, *India Tracts* (Fig. 1). Built at his own expense during his two-year tenure as governor of the city, the brick and plaster obelisk was dedicated to the '123 Persons, [who] were by the Tyrannic Violence of Surajud Dowla, Suba of Bengal, Suffocated in the Black Hole Prison'. On one side the names of some of those who died were carved, together with a reference to Holwell himself: 'This Monument is Erected By Their Surviving Fellow Sufferer, J. Z. HOLWELL'. On the other, an inscription connected the Black Hole with the subsequent military action: 'This Horrid Act of Violence was as Amply as Deservedly Revenged on Surajud Dowla By his Majesty's Arms under the Conduct of Vice Admiral Watson and Col! Clive Anno, 1757' (*India Tracts*: frontispiece). To record this act of civic generosity, Holwell had his portrait painted standing at the base of the half-built monument, directing the works. A print of the painting, which once hung on the walls of Government House, Calcutta, is to be found in the archives of the India Office Library in London (Fig. 2). The brightly-lit, fully dressed figure of Holwell (wearing a 'purple red coat and yellowish waistcoat' according to a description of the original painting) points to a plan of the obelisk, instructing a half-naked Indian labourer who stoops over a basket, indistinct in the monument's shadow.[14] The respective postures of Holwell and the workman, their dress and the play of light and shade, all emphasise the dramatic reversal of power that succeeds the Black Hole episode. Holwell is manifestly back in charge.

'Unconscious builders of Empire'

Architect of his own reputation, Holwell wrote and built his way into the history books. Later writers accepted the connection he established between the Black Hole and Plassey, largely because of the significance which the battle had acquired: British rule in India has traditionally been dated from 1757, with the battle of Plassey symbolising the inauguration of empire. In this version of colonial history, the Black Hole massacre justifies British military intervention and the establishment of centuries of political and territorial control. The most famous retelling of the Black Hole story was undoubtedly that contained in Macaulay's essay on Clive, first published in the *Edinburgh Review* of January 1840. For Macaulay, the Black Hole was 'that great crime, memorable for its singular atrocity, memorable for the tremendous retribution by which it was followed'.[15] Like many of Macaulay's confident pronouncements, this became the authorised version of events. Macaulay's collected *Critical and Historical Essays* (1843) were immensely and enduringly successful throughout the nineteenth century and into the twentieth; editions for school use were issued as late as the 1960s.

Macaulay may have turned the story into a founding myth of empire, but earlier writers also saw the Black Hole as a turning point in Indian history. A correspondent to the *Asiatic Journal* of February 1817, for example, recalls a visit to the Old Fort of Calcutta in 1812, before the building was demolished to make way for some Company warehouses. The writer (who goes under the name of 'Asiaticus') joined a party expressly to visit the 'melancholy spot' of the Black Hole, a room which bore 'the appearance of an oven'.[16] On leaving, the writer remarks of Holwell's monument:

> It serves as the first attraction to a stranger arriving in Calcutta; and he pauses with no little exultation to review in his mind the astonishing events which in so short a space of time have succeeded this wanton act of power – events which have secured us an empire second in riches to none in the world, and which have placed at our disposal the lives of millions of fellow-creatures.[17]

British power in India is conceived in dramatic terms as a *peripetaia* or sudden reversal of fortune: from a room crammed with British bodies to an immense and wealthy empire. Siraj-ud-Daulah may have had 146 captives at his disposal, but the Company now has millions of Indian lives. Political manoeuvres and military aggression are elided in the unspecified 'astonishing events' which have transformed the state of affairs. Holwell's monument functions as a triumphalist symbol of Company control.

Yet this obelisk, phallic sign of British power, is at the same time, inescapably, a monument to British impotence and death. The confident narrative of Empire is produced by the narrative of insecurity, but also undermined by it. The need to proclaim power is itself a symptom of fear, as Frantz Fanon has observed: '[the settler] is an exhibitionist. His preoccupation with security makes him remind the native out loud that he alone is master'.[18] The Black Hole story locates a sense of helplessness at the very start of the narrative of colonial power in India. Despite all attempts to still this fear, it is liable to surface, like a half-repressed traumatic memory. The heroine of an anonymous novel of 1789, *Hartly House, Calcutta*, is particularly prone to this anxiety. Writing to a friend in England, Sophia describes a tour of the Old Fort of Calcutta, which provides the occasion for a potted history of the city. The Black Hole, which occupies most of her short narrative, elicits the parenthetical aside '(I shudder to name it)', and the anxiety which the story generates causes her to cut short her sight-seeing trip: 'The recollection of what I have related, so affected my spirits, that I begged to return home; and, having committed my morning's excursion to paper, shall endeavour to remember the concluding part of it no more'.[19] The horrors of the story demand that it be both told and forgotten, both written and erased. Inevitably, the story resurfaces. Sophia is later startled by the sound of gunshot and explains that her sense of panic is caused by the persistent memory of the Black Hole.[20]

Colonial historiography attempts to contain the horror of the Black Hole by supplying a form of narrative closure in the revenge of Plassey and the death of Siraj-ud-Daulah. But the fear which the story generates seems to be always in excess of this, to be uncontainable. For the end of one story is the beginning of another – the much longer story of empire. Colonial regimes are haunted by a sense of insecurity; Fanon writes that the settler, when he meets the native's eyes, 'ascertains bitterly, always on the defensive "They want to take our place." It is true that there is no native who does not dream at least once a day of setting himself up in the settler's place'.[21] This fantasy of the inversion of roles is shared by both colonised and coloniser. Elaborating on Fanon, Homi Bhabha argues that the identities of coloniser and colonised are not discrete and separate, not organised around a clear-cut Self/Other opposition, but rather disturbingly fused, intimately connected. The coloniser is troubled by the recognition of similarities with the native:

> the image of post-Enlightenment man [is] tethered to, *not* confronted by, his dark reflection, the shadow of colonized man, that splits his presence, distorts his outline, breaches his boundaries, repeats his action at a distance, disturbs and divides the very time of his being. The ambivalent identification of the racist world ... turns on the idea of man as his alienated image; not Self and Other but the otherness of the Self inscribed in the perverse palimpsest of colonial identity.[22]

Following Bhabha's suggestion, we might direct our attention to the inversion of roles in the Black Hole story. The British are easily reduced to powerlessness by Muslim tyranny; they are placed in much the position that contemporary histories assign to the Hindu – 'the most enervated inhabitant of the globe', according to Robert Orme, writing a few years after Holwell.[23] The helpless victims of the Black Hole offer an 'alienated image' of Indianised impotence. The horror of the story resides in the recognition that there is no fixed dividing line between Self and Other, between domination and subordination. The narrative reveals 'the dynamic of powerlessness' which Sara Suleri locates 'at the heart of the imperial configuration'.[24] In the darkness of the Black Hole, identities are alarmingly unstable. The very name of the prison – the conventional term for a detention cell in a military barracks – seems charged with significance: 'the fearful name of the Black Hole' (to quote Macaulay) comes to signify an indeterminate no-place where white captives turn black.[25]

And, indeed, where black tyrants turn white. The assignment of the role of oriental despot to the Nawab, and of righteous avenger to Clive may have appeared less self-evident to readers in the decades following the first publication of the *Genuine Narrative*. Clive's military victories initially secured him the status of national hero, but by 1772 he was attacked in the press and investigated by Parliament, as charges of British profiteering and extortion in Bengal became widespread. The Company was accused of cruelty, tyranny and oppression. 'Nabob', an Anglicised form of Nawab (the Indian title of rank held by Siraj-ud-Daulah, among others) became a term of abuse directed against Clive in particular, and more generally against the British who returned home hugely enriched from India. The question which inevitably poses itself is: who, here, is the despot?

Such a question undermines the structure of absolute difference between East and West to reveal an ambivalence which, Bhabha argues, threatens the authority of colonial command.[26] In order to contain this threat, writers like Macaulay, intent on redeeming Clive's reputation, insist on Siraj-ud-Daulah's despotic nature even more emphatically than Holwell. When Macaulay introduces the young Nawab, he announces, 'Oriental despots are perhaps the worst class of human beings; and this unhappy boy was one of the worst specimens of his class' (*Essays*: 504). Having established a separate generic category, Macaulay enumerates the personal failings which, encouraged by an inadequate education, confirm the Nawab as oriental despot: feeble intellect, selfishness, self-indulgence, addiction to debauchery.

The sadism which Holwell ascribes to the prison guards becomes Siraj-ud-Daulah's own in Macaulay's account:

> It is said that he had arrived at the last stage of human depravity, when cruelty becomes pleasing for its own sake, when the sight of pain as pain, where no advantage is to be gained, no offence punished, no danger averted, is an agreeable excitement. It had early been his amusement to torture beasts and birds; and, when he grew up, he enjoyed with still keener relish the misery of his fellow-creatures.
>
> (*Essays*: 504)

Although Macaulay's Nawab, sleeping off a debauch, is not present at the site of the Black Hole, he is clearly implicated in the event.

The explicit aim of Macaulay's essay is to exonerate Clive, to place his name 'high on the roll of conquerors' and 'in the list of those who have done and suffered much for the happiness of mankind' (*Essays*: 549). The idea of British guilt cannot, however, be altogether banished; it is invoked, inadvertently perhaps, at the very moment that the British seem most helpless. In the preamble to his account of the Black Hole suffering, Macaulay builds to a rhetorical climax: 'Nothing in history or fiction, not even the story which Ugolino told in the sea of everlasting ice, after he had wiped his bloody lips on the scalp of his murderer, approaches the horrors which were recounted by the few survivors of that night' (*Essays*: 505). Ugolino's story is of the terrors he endured in prison, forced to watch his sons die of starvation before him, and then (although the text is ambiguous) driven by hunger to feed off their corpses. The parallel points to the taboos that are broken and the ties of affinity that are severed in the Black Hole; but the analogy also suggests that the prisoners themselves are in some way implicated in wrong-doing. For Ugolino is himself a traitor, encountered, gnawing at the brains of his untrustworthy fellow conspirator, in the depths of Dante's *Inferno*.[27] The hellish conditions of the Black Hole seem to rub off on the captives. The spectre of 'colonial guilt', to borrow Suleri's term, haunts even this founding myth of empire.[28]

Clive's infamy casts a shadow of guilt over the story retrospectively, but one way to exorcise it is to turn the captives into national martyrs. In 1797 *A Collection of Poems written in the East Indies* was published in Calcutta by Sir John Horsford, who served with British forces in India, and mainly wrote on military themes. The collection includes 'Dum-Dum', a poem which takes its title (and thumping rhythm) from the name of the site where the treaty was signed after the recapture of Calcutta in 1757. The poem celebrates the force of 'our conqu'ring arms' over the Nawab, but is called back to the scene of suffering at the Black Hole by the 'awful shades of murder'd victims':

> Thrice forty patriot men – a martyr'd band,
> Drove to destruction by a vile command,
> Who in the gloom of smothering dungeons laid,
> Implor'd th'implacable SURAJAH's aid;
> But deaf to misery's expiring pray'r,
> He stopp'd Heav'n's common benefit, the air;
> Insan'd by thirst and agoniz'd at heart –
> I see their eyes from their blank sockets start!
> To monstrous bosoms soft entreaty's vain,
> They fell in struggles of convulsive pain[29]

There is not the slightest suspicion of 'colonial guilt' here. Horsford lays the blame for the massacre directly on Siraj-ud-Daulah, and the victims maintain their sense of community throughout: the 'band' of 'patriot men' die, not fighting each other, but 'in struggles of convulsive pain'. The focus is on the suffering body, but the pain is sanctified through martyrdom. Horsford's canonisation of the Black Hole dead anticipates the commemoration of the British who died, a century after the battle of Plassey, in the Indian Rebellion of 1857. As Jenny Sharpe has noted, those who died at rebel hands were represented as martyrs, and (as for the Black Hole) monuments were erected at the sites of their deaths which recorded their sacrifice and functioned as 'spectacular signs of Indian savagery to be read by future generations'.[30]

By the time of the Indian Rebellion, however, the Black Hole monument could no longer be read. Holwell's brick and plaster obelisk had decayed and was taken down in 1821. But it was re-erected in 1902, carved out of marble and designed to last for generations. The replica monument was a 'personal gift to the city of Calcutta' from Lord Curzon, Viceroy from 1898–1906, and enthusiastic patron of historical research into the Black Hole. The obelisk was not an exact copy of Holwell's; Curzon's research had added 40 names to Holwell's short list of British dead, and out of concern for Muslim sensibilities, had left out the part of the inscription concerning Siraj-ud-Daulah's personal responsibility as 'calculated to keep alive feelings that we would all wish to see die'.[31] Unveiling the monument, Curzon honoured 'the brave men whose life-blood had cemented the foundations of the British Empire in India'.[32] For Curzon, the Black Hole does not represent the threat of native power, or the vulnerability of the British, but rather the glorious origins of imperial expansion. Reproducing Horsford's figure of the 'martyr'd band', he sanctifies the site as a holy place of empire:

> if among these forerunners of our own, if among these ancient and unconscious builders of Empire, there are any who especially deserve commemoration, surely it is the martyr band whose fate I recall and whose names I resuscitate on this site; and if there be a spot that should be dear to the Englishman in India, it is that below our feet, which was stained with the blood and which closed over the remains of the victims of that night of destiny, the 20th of June, 1756. It is with these sentiments in my heart that I have erected this monument, and that I now hand it over to the citizens of Calcutta, to be kept by them in perpetual remembrance of the past.[33]

Curzon thus constructs a continuous history of the Raj from 1756 into the early twentieth century which elides the insecurities, anxieties and hesitancies of colonial rule.

Nationalist contestations

Curzon's heroic version of the Black Hole did not go unchallenged. The growth of opposition to the Raj was accompanied by the nationalist project to rewrite India's history. In the first decade of the twentieth century, Akshay Kumar Maitra, a pioneer archaeologist and historian of Bengal, published a book and a number of essays in Bengali journals that aimed to redeem Siraj-ud-Daulah from his colonial notoriety. The Nawab was adopted by the growing Indian nationalist movement as a symbol of Indian resistance to the British. This nationalist contestation of colonial historiography found an unlikely ally in J. H. Little, a British schoolmaster, who began a lively scholarly controversy in *Bengal Past and Present* in 1915, and continued in the following year on the letters page of the Indian newspaper, *The Statesman*. Little set out 'to prove that the Black Hole incident was a gigantic hoax'.[34] Drawing on the work of Maitra, Little claimed that the *Genuine Narrative* was full of inaccuracies and lies, and that a Persian history of the 1780s was a more reliable source. The *Siyar-ul-Mutakharin* (*Review of Modern Times*) by the Mughal noble, Ghulam Husein Khan, omitted all mention of the Black Hole, and offered instead a narrative of the brave, if desperate, defence of Calcutta mounted by the unarmed British residents: 'these unfortunate men, without losing courage marched up to their murderers and, with empty bottles, and stones, and brickbats, fought them to the last man, until they were all killed'. Little comments, 'we seem to recognise our country men in that story but do we recognise them in the howling, frenzied mob fighting with each other for water or for a place at the window and ruthlessly trampling down the weak?'[35] Little focuses on the elements of Holwell's narrative which trouble his sense of national identity – the unmanly hysteria, the self-interested battle for survival – ignored by Curzon in his imperial retelling. A heroic version of events is offered in its place, a story suitable for a Britain at war, which 'presents to the British nation a band of heroes not unworthy to rank with those who turned at bay in the retreat from Mons, and those who held the trenches at Ypres or those who stormed the blood-stained heights of Gallipoli'.[36]

Of course there was more than one national identity at stake in the Black Hole story. Responding to Little's article, Professor E. F. Oaten reluctantly found inadequate evidence for the revision; reluctantly, because he regarded Holwell's account of the Black Hole as politically dangerous, and welcomed the prospect of a convincing and less inflammatory alternative:

> In approaching the mystery of the Black Hole I confess myself frankly prejudiced. I want to be able to disbelieve the story. ... For there are certain happenings of the past the mere memory of which brands and sears the sensitive places of our common human nature; history, too, places ... certain dreadful barriers between nations and races, which only time can remove. For this reason, I should regard any one who could prove that Holwell's Narrative is a tissue of lies as one of the truest servants of our Indian land; but for the same reason I would enter a caution against the subject being too frequently dragged to light, and made a topic of newspaper controversy in a land such as modern India, unless the cogency of the aggressive argument is indubitable, or new evidence can be adduced. It is emphatically not a matter for leading articles in newspapers, or for polemic letters from politicians and professors, however distinguished.[37]

This, then, is a narrative that the British could no longer tell (at least not publicly, where Indians might read it). Over-burdened with symbolic meaning for both the Indians and the British, the story of the Black Hole had become an ideological flash-point.

The explosion came during the next World War, in 1940. The nationalist leader, Subhas Chandra Bose, who opposed the British decision to involve India in the war, launched a *satyagraha*, or non-violent campaign, against the Black Hole monument. Writing in the nationalist journal *Forward Bloc*, he announced:

> The third July, 1940, is going to be observed in Bengal as Sirajuddowla Day – in honour of the last independent King of Bengal. The Holwell Monument is not merely an unwarranted stain on the memory of the Nawab, but has stood in the heart of Calcutta for the last 150 years or more as the symbol of our slavery and humiliation. That monument must now go.[38]

On the eve of the protest day, Bose was arrested, but the *satyagraha* went ahead. A Sirajuddowla Day meeting at Calcutta town hall passed several resolutions, including a call for the historians of Bengal 'to vindicate the ill-fated Nawab by giving a true account of his life and work', and a request that government universities and textbook committees 'see that all false accounts and mischievous statements relating to the unfortunate Nawab be deleted from all Text Books'.[39] These attacks on colonial historiography were accompanied by direct action. Over the following weeks, a steady stream of volunteers, some holding small hammers, advanced on the heavily guarded monument, only to be arrested by police. The nationalist press kept a running tally of the numbers of arrests, reaching 236 by mid-July, when a government order enforced a news black-out. On July 23 1940, however, the government capitulated: the Chief Minister of Bengal announced the removal of the monument.

Relocated in the churchyard of St John's, Calcutta, the monument now stands largely disregarded. But the obelisk is not the only memorial to Holwell's account, for the Black Hole returns to haunt the narratives of India in various forms. The horror tales of the 1857 Rebellion replay its claustrophobic carnage in the prison house at Cawnpore, and in the besieged Residency of Lucknow. Likewise, the nightmarish sand crater of the living dead in Kipling's story, 'The Strange Ride of Morrowbie Jukes', powerfully recalls the night of frenzied incarceration. More generally, black holes and prison cells are places of terror and torture for both Indian and British protagonists in a number of colonial and postcolonial novels: the Marabar caves in Forster's *Passage to India*, Hari Kumar's cell in Scott's *The Jewel in the Crown*, and Rushdie's Widows' Hostel in *Midnight's Children*. This primal scene of colonial terror is revisited, over and over again.

Contemporary historians, however, have little time for the Black Hole. The consensus seems to be that there was a mass imprisonment, but that the loss of life was relatively small-scale; the incident did not provoke an immediate British response, and it was no more than a fairly commonplace accident of war. So much for 'facts'. The study of the Black Hole reminds us forcibly that history is also narrative; that as Gayatri Spivak has noted, ' "events" are never not discursively constituted and that the language of historiography is always also language'.[40] In the case of the Black Hole, we could add that the language of historiography is also the language of national identity.

Notes

1 From Thomas Twining, *Travels in India A Hundred Years Ago*, ed. W. H. G. Twining (1893) quoted in Lord George Curzon, *British Government in India*, 2 vols. (London: Cassell, 1925), I, p. 172.

2 See Brijen K. Gupta, *Sirajuddaullah and the East India Company 1756–7* (Leiden: E. J. Brill, 1962), pp. 71–2 for an outline of the debate about the authenticity of the Black Hole story.

3 Natalie Zemon Davis, *Fiction in the Archives: Pardon Tales and their Tellers in Sixteenth-Century France* (Cambridge: Polity Press, 1987), p. 3.

4 John Zephaniah Holwell, *India Tracts*, 3rd edn. (London: T. Becket, 1774), title page; page numbers given in the chapter hereafter are taken from this edition. Epigraph from Virgil, *The Aeneid* II, 1. 5–8.

5 Virgil, *The Aeneid*, trans. W. F. Jackson Knight (Harmondsworth, Penguin, 1956), p. 51.

6 Mary Louise Pratt, *Imperial Eyes: Travel Writing and Transculturation* (London: Routledge, 1992), p. 87; see also Peter Hulme, *Colonial Encounters: Europe and the Native Caribbean 1492–1797* (London: Methuen, 1986; reprinted London: Routledge, 1992), pp. 228–9 on the alliance of sentimentality and travel literature.

7 For the voyeuristic elements in later nineteenth-century British accounts of *sati*, see Lata Mani, 'Cultural Theory, Colonial Texts: Reading Eyewitness Accounts of Widow Burning', in L. Grossberg, C. Nelson, P. Treichler (eds.), *Cultural Studies* (New York: Routledge, 1992), p. 400. For earlier European accounts of *sati*, see my book, *India Inscribed: European and British Writing on India 1600–1800* (Delhi: Oxford University Press, 1995), pp. 51–68.

8 Tea was to become an emblem of *Indian* suffering and exploitation in the rhetoric of Edmund Burke in his opening speech in the impeachment of Warren Hastings in 1788, see *The History of the Trial of Warren Hastings*, 5 parts (London, 1796), I, p. 8.

9 In G. A. Henty's 1884 rewriting of the Black Hole scene in his boys' adventure story, *With Clive in India, or the Beginnings of an Empire*, a greater sense of decorum is observed: the sweat-sodden shirt becomes a shawl drenched in water. The shawl belongs to Ada, a girl captive introduced for Henty's hero, Charlie, to protect (and finally marry). The feminised helplessness of Holwell's captives is displaced onto the weak, fainting Ada, whom Charlie valiantly tends throughout the night.

10 Pratt, *Imperial Eyes*, p. 87.

11 Edward Ives, *A Voyage from England to India* (London: Edward and Charles Dilly, 1773), p. 87.

12 Ives, *Voyage*, pp. 179–80.

13 Ives, *Voyage*, p. 87.

14 Article by M. J. Cotton, first printed in the *Pioneer*, January 20 1891; reprinted in *The Hindoo Patriot*, December 20 1902, p. 3.

15 Thomas Babington Macaulay, *Critical and Historical Essays*, 2 vols. (London: Dent, 1907), I, p. 505. Page numbers given in the chapter hereafter are taken from this edition.

16 *Asiatic Journal* III (1817), p. 104.

17 *Asiatic Journal* III (1817), p. 105.

18 Frantz Fanon, *The Wretched of the Earth*, trans. Constance Farrington (Harmondsworth: Penguin, 1963), p. 42.

19 *Hartly House, Calcutta* (London: Pluto Press, 1989), p. 62.

20 *Hartly House, Calcutta*, p. 219.

21 Fanon, *The Wretched of the Earth*, p. 30.

22 Homi Bhabha, *The Location of Culture* (London: Routledge, 1994), p. 44.

23 Robert Orme, *A New History of the Military Transactions of the British Nation in Indostan*, 2 vols. (London: John Nourse, 1763), I, p. 5.

24 Sara Suleri, *The Rhetoric of English India* (Chicago: University of Chicago Press, 1992), p. 3.

25 Macaulay, *Critical and Historical Essays*, p. 505.

26 Bhabha, *The Location of Culture*, pp. 97–8.

27 Dante, *Inferno*, Canto XXXIII, 1–90.

28 Suleri, *The Rhetoric of English India*, p. 53.

29 Sir John Horsford, *A Collection of Poems written in the East Indies* (Calcutta: Joseph Cooper, 1797), pp. 12–13.

30 Jenny Sharpe, *Allegories of Empire: The Figure of Woman in the Colonial Text* (Minneapolis: University of Minnesota Press, 1993), pp. 81, 85.

31 Curzon's speech, delivered at the unveiling of the Black Hole monument, quoted in Alok Ray (ed.), *Calcutta Keepsake* (Calcutta: RDDHI-India, 1978), p. 99.

32 Ray, *Calcutta Keepsake*, p. 99.

33 Ray, *Calcutta Keepsake*, pp. 101–02.

34 J. H. Little, 'The Black Hole – the Question of Holwell's Veracity', *Bengal Past and Present*, XI (1915), p. 76.

35 'The Black Hole: Full Proceedings of the Debate', *Bengal Past and Present*, XII (1916), p. 146.

36 Little, 'The Black Hole', *Bengal Past and Present*, XI (1915), p. 76.

37 'The Black Hole: Full Proceedings', *Bengal Past and Present*, XII (1916), p. 150.

38 Bose, Subhas Chandra, *Crossroads, being the Works of Subhas Chandra Bose, 1938–1940* (Calcutta: Netaji Research Bureau, 1962), p. 324.

39 *Amrita Bazar Patrika*, July 4 1940, p. 5.

40 Gayatri Chakravorty Spivak, 'A Literary Representation of the Subaltern: Mahasweta Devi's *Stanadayini*', *Subaltern Studies*, V (1987), p. 92.

Bibliography

Bhabha, Homi, *The Location of Culture* (London: Routledge, 1994).

'The Black Hole: Full Proceedings of the Debate', *Bengal Past and Present*, XII (1916), pp. 136–71.

Bose, Subhas Chandra, *Crossroads, being the Works of Subhas Chandra Bose, 1938–1940* (Calcutta: Netaji Research Bureau, 1962).

Curzon, Lord George, *British Government in India*, 2 vols. (London: Cassell, 1925).

Davis, Natalie Zemon, *Fiction in the Archives: Pardon Tales and their Tellers in Sixteenth-Century France* (Cambridge: Polity Press, 1987).

Fanon, Frantz, *The Wretched of the Earth*, trans. Constance Farrington (Harmondsworth: Penguin, 1963).

Gupta, Brijen K., *Sirajuddaullah and the East India Company 1756–7* (Leiden: E. J. Brill, 1962).

Hartly House, Calcutta (London: Pluto Press, 1989).

Henty, G. A., *With Clive in India, or the Beginnings of an Empire* (London: Blackie & Son, 1884).

The History of the Trial of Warren Hastings, 5 parts (London, 1796).

Holwell, John Zephaniah, *India Tracts*, 3rd edn. (London: T. Becket, 1774).

Horsford, Sir John, *A Collection of Poems written in the East Indies* (Calcutta: Joseph Cooper, 1797).

Hulme, Peter, *Colonial Encounters: Europe and the Native Caribbean 1492–1797* (1986; London: Routledge, 1992).

Ives, Edward, *A Voyage from England to India* (London: Edward and Charles Dilly, 1773).

Little, J. H., 'The Black Hole – the Question of Holwell's Veracity', *Bengal Past and Present*, XI (1915), pp. 75–104.

Macaulay, Thomas Babington, *Critical and Historical Essays*, 2 vols. (London: Dent, 1907).

Mani, Lata, 'Cultural Theory, Colonial Texts: Reading Eyewitness Accounts of Widow Burning', in L. Grossberg, C. Nelson, P. Treichler (eds.), *Cultural Studies* (New York: Routledge, 1992), pp. 392–408.

Orme, Robert, *A New History of the Military Transactions of the British Nation in Indostan*, 2 vols. (London: John Nourse, 1763).

Pratt, Mary Louise, *Imperial Eyes: Travel Writing and Transculturation* (London: Routledge, 1992).

Ray, Alok, *Calcutta Keepsake* (Calcutta: RDDHI-India, 1978).

Sharpe, Jenny, *Allegories of Empire: The Figure of Woman in the Colonial Text* (Minneapolis: University of Minnesota Press, 1993).

Spivak, Gayatri Chakravorty, 'A Literary Representation of the Subaltern: Mahasweta Devi's *Stanadayini*', *Subaltern Studies*, V (1987), pp. 91–134.

Suleri, Sara, *The Rhetoric of English India* (Chicago: University of Chicago Press, 1992).

Teltscher, Kate, *India Inscribed: European and British Writing on India, 1600–1800* (Delhi: Oxford University Press, 1995).

Virgil, *The Aeneid*, trans. W. F. Jackson Knight (Harmondsworth: Penguin, 1956).

2

Towards an Anglo-Indian poetry? The colonial muse in the writings of John Leyden, Thomas Medwin and Charles D'Oyly

NIGEL LEASK

This essay sets out to explore the question of whether it is possible to discern, in the writings of early nineteenth-century British poets writing in the Indian subcontinent, the lineaments of a distinctively Anglo-Indian poetry. The recent spate of interest in romantic orientalism has by now confirmed (although not without a note of caution) Raymond Schwab's suggestion that European romanticism – and poetry in particular – was strongly influenced by the 'oriental renaissance' instigated by Sir William Jones and the scholars of the Asiatic Society of Bengal and its cognate institutions in Asia and Europe.[1] In his influential *Essay on the Poetry of the Eastern Nations*, Jones had recommended that emulation of the metaphorical naturalism and expressive power of Asian poetry might rejuvenate the stale conventions of European neoclassicism; 'we should be furnished with a new set of images and similitudes; and a number of excellent compositions would be brought to light, which future scholars might explain, and future poets might imitate'.[2] Jones sought to implement this desideratum in his translations from Sanskrit and Persian poetry and drama, as well as in the nine *Hindu Hymns* which he began to publish in the *Asiatic Miscellany* in 1785. The importance of Jones's work for metropolitan romanticism has been thoroughly studied by Schwab, Garland Cannon and other recent scholars.[3] But despite this critical interest in the relationship between literature and imperialism in the metropolitan culture of the early nineteenth century, little attention has been paid to the phenomenon of *Anglo-Indian* literature in the romantic period. The present essay sets out to redress this deficiency (and in so doing, to question a commonly-held belief that Anglo-Indian poetry begins with Kipling) by surveying the work of three Anglo-Indian poets in the 1800–1830 period.

Any perceptive student of late-eighteenth-century English literature will be aware that Anglo-Indians occupied quite a distinctive niche in the literature of this period. In the novels, and particularly the plays, of these years, as well as in the powerful impeachment rhetoric of Edmund Burke and R. B. Sheridan, Anglo-Indians were commonly represented in a negative light as vulgar 'nouveaux-riches', returning home laden with dubiously-acquired wealth to threaten the stability and moral probity of British society. But not all Anglo-Indians were money-grubbing *arrivistes*, 'Nabobs' on the make, or reformed rakes like William Hickey.[4] Victor Jacquemont, a French visitor to Calcutta in the late 1820s, admitted that 'people do not come here to live, and enjoy life; they come ... in order to gain something to enjoy life elsewhere'. But having paid lip-service to this customary view of the Anglo-Indians, he was forced to admit that there was also a burgeoning cultural life in the principal cities of British India, somewhat akin to the provincial centres of Britain and Europe: 'for a truly small number of Europeans, there are journals without number, both political and literary; there are learned societies ... of every determination – craniological, phrenological, horticultural, literary, medical, Wernerian, and I know not how many besides'.[5] The richness and strangeness of India may have induced an experience of sublime vertigo in the colonising mind,[6] but it also provided an intellectual challenge and a stimulus to European artists and poets seeking a diversion from the tedium of military, civil or commercial life.

Jacquemont's remarks on this small but thriving colonial literari are born out by journals like *The Asiatic Miscellany*, *The Asiatic Journal* and the *Calcutta Journal*, packed with occasional pieces by aspiring amateur poets eager to show off their imitations of the latest metropolitan models, but also to express their sense of the idiosyncracies and ennui of colonial life. This body of poetry is the product of British soldiers, civil servants and lawyers writing in their spare time (few women writers are in evidence before 1830), a fact which is often reflected in its poor literary quality. For this reason, it has proved of more interest to historians than literary critics, only significant inasmuch as it offers a documentary record of the social life of early British India. Considerably more attention has been directed to Anglo-Indian painters of the same period (although more to professionals like

William Hodges, the Daniells and Henry Salt than to the much larger body of amateur draftsmen and watercolourists), and the 'Indian Picturesque' is by now an established sub-genre of nineteenth-century Art History. Given the reluctance of academic criticism to address the problem of amateur literature, it is perhaps unsurprising that scholars of orientalist poetry have ignored the Anglo-Indians and chosen rather to dwell upon home-based professionals writing about India, romantic poets like Thomas Beddoes, Robert Southey, Percy Shelley and Tom Moore. Whilst there is no denying that much early Anglo-Indian poetry *is* highly derivative, it is worth noting that amateur poetry tends to be so by definition, lacking the confidence to rethink style and genre even when it seeks to adapt conventions to particular social or cultural milieux.

Outlining a distinctive tradition of early nineteenth-century Anglo-Indian poetry might be easier if it were possible to argue that it was inaugurated by the poetry of Jones himself. As a British poet actually working in the colonial 'contact zone'[7] Jones clearly has something in common with the Anglo-Indian poets I will be discussing in this essay. Moreover, Jones was technically-speaking an amateur poet insofar as he was by profession a lawyer and linguist rather than a poet. And yet, as Javed Majeed has pointed out, because Jones's Indian poetry (particularly the *Hindu Hymns*) was largely concerned with exploring the cultural syncretism outlined in his essay *On the Gods of Greece, Italy and India*, and was as such part of his larger project of legitimising British rule in an Indian idiom, it is remarkably different in theme and style from the amateur Anglo-Indian poetry which followed it.[8] There is a strongly public, neo-Augustan quality to Jones's poetry which marks it out as participating in his overall scholarly and legislative programme. Jones tends to substitute Hindu mythological machinery for the neoclassical pantheon which had long dominated European poetry, without significantly transforming poetic style and diction. Whilst there is no denying that the *Hindu Hymns* represent an important link between the neoclassical Pindaric Ode and the romantic great ode (Jerome McGann opens his recent anthology of *Romantic Period Verse* with the 'Hymn to Na'ra'yena'),[9] it is also the case that they are far removed from the subjectivist idiom of sensibility which was beginning to hold sway in the metropolis, and which would provide the dominant literary model for Anglo-Indian romantic poets.

Just as the European picturesque style, with its sedate, melancholy representation of Indian landscape, dominated painting in India throughout the romantic period,[10] the subjective emphasis and abject tone of the sensibility idiom dominated Anglo-Indian poetry of the same period. Mary Louise Pratt has argued that in both travel writing and imaginative literature sensibility 'consolidated itself quite suddenly in the 1780s and 1790s' as the 'domestic subject of empire found itself enjoined to share new passions, to identify with expansion in a new way, through empathy with individual victim-heroes and heroines'.[11] As the present essay will show, the Anglo-Indian poetry of sensibility, which loosely coincided with the 'orientalist' phase of colonial rule, began to lose ground after about 1820 to anti-orientalist burlesque modelled on the satirical style of Pope, Butler and (most significantly) Byron's *Don Juan*. This raises the important question as to whether Anglo-Indian poetry, by nature of its geopolitical self-consciousness, is distinguishable from the changing styles of metropolitan poetry which provided it with its dominant models. Put in more polemical fashion, this is tantamount to asking whether it can be said to participate in what Sara Suleri describes as the 'rhetoric of British India' which 'breaks down the dividing lines between domination and subordination'.[12] If such a thesis is to be sustained, it must be shown firstly that Anglo-Indian poetry revised metropolitan styles in response to its colonial context, and secondly that it was in some significant way influenced by Asian poetry in a manner which distinguished it from 'orientalist' poetry written in metropolitan Britain.

To take the second question first. We have already noted Jones's exhortation to European poets to imitate oriental style and imagery, and there is no doubt that the practice of translation from Persian, Sanskrit and indigenous Indian poetry was a familiar exercise for both Anglo-Indian and European poets of the period.[13] However, it is also the case that the translation of Asian poetry into English (like the 'translation' of Celtic or medieval poetry by James Macpherson or Thomas Percy) mediated 'primitive' poetic discourse in terms of contemporary eighteenth-century literary conventions, and Jones himself was no exception to this rule. For this reason, one has to look hard for the direct influence of Asian poetic styles upon Anglo-Indian poetry, other than those which had already been encoded within the metropolitan discourse of the primitive or the exotic. In considering what was *different* about Anglo-Indian poetry, it thus becomes necessary to distinguish influence at the formal level of style and expression (probably negligible, despite the frequency of poetic translations) from the manner in which metropolitan conventions were inflected by the colonial context. In the analogous field of painting, this might be linked to the question of the impact of the topographical tradition of representation upon picturesque conventions. In the 'sister art' of poetry, the colonial context signifies at the level of a rhetoric of evocation known in artistic parlance as 'costume', 'the manner, dress, arms, furniture, and other features proper to the time and locality in which the scene is laid'.[14] In the case of Anglo-Indian poetry, as we shall see, this resulted in the re-inflection of the plots and settings (but not the distinctive mood) of sensibility and satirical poetry in terms of the colonial context, and particularly the ethnographic imperative which loaded the familiar poetic vehicle with indigenous words and 'costume' unfamiliar to a metropolitan readership.

It is perhaps ironic that no Anglo-Indian poet dared emulate the manner and style of Indian poetry with the boldness of Robert Southey in his Hindu epic of 1810 *The Curse of Kehama*, a poem which was severely censured by critics for abolishing the cordon sanitaire between European aesthetic proportions and the oriental 'grotesque' style. The fact that Southey (just as much as his fellow-Laker Wordsworth) was a professional poet seeking to experiment with Sir William Jones's desideratum about imitating the 'poetry of the Eastern Nations', whereas the Anglo-Indian poets I will be discussing were amateurs satisfied with successful imitation of current European models, goes a long way to explaining the paradox. Nevertheless it would be misleading to argue that Anglo-Indian poets were simply oblivious to the Indian context in which they were writing because of their anxiety successfully to emulate metropolitan models. Like the amateur picturesque water-colours and sketches produced in such profusion in early British India, magazine and coterie poetry wasn't simply an occasion for amateur poets to show off their mastery of the latest European styles. The subjects which they chose to address in their amateur poetry reflected their sense of the distinctiveness of life in British India. Moreover, in the field of poetry (if not in painting) the restraints of convention could be enabling as well as restricting in representing cultural encounter. The in-built concern of the poetry of sensibility with intersubjectivity, with bridging the 'artificial' divisions of gender, class and race, as well as its focus on private and domestic emotions, provided aspiring literati with a literary framework for expressing the concerns of life in an alien cultural context. As in the case of painting, the representation of native peoples and of an exotic 'costume' without exact precedent in the European artistic tradition gave a distinctive ethnographic flavour to much Anglo-Indian poetry which differentiated it from the often-generalised orientalism of European romanticism. At the same time, the emphasis on alienation and loss characteristic of sensibility plotted the colonial encounter as an experience of frustrated desire and unhappy romance.

For John Leyden (1775–1810), Thomas Medwin (1778–1869) and Charles D'Oyly (1781–1845) poetry was not, therefore, as it had been for Jones, a vehicle for legitimising British rule in an indigenous idiom, but rather a mode of representing the poignancies or absurdities of quotidien life in colonial society. As we will see, the melancholy scene of exile and alienation which suffuses the poetry of Leyden and Medwin adapts the literary conventions of sensibility to the colonial context. In the shift from sensibility to high romanticism marked in the transition from Leyden to Medwin, longing for loved ones left at home is displaced onto an eroticised Indian woman; in the typical plot, although the love is reciprocated, it inevitably fails and is translated into the idiom of bereavement. Cultural encounter is thus represented in the feminised terms of the private passions rather than the heroic register of imperial reason. Even when Medwin ranges over conventional male topics such as hunting and war, he is evidently more absorbed by the alienated sensibilities of his heroes and heroines, the erotics rather than the politics of the colonial situation. By 1820, however, a change is perceptible. In tandem with the ideological assault on orientalism signalled by works like James Mill's *History of British India* (1817), the romance plot gives way to a burlesque vision which begins to replace transcultural desire with racial disdain, although European orientalism is often just as much the satirical target as Indian characters and customs.

The three poets upon whom I will focus were amateurs with connections to more celebrated artistic and literary circles in Europe, particularly Leyden (friend of Walter Scott) and Thomas Medwin (cousin of Percy Shelley and later author of the scandalous *Conversations of Lord Byron*). Of the three writers, Leyden is the best known; an established minor poet before arriving in

India in 1802, his Chair of Hindostani at Fort William College and his fellowship of Jones's Asiatic Society of Bengal, as well as his philological contributions to the journal *Asiatick Researches*, made him a well-known figure both in scholarly and literary circles. As far as I know, Medwin's Indian poetry has never been mentioned by any student of either romantic or Anglo-Indian literature, despite the fact that it was 'proof-read' and corrected by Percy Shelley in 1820. D'Oyly, better known as a 'gentleman painter' (to quote Bishop Heber's description)[15] and illustrator of the popular *Indian Field Sports* (1829), has only occasionally been footnoted in his role as poet. There may be some justice in the *Dictionary of National Biography*'s judgement that D'Oyly's (illustrated) burlesque *Tom Raw the Griffin* 'is more meritorious from an artistic than from a literary point of view'.[16] Nevertheless, like Medwin's 'Julian and Gizele', it does offer us a particularly rich account both of conflicting orientalist and anti-orientalist mentalities in early-nineteenth-century British India, as well as the continuing influence of metropolitan literary models (in this case, Byron's *Don Juan*) on amateur poets after 1820.

Anglo-Indian romanticism: John Leyden and Thomas Medwin

Dr John Leyden, the rough-spoken son of a Border shepherd, educated at Edinburgh University (a breeding ground for orientalists like Alexander Hamilton, James Mackintosh, Alexander Murray, Mountstuart Elphinstone and Vans Kennedy),[17] might be designated the first significant Anglo-Indian poet after Jones. Before his departure for India in 1802, Leyden had shown his formidable talents as a polyglot by contributing poetry translated from Norse, Hebrew, Aramaic and Persian to the *Edinburgh Magazine*. He had also contributed a Gothic ballad to Matthew Lewis's *Tales of Wonder* (1801) and assisted Walter Scott in his folkloristic inquiries in preparing *The Minstrelsy of the Scottish Borders*; the essay on 'The Fairies of Popular Superstition' in that volume is Leyden's work. His major poetic achievement was a long philosophical effusion entitled *Scenes of Infancy: Descriptive of Teviotdale* (1802), modelled on the work of another Border poet, James Thomson's *The Seasons*. Notwithstanding its parochial title, *Scenes of Infancy* reveals the mixture of cosmopolitanism and colonialism which permeated contemporary Scots

culture. Leyden's Tory populism is evident in his celebration of
the stalwart Border peasantry fighting 'unconquer'd Gallic legions
on the Nile' in Abercromby's army.[18] Despite the sentimental
celebration of his native Teviotdale, a sinister Miltonic trope of
exoticism is already evident in a poem written before Leyden's
own departure on colonial service:

> Land of my father! – though no mangrove here
> O'er the blue streams her flexile branches rear,
> Nor scaly palm her finger'd scions shoot,
> Nor luscious guava wave her yellow fruit,
> Nor golden apples glimmer from the tree –
> Land of dark heaths and mountains! thou art free! (PR: 374)

Leyden's linguistic, ethnographical and literary interests were
powerfully stimulated by his arrival in India, particularly as he
was quickly appointed as surgeon to Colonel Mackenzie's survey
of the Company's newly acquired territories of Mysore and Coorg.
In a letter home written in the early 1800s, he described his
romantic adventures (marred only by the obligatory liver complaint) in Coorg and Malabar, which he likened to the Scottish
highlands: 'you would undoubtedly imagine I wanted to impose
on you were I to relate what I have seen and passed through.
No! I certainly shall never repent of having come to India. It has
awakened energies in me that I scarcely imagined I possessed,
though I could gnaw my living nails with pure vexation, to think
how much I have been thwarted by indisposition' (PR: xli).
Leyden's perceptions of India are marked by constant cultural
comparisons with his native Scotland; for example, revealing a
Border shepherd's disdain for the urbanised Englishman, Leyden
lavished 'a mountaineers ... approbation' upon the 'frank, open
and bold demeanour' of the Tamil natives, which he contrasted
with the 'mean and cringing aspect of all the native Hindoos'
(PR: xli). His training as an antiquarian came in useful in
deciphering ancient Canara inscriptions at Mahabalipuram, and
his interest in folklore found boundless scope in the rich cultural
melting-pot of Southern India. Leyden's tour of Mysore retraced
the symbolic itinerary of a Highland tour undertaken shortly
before his departure from Scotland in search of Ossianic fragments, its ethnographic concerns writ large in the exotic Asiatic
setting. However, his muse was still largely directed towards his
native Scotland. In a well-known anecdote, Sir John Malcolm
borrowed Leyden's copy of *Scenes of Infancy* and returned it
with the following lines pencilled in the margins:

> Thy muse, O Leyden, seeks no foreign clime,
> For deeds of fame, to twine her brow with bays,
> But finds at home whereon to build her rhyme,
> And patriot virtues sings in patriot lays ...

Leyden entered the poetic contest by returning the following lines to Malcolm, in which he stressed the patriotic function of sentimental memories of home in cementing the homosocial bonds of Anglo-Indian identity:

> Soft as I traced each woodland green,
> I sketched its charms with parting hand;
> That memory might each fairy scene
> Revive within this Eastern land.[19]

This is evident in the poetry he began writing shortly after arriving in India, in which Indian landscapes often figure as palimpsests for his native hills. Although stylistically influenced by the lyrical poetry of sensibility associated at home with the names of Robert Burns, Charlotte Smith and William Bowles, Leyden's verses show a recurrent sense of their Indian context. Conventional modes of sensibility are re-inflected by Leyden's sense of location, as in his rewriting of Burns' 'Ae fond Kiss' in 'To Aurelia' (1802) in which the languishing lovers are condemned 'to pine on India's shore', or the melancholy 'Ode on Leaving Velore' (1804), in which the Indian landscape is suffused with memories of departed youth in Teviotdale (PR: 140, 159). The patriotism which Sir John Malcolm applauded in *Scenes of Infancy* is at times, however, interestingly combined with a critique of colonialism often associated with the literature of sensibility. In 'Ode to an Indian Gold Coin, written in Cherical, Malabar' Leyden's sentimental nostalgia for home is combined with an indictment of imperialist greed worthy of the attack on British rapacity in India contained in his friend and fellow-Scot Henry Mackenzie's sentimental novel *The Man of Feeling* (1771); 'when shall I see a commander return from India in the pride of honourable poverty?'.[20] Here the exotic landscape is suddenly alienating, returning to the 'satanic' exotic of *Scenes of Infancy*. The poem's characterisation of the coin as a 'vile yellow slave' is particularly significant, as the wealth expropriated by colonialism is stigmatised by its metaphorical association with racial inferiority and chattel-slavery. Leyden has reified his own bondage to imperial service into the acquisitive urge, displacing it onto the coin, which is then figuratively blamed for having sundered him from the pleasures of virtuous and enamoured youth:

By Cherical's dark wandering streams,
Where cane-tufts shadow all the wild,
Sweet visions haunt my waking dreams.
Of Teviot lov'd while still a child,
Of castl'd rocks stupendous pil'd
By Esk or Eden's classic wave,
Where loves of youth and friendship smil'd,
Uncurs'd by thee, vile yellow slave!

... For thee, for thee, vile yellow slave,
I left a heart that lov'd me true
I cross'd the tedious ocean-wave,
    To roam in climes unkind and new.   (PR: 163)

Although in his short career in India Leyden also penned the statutory translations from the Persian poets Hafiz, Sadi and Anwari, as well as patriotic occasional pieces like 'The Battle of Assaye' (1803) and 'Verses on the Death of Nelson' (1809), his best (and best-known) Indian poem is the 1803 'Song of the Telinga Dancing Girl. Addressed to an European Gentleman, in the Company of Some European Ladies'. It is a short poem, and deserves quotation in full:

Dear youth, whose features bland declare
A milder clime than India's air,
These ardent glances hither turn!
For thee, for thee alone, I burn.

Ah! if these kindling eyes could see
No dearer beauty here than me,
I vow by this impassion'd sigh,
For thee, for thee, would Rad'ha die!

Ah me! wher'er I turn my view,
Bright rivals rise of fairer hue,
Whose charms a milder sun declare –
Ah! Rad'ha yields to sad despair.   (PR: 155)

The poem represents a specular displacement of desire common in the poetry of sensibility. Its thematic of frustrated female longing appears to allude to Alexander Pope's *Eloisa to Abelard*. (Pope was one of Leyden's favourite English poets, as is evident from the frequent Popean touches in his poems).[21] If Abelard's 'coldness' is a result of his castration, Rad'ha's European love-object is cold rather because of his race and the fact that he is 'protected' by European women. Rad'ha's futile 'burning' picks up on Eloisa's; 'Ev'n thou [i.e. Abelard] are cold – yet Eloisa loves. / Ah hopeless, lasting flames! like those that burn / To light the dead, and warm th'unfruitful urn'.[22] Pope's metaphors of heat and cold are given new significance by the poem's Asian context, where, linked to the commonly-held Enlightenment notion of the climatic determination of cultural characteristics, there is a suggestion that 'natural' ethnic or racial qualities prevent the reciprocation of Rad'ha's desire.

And yet there is a sense in which the poem contradicts this ideological burden; the European disavowal of desire for the native woman is complicated by the narcissistic male fantasy of drawing the gaze of the Other. Miscegenation was of course fairly commonplace in early colonial India, although (as the poem implies) the advent of increasing numbers of European women began to work against a feared 'creolisation' of European men. The screen of fair, mild European women who shelter Rah'da's love-object render her desire transgressive and enforce distinctions of race and character, preventing Rah'da from soliciting his gaze. In her remarks on the role of the courtesan in Anglo-Indian literature, Sara Suleri quotes a diary entry by one 'Mrs Sherwood': 'The influence of these nautch-girls over the other sex, even over men who have been brought up in England, is not to be accounted for ... all these Englishmen ... had had mothers at home etc etc'.[23] Leyden's treatment of the subject is in marked contrast to Suleri's Anglo-Indian women writers, except insofar as the poem can be read as a warning to European wives, fiancées and mothers. The withheld European male gaze of Leyden's poem is reinstateable from the point of view of a reading which *enjoys* the desire of the Telinga girl. However the poem is read, its thematisation of race and sexuality are far more unstable than in some later colonial representations of transcultural desire. Compare it for example with Rider Haggard's description of the African girl Foulata's love for the Englishman Goode near the end of *King Solomon's Mines*: 'I love him ... and am glad to die because I know that he cannot cumber his life with such as I am, for the sun may not mate with the moon, nor the white with the black'.[24] In contrast to Leyden, Rider Haggard places the sentence of prohibition in the mouth of the desiring woman herself, in allowing it to kill off and proscribe her desire for the white man.

The study of languages soon usurped the place of poetry in Leyden's Indian career, particularly after his election to the prestigious chair of Hindostani at Fort William College in 1807. In 1808 he published a *Dissertation on the Languages and Literature of the Indo-Chinese Nations* in the *Asiatick Researches*,[25] as well as working on a history of the Moghul Emperor Baber, which was published posthumously in 1826. In the course of adding Sanskrit, Pali, Prakrit, Urdu, Hindi, Tamil, Teluga, Canarese, Malayalma and Malay to his already impressive repertoire of languages, Leyden complained that 'We are here in the peninsula exactly in the situation of the revivers of literature in Europe, and likewise exposed to the same difficulties in respect of the incorrectness of MSS, the inaccuracy of teachers, and the obstacles that must be encountered in procuring either'.[26] Leyden clearly perceived the collation and revival of Indian classical literature as analogous to the labours of European antiquarians and folklorists like James Macpherson, Thomas Percy and Sir Walter Scott, piecing together fragmented traditions and recovering a genealogy for modern literature. His view of this scholarly enterprise as a heroic vocation is particularly appropriate in the light of his premature death in 1811; having accompanied Lord Minto's military expedition to Java as official philologer, he died of a 'poisonous sickness' after searching through a captured Dutch library basement in Batavia in search of rare oriental manuscripts. Tributes poured in from his literary compatriots like Sir John Malcolm and Sir Walter Scott, and James Hogg, 'the Ettrick Shepherd', penned an epitaph alluding to several of Leyden's poems:

> Sad were those strains when hymned afar
> On the green vales of Malabar,
> O'er seas beneath the golden morn,
> They travell'd on the monsoon borne
> Thrilling the heart of the Indian maid
> Beneath the wild banana's shade –
> Leyden! a shepherd wails thy fate,
> And Scotland knows her loss too late.[27]

The Indian writings of Thomas Medwin exhibit many features in common with Leyden's orientalism, although their account of colonial disappointment and exile is now filtered through a Byronic and Shelleyan '*Weltschmerz*' shorn of the patriotic tones of some of Leyden's poetry. The Anglo-Indian poet is now much less sure of where home is, and tends to hover in a condition of liminal anxiety, having displaced his affections onto an indigenous woman whose possession always evades him. This sense of alienation is evident in a fragment of Medwin's journal published in *The Angler in Wales* in 1834, written whilst his regiment, the 24th Light Dragoons, was stationed at Boorwa

Sangar in 1817. A self-hating 'Julian' (the Shelleyan pseudonym adopted by Medwin in his semi-fictionalised account of his Indian adventures in *The Angler*) is afflicted by a Byronic sense of remorse whilst contemplating the fragility of British power in India. As he ruminates upon a well-tended garden of English plants in the dusty cantonment, he writes:

> We are exotics in the animal, as many of [the English flowers] are in the vegetable kingdom, ... [I] sighed and exulted over the concluding paragraph from Gibbon, whilst speaking of the overthrowal of the Moghul Empire 'Since the reign of Aurungzebe, their empire has been dissolved – their treasures of Delhi rifled by a Persian robber, and the riches of their kingdom are now possessed by a company of Christian merchants, of a remote isle in the *Northern* ocean.' The train of thought gendered by the recollection of this remarkable sentence, threw a gloom over my mind.[28]

The self-denominated 'exotic' Julian/Medwin was maybe *entitled* to a genuine sense of remorse. He had recently seen action in the Pindari wars with Lord Hastings' grand army, participating in the siege and bombardment of Hathras by seventy-one mortars and howitzers and thirty-four 18 and 24-pounder battering guns, a military siege-technology greater than any yet deployed in the subcontinent. The defeat of the Pindaris and their Maratha allies in 1817–18 effectively destroyed the last organised resistance to British hegemony in the Indian subcontinent, although one looks in vain in Medwin's poetry for the jingoism evident in Leyden's 'Battle of Assaye' (concerning an earlier Maratha war) or 'Verses on the Death of Nelson'. Julian's autobiographical narrative in *The Angler in Wales* provides the framework for the poem 'Julian and Gizele': the unlikely setting probably explains why Medwin's best Indian poem has gone unnoticed.

In the course of his sojourn in India, Julian finds a means of easing his shell-shocked colonial conscience, temporarily relieving himself of his corrosive guilt by falling in love with a young Hindu woman whom he rescues from death by *sati* on the banks of the Sutlej river. Medwin's representation of *sati* here is a recurrent theme in early-nineteenth-century British writing about India, a practice which, as Gayatri Spivak and Lata Mani have shown, was a major thorn in the side of British orientalist policy. Spivak writes of the British obsession with *sati* that it is a case of 'White men ... saving brown women from brown men ... The protection of women ... becomes a signifier for the establishment of a *good* society, which must ... transgress mere legality'.[29] It is perhaps significant that whereas Leyden's poetic persona finds his desire being solicited by the Telinga dancing girl (whose accomplishment 'allows her a greater intellectual and erotic liberty than the Englishwoman could hope for'),[30] Medwin's is now represented as the rescuer and protector of the native woman. Julian's 'Gizele' becomes devoted to her English rescuer: 'she tended me during the days and nights of howling, and would allow no doctor to approach me, and with the healing medicine of her spirit charmed away the fiend that preyed on me. But she died ... After her death I became a Manichaean, and supposed the world governed by some malignant genius' (*Angler* II: 83). Loss, bereavement, exile and the failure of transcultural desire are the leitmotifs of Medwin's Indian poems. Notwithstanding a brief respite from this misery induced by his reading of Shelley's hope-inducing *The Revolt of Islam*, Julian remains possessed by the blue devils, and he begins to take instruction from a Guru at Benares, before his disconsolate return to England, a broken man. In the absence of any detailed contemporary evidence, we will never know the extent to which Julian's experiences in India corresponded with Medwin's, although Medwin was so obsessed by this tragic narrative that he worked and reworked it in different forms over the next thirty years.

Like many Indian army officers in the 1810s, Medwin was a learned orientalist, as is evident from his articles (in French) on the Ellora temple-carvings published in the Genevan journal *Bibliothèque Universelle* in April and September 1821. In contrast to Leyden, however, it was not as a 'reviver of oriental learning' but rather as an amateur poet of contemporary British India that Medwin would make his début in the literary world. His first poetic offering seems to have been a mock-heroic poem entitled 'Schacchia-Macchia; or, a Game at Chess', serialised in the poetry section of the *Asiatic Journal* between March and June 1818. This was a bravura piece poeticising the rules of chess, based on Pope's mock-heroic treatment of the game of ombre in *The Rape of the Lock*: as such it is of little significance to the development of Anglo-Indian poetry. Around about 1818, however, a number of imitations of Byron's *Eastern Tales* and Moore's *Lalla Rookh* begin to appear in the journals, such as Hamilton Sydney Beresford's 'The Warrior Prophet', and James Atkinson's 'The Aubid; an Eastern Tale', both published in the *Asiatic Journal* in October and November 1818. Medwin was quick to

adapt his poetic talents to the new fashion, and went on to produce the most successful poetic treatments of colonial life in India
in sustained narrative style, primarily inspired by the works of
Byron and Shelley. His 1821 collection *Sketches from Hindostan*
reworked the earlier *Oswald and Edwin: an Oriental Sketch*
(February 1820) in its opening poem 'The Lion Hunt', and its
principle offering 'The Pindarees' germinated from section xxiii
of the 1820 poem. Both these earlier works were corrected and
edited by Shelley himself, who thought the 1820 poem (not, I
think, without a note of disdain) was 'highly fit for popularity,
considered in its subject; there being a strong demand in the
imagination of our contemporaries for the scenery & situations
which you have studied. I admire equally the richness & variety
of the imagery with the ease & profusion of language in which
it is expressed'.[31] Shelley was, however, worried by the obtrusion
of unfamiliar Indian words and 'costume' into Medwin's verse.
Disregarding his cousin's scruples, Medwin went on to extend
and elaborate 'The Pindarees' into 'Julian and Gizele', published
with copious notes in the *Angler in Wales* in 1834. Finally,
Julian's tragic love-story was reworked one last time as a
magazine piece with a farcical turn entitled *A Bengal Yarn* in
1842.[32]

Despite their appearance of being mere pastiche versions of
Byron's *Eastern Tales*, appropriating Byron's verse couplets as
well as elements of character and narrative, Medwin's Indian
poems are also strongly influenced by the poetry of Shelley,
especially in the manner in which they adapt the male and female
protagonists of *Alastor, The Revolt of Islam* and *Prometheus
Unbound* to their author's own experience of India. The character
of Edwin in 'The Lion Hunt' is evidently based on a version of
the *Alastor* 'poet-protagonist', and Medwin's epigraph cites lines
429–30 of Shelley's poem: 'He sought in Nature's dearest haunt
some banks, / Her cradle and his sepulchre'. The poem's ostensible theme, its exploration of doomed male friendship between
the lion-hunters Edwin and Oswald, collapses under the strain
of its evidently greater fascination with the 'hybrid' character
of Oswald. If Edwin is like the visionary wanderer of 'Alastor',
Oswald is closer to Byron's Giaour or Conrad the Corsair: 'But
on his brow a cloud of mystery hung, / ... And in his very smile
you might detect / A sneer, for those he knew not to respect'.
Like Byron's protagonist Alp in 'The Siege of Corinth', Oswald
has 'gone native' in religion and manners:

Though Christian born, he followed Brahma's laws;
His faith ascribed to many a various cause.
And Oswald practised strictest abstinence;
The Yoga's [sic] life – without the priest's pretence.[33]

The narrator tells of speculation amongst the British community as to the cause of Oswald's 'conversion' to Hinduism – he is considered to be either a dedicated Sanskritist (like Colonel Pollier of the East India Company, the first European to succeed in collecting copies of all four Vedas), seeking to 'cheat the Brahmins of their Veda lore', or, in anticipation of Kipling's *Kim*, a political spy involved in the 'great game of Asia'.[34] But consensus has it that the cause of his 'strange apostacy' is his love for Seta, a high-caste Hindu girl, an affair which is downplayed in a hunting poem concerned with male friendship. Medwin's poem recalls itself to the matter in hand – the hunt – and to the fate of Edwin rather than the more compelling character of Oswald, returning to the task of bringing the lion to bay. It ends rather abruptly with Edwin being himself eaten by his quarry (apparently an essential element of Anglo-Indian sporting narratives), and Oswald's morbid reflections on bereavement.

The central theme of Oswald and Seta is developed in the second part of 'The Pindarees', which followed it in the 1821 volume. Seta's village is raided by the Pindaris, and Oswald (like Medwin a cavalry officer), sets off on a retaliatory raid, despite Seta's exhortations that he should not go. The Pindaris are defeated and suffer heavy losses, and Seta's brother Singha, one of Oswald's sepoys, is killed in the fighting. News gets back to Seta that Oswald has perished as well as Singha, and she dies of a broken heart. When Oswald returns, 'an empty urn is all that fills his arms' and he gradually pines away: 'the store that fed the lamp, diminished more and more; / Till in the socket glimmering, it but threw / On the dark future a despairing hue'.[35] The poem as a whole is indebted to Byron's *Corsair*, its description of Zalim's Pindari band a pastiche of Conrad's pirate band (exchanging Levantine for Indian 'costume'), and Seta's exhortations and tragic death being closely based on the story of Conrad and Medora.

But the character of Oswald now owes more to Shelley than to Byron, in particular to the protagonist of *Alastor*. Medwin's poem seems to illustrate the dictum of the Preface to *Alastor*, to the effect that, 'that Power which strikes the luminaries of the world with sudden darkness and extinction, by awakening them to too exquisite a perception of its influences, dooms to a slow and poisonous decay those meaner spirits that dare to abjure its dominion'. Referring to Oswald's bereavement and alienation, Medwin asks 'Who that has owned in all their thrilling force / Would seek an unendearing intercourse / With those, who make of life a cold pursuit; / And laugh at passions in their bosoms mute?' [36] By concentrating upon the sympathetic rather than the critical element of Shelley's treatment of his protagonist, Medwin represents the imperialist project (symbolised by the uncertain and ephemeral 'possession' of Seta) as a heroic vocation for which the price to be paid is alienation from kith and kin, and even a form of hybridity or semi-absorption in the Other. Alienation and absorption on the imperial frontier have replaced the sentimental homesickness of Leyden's poems. In 'The Lion Hunt', the Briton who has stayed at home is possessed of 'A brain of figures and a heart of ice; / With microscopic eyes to grope his way, / And scales of gold his every thought to weigh'.[37] In this new Anglo-Indian disdain for the sedentary and home-bound, we see before our eyes the transmutation of the romantic visionary quest poem into the nineteenth-century epic of empire, as romantic idealism becomes imperial heroism.

In his reincarnation as Julian in *The Angler in Wales*, the 'Byronic' Oswald of 'The Lion Hunt' has undergone a further shift in the direction of Shelley (the very name evokes Shelley's self-dramatisation in his poem 'Julian and Maddalo'). Julian retains Oswald's 'hybrid' character; as his interlocuter Stanley remarks 'I found my old friend a person neither English nor Indian, Christian nor Hindu' (*Angler* I: 51). Forced to return to England for his health's sake, he cannot settle, denying that Britain is any longer his native country and expostulating 'Call it exile – call it what you will, India was *my* country. There I had friends, a home, congenial employments – pursuits to rouse the mind to energy: here all is torpor – stagnation – death!' (*Angler* I: 265). Nonetheless, Julian, speaking as the protagonist of Shelley's 'Alastor' might have done on his stony death-bed in the Caucasus, admits that he had paid a high price for the stimulus of the contact zone. He curses 'the depraved imagination [which] drove me from [the arms of the blissful protection of those to whom I owe my being] – a cursed destiny urged me to venture on a world of which I was ignorant, and for which I was unfitted – a fiend ... dragged me with unmeaning steps over half the globe' (*Angler* II: 64–5). His overland journey to India, through

the Don country, over the Caucasus into Georgia, thence traver-
sing the Persian empire, and crossing the desert 'to Bushire ...
to Head-quarters in the United Provinces' nearly follows the
itinerary of the hero of 'Alastor'. However, Julian's destination,
a British military cantonment in Kanpur, casts the harsh light of
contemporary history on the mysterious, oriental journey pursued by Shelley's character in search of 'the thrilling secrets of
the birth of time'. Needless to say, Julian's obsessive pursuit of
the Indian ideal takes a toll on his health similar to that of his
Shelleyan prototype; Julian's 'winter of strange sorrows' had
'prematurely furrowed his brow and thinned his hair which had
become almost grey' (*Angler* I: 4; II: 293).

Medwin's reworking of 'The Pindarees' in 'Julian and Gizele'
elaborates the earlier poem's division of its Indian subject-matter
by means of the ideological strategies of *criminalisation* and
eroticisation. Whilst his account of the Pindaris seeks to evoke
in its readers the same *frisson* as other primitive rebels like
Schiller's Robbers, Byron's Corsairs, or Phillip Meadows Taylor's
Thugs, Medwin contributes to the colonial construction of tribal
peoples (the poem's Goorkhas, Thugs, Brinjarries and Arab
nomads who compose the Pindari band) as criminal renegades.
C. A. Bayly describes how in the years after 1812 the Company's
development of a cavalry arm (of which Medwin's regiment was
part) and improved siege technology, such as that used at the
siege of Hathras, allowed it to strike at what Wellesley termed
the 'freebooting system' threatening the land revenue yield in
western and central India, its main source of income.[38] The
importance of private property in land and the 'independence' of
the Indian peasant was gravely threatened by 'nomadic' elements
such as the Pindaris, represented by Medwin as romantic
criminals striking at the rule of law:

> 'Tis nature's ordinance, – man preys on man;
> Our's not the fault, – condemn the general plan!
> Call us Pindarries, Cossacks – to the strong,
> All that the weak protect not, should belong.   (*Angler* II: 303)

In these years, according to Bayly, the British 'were seeking not
simply an increase of their revenues but a monopoly of all sources
of political authority throughout Indian society ... If other chiefs
[i.e. outside the arbitrarily designed category of 'native princes']
resisted they were rebels, or plunderers, or bandits, defined
out of existence by a power which perceived itself to be unitary

and unchallenged as no other had done before it'.[39] Medwin's representation of the Pindaris as nomadic criminal elements borrows from Shelley's description of the diverse Asiatic desperadoes composing Othman's counter-revolutionary army in canto x of *The Revolt of Islam*. The criminal nature of the Pindari nomads calls for the suspension of British civility and the deployment of an equivalent savagery. When Julian's punitive band discover the carnage wrought by the Pindaris on Gizele's native village, their thirst for revenge is aroused; the British force decimates the rebels and Julian kills Zalim their leader with his own hands: 'No quarter's given; 'twere vainly asked of those / Who treat as fiends in human shape their foes' (*Angler* II: 315).

The second important element of Medwin's poem is its eroticisation of the Indian Other, again strongly influenced by the Shelleyan eros of 'Alastor' and 'The Revolt of Islam'. In the 1820 'Pindarees', Oswald has saved Seta from the depredations of the Pindaris, who like true romantic chauvinists know only one way to treat women. In 'Julian and Gizele', however, Julian has saved his lover from death by *sati*, exemplifying the process described by Spivak as 'white men saving brown women from brown men'. The interference of a non-caste Hindu has of course resulted in Seta's loss of caste, and she becomes dependent on the Englishman. By the time he came to adapt the earlier poem (i.e. 1834), *sati* has replaced Pindari banditry at the top of the agenda of Indian incivilities to be reformed by the British 'Guardian State'. Although Medwin's horrific footnote description of the voluntary, unintoxicated, adult *sati* he had witnessed at Mandula concluded that 'no instance of heroism could be greater than this', Gizele's account of her *sati* here contains all the stereotypes noted by Lata Mani:[40]

> ... I did not, could not pine,
> For *that*, whose loss has made me thine –
> Link'd as it were – is – must be now,
> With those who urged the barbarous vow;
> For though betrothed, I was a child,
> And therefore easily beguiled,
> And till I reach'd the fatal pyre,
> I knew not what a Suttee's rite.   (*Angler* II: 307)

Gizele is represented as an embodiment of Indian antiquity, her sensuality distinguishing her at once from Byron's personification of a morbid, sepulchral Greek antiquity in the character of the Corsair's beloved Medora. Gizele's innocent love of nature, her 'saumur' (thrush) and 'favourite tree' evoke the nature-loving heroine of *Sacontala* (in Jones's translation of *The Fatal Ring*), and her Vedantin religion evokes Luxima in Sydney Owenson's (alias Lady Morgan) 1811 Indian novel *The Missionary*. Her very figure and colouring are described in terms of the classical Indian (albeit, in this case, Moghul) architecture and sculpture of which Medwin was a well-informed student:

> a shape of Ind
> In infant slumberings on a couch reclined:
> Pale as the Tajh's marble was her cheek,
> Her features and her form half breathing speak,
> The love that animated them, each line
> Might pass in sculpture's language for divine.   (*Angler* II: 306)

Gizele's long declaration of her love for Julian, as she exhorts him not to set off on the punitive raid against the Pindaris, whilst in *narrative* terms deriving from Medora's speech to Conrad, rather takes its idiom and breathless syntax from Shelley's *Alastor*, canto vi of *The Revolt of Islam* or *Epipsychidion* 11.575–91:

> 'Twas you first taught this heart of mine
> To throb in ecstasy with thine,
> To beat in mystic ebb and flow,
> Self-conscious of thy joy, or woe.
> … Why said I two? We are but one –
> One heart – one mind – one soul – one breath –
> And shall we not be one in death?   (*Angler* II: 308)

Only in death can the lovers be united, it transpires, for Gizele (like Medora) dies on account of a tragic piece of misinformation. The conclusion of Medwin's poem enforces the tragic self-representation of British orientalist discourse, and the futility of its erotic desire to possess the Other. As Suleri writes, ' "India" becomes an absent point towards which 19th century Anglo-Indian narrative may lean but which it may never possess, causing both national and cultural identities to disappear in the emptiness of a representational mirage'.[41] The savagery of Julian's reprisal against the Pindaris is intrinsically connected to the death of his Hindu lover, in an allegory of the way in which the violence of one aspect of British imperialism in India – of imperialism *per se* – always qualifies its desire to 'reconstruct' the purity and integrity of its desired object. Julian himself is left vacillating between a corrosive nostalgia for his lost love, and an inability

to return to his own cultural base: 'Estranged from man henceforth he ran his race. / Year after year, waning lingering moons
away, / And Julian's hair turn'd prematurely grey' (Angler II:
317–19). Medwin's poems elegise the 'orientalist' project as
it is eclipsed by the new imperial guardians, their increasing
aggression towards Indian culture enhanced by disdain rather than
problematised by desire. It is for this reason perhaps all the more
surprising that in Medwin's late reworking of the familiar plot
in the 1842 'A Bengal Yarn', the orientalist 'Major B–' is ridiculed
by the narrator, and cheated by the child-bride (again called Seta)
whom he has rescued from sati. Seta decamps into the jungle
with all 'B's' property, and when the Major pursues her he is eaten
by a tiger. Seta returns and, using her late husband's wealth, buys
herself back into Hindu respectability by employing a yogi to
perform extravagant penance on her behalf. The moral of this
farcical story is not simply that 'native women make bad wives'
but rather that orientalist reverence for native culture is delusory;
Medwin's own former romance narrative has been converted to
burlesque.

Anti-orientalist burlesque: Sir Charles D'Oyly

The decline of British orientalism in the years after 1820 is
epitomised by two significant transitions in the culture of British
India, one institutional, the other literary. In his study British
Orientalism and the Bengal Renaissance, David Kopf describes
the decline and fall of Calcutta's Fort William College in the
1820s and 1830s, the transfer of many of its functions to the
Company's new College at Haileybury, and its eventual closure
in 1854.[42] Under the direction of a chain of brilliant scholars of
the calibre of Henry Colebrooke, William Carey and John Leyden,
the college had a list of distinguished alumni like Charles
Metcalfe, William Bayley, John Digby and Charles Trevelyn;
as Kopf argues, its patronage had contributed to the formation
of a Bengali intellectual elite which would spearhead the Bengali
Renaissance of the mid-nineteenth century. But by 1822 the
writing was on the wall, a fact exemplified by Holt Mackenzie's
complaints about a wave of student indiscipline and a lapse in
'studies and proficiency'.[43] In 1827, on the eve of Lord William
Bentinck's assumption of supreme office in British India, the
College Council expelled thirteen students for idleness and sent

them to remote stations in East Bengal and Orissa.[44] Apart from the challenge of the anti-orientalist ideologies of evangelicalism and utilitarianism, the lower echelons of the Company's service were reacting against what seemed to be a fossilised and elitist institution. Unsurprisingly, Mill's *History of British India*, which would later exert such an influence on the syllabus at Haileybury, was severely attacked by orientalists in the *Calcutta Journal* in 1819, foreseeing its damaging implications for Fort William College.

The student rebels had a point. On the one hand, success in oriental languages was remunerative; 5,000 rupees were paid to any student who already knew Sanskrit or Persian and who passed a demanding examination in Hindu or Islamic law, and lucrative appointments were awarded to the highest achievers. But the price of success was also high: John Leyden had earlier discovered the obstacles awaiting the aspiring orientalist from humble backgrounds like his own. Professional advancement in the Company, which depended on a knowledge of Indian languages and culture, was almost beyond his financial means; 'the expense of native teachers would prove almost insurmountable to a mere assistant surgeon, whose pay is seldom equal to his absolutely necessary expenses', he complained, 'and besides ... it was necessary to form a library of MSS at most terrible expense, in every language to which I should apply, if I intended to proceed beyond a mere smattering'.[45] Leyden was fortunate in being sponsored by Lord Minto (whose family hailed from his native Teviotdale), and thereby gaining a chair at Fort William College. But other men of humble origin who couldn't meet the considerable expense weren't so lucky. Undistinguished results led to the fate of becoming a 'Mofussilite', in Anglo-Indian parlance a civilian (as non-military Company servants were called) assigned to a remote station in the interior of the country. Civilians from unprivileged social backgrounds more often than not found themselves caught in a vicious circle which blocked professional advancement.

The literary expression of this growing sense of professional frustration was evident in a wave of satirical poetry attacking orientalism and the Company's elitism as two sides of the same coin. Anglo-Indian literary satire seems to have risen in popularity in the course of the 1810s, as a glance at the *Asiatic Journal* for these years indicates. In 1816 the journal published excerpts entitled 'Dulness in India' and 'Indian servants' from a satirical poem entitled simply 'Calcutta' by Captain Majendie, son of the Bishop of Bangor.[46] A similarly negative reaction to India was evident in the anonymous Hudibrastic poem entitled 'The Grand Master, or Adventures of Qui Hi? in Hindostan' (1816). Qui Hi was a military officer in India, a 'poor bastard' of humble origins, robbed of all his possessions upon arrival in India, who ran up increasing debts whilst stationed at an obscure military station. He ended up being thrown into prison in Bombay with his native wife and child, where he drank himself to an early death. But despite its down-spiralling plotline, 'Qui Hi?' does represent Indian culture in a favourable light when compared with later satires like *Tom Raw*, appealing for example to the Hindu deities to redress the wrongs of Britain's Indian subjects, and reserving its venom for the Company itself, the oppressive 'Grand Master' of the title.

In the same years there is an evident critical reaction against poetry written in the sentimental vein of the early Byron. For example the *Asiatic Journal* reviewed G. A. Vetch's *Sultry Hours: Containing Metrical Sketches of India* in November 1821 (Vetch was another officer in the Bengal Military Service) and saw fit to complain 'How much has Lord Byron to answer for!' in corrupting the author, formerly an ambitious and upstanding youth who 'reads *Childe Harold*, and forthwith writes sonnets to the moon, monodies on canary-birds, and Hebrew Melodies!'.[47] The appearance of Byron's *Don Juan* in Calcutta in 1819, however, aroused quite a different mood, transforming the dominant style of Anglo-Indian poetry and giving a powerful impetus to anti-orientalist satire. *Don Juan* of course marked a major transformation in Byron's own poetic career and a rethinking of his earlier orientalism, returning critically upon the trail of the 'Pilgrim of Eternity' and converting what was once romantic to burlesque. The pathos of the earlier poetry is replaced in *Don Juan* by an urbane irony re-traversing (at least in the first nine cantos) the Levantine landscape of the *Eastern Tales*. The characters, some of the episodes, the oriental 'costume' are all there; yet the familiar pathos is comically subverted by the jingling, Italianate *ottava rima* and the 'conversational facility' of the narrator into a restless critical indictment of the cant and legitimacy of the post-Napoleonic status quo. Kopf has described how students at Fort William College rapidly 'Byronized' their dissatisfaction with the status quo in poems like 'Sir Anthony Fudge to his Friend, Sir Gabriel, # 36 Writer's Building Calcutta' (1820) (the

Writer's Building was the Fort William College dormitory), 'Ruin: A Familiar Tale of the East' (1821), and 'Rinaldo, or the Incipient Judge. A Tale of the Writer's Building' (1822).[48] Rinaldo, a hard-drinking, horse-loving dandy prefers wining and dining his mistress to studying oriental languages:

> He studied Persian for a year or more,
> And Hindoostanee at the same time read;
> He did not relish much the bore
> Of filling with these languages his head,
> But by degrees he so improved his store
> Of 'vox et nil praetera', that he made
> Proficiency in Oriental knowledge
> Sufficient to pass out, last year.

Sufficient to pass out, but not to avoid the fate of 'mofussilite' exile:

> Mofussil is indeed a mopish place
> Particularly to a man of taste
> And spirit, like Rinaldo, with a face
> Adapted to attract; as he is placed,
> Where he cannot show off his knowing grace,
> To any purpose, and is doom'd to 'waste'
> Like flow'rs, 'his sweetness in the desert air,'
> Without the chance of waiting on the fair.

In Kopf's words, the indifference of the Rinaldo type to all things Indian demonstrated that his costly orientalist education at Haileybury and Fort William College 'designed to produce a competent, serious-minded administrator, certainly had been a costly failure'.[49]

The most successful anti-orientalist satire in the Byronic vein was published anonymously in 1828 with the title *Tom Raw the Griffin: A burlesque poem in 12 cantos ... descriptive of The Adventures of a Cadet in the East India Company's Service from the period of his quitting England to his obtaining a Staff Situation in India*.[50] I mentioned above that the author was the artist Sir Charles D'Oyly (1785–1845), who here assumes the pseudonym of 'Mr Quilldrive', although the poem seems to have been collectively-authored by D'Oyly's literary coterie in Calcutta. The fact that the poem was something of an afterthought, written as a commentary on D'Oyly's twenty-five satirical aquatints, is reflected in the flippant, professedly 'amateur' tone of the verse, which falls far short of the high quality of the plates. These provide a Hogarthian (or rather Cruikshankian) commentary upon

Tom's variegated fortunes in India, 'a country very little known in our native land' (*Tom Raw*: v). Although *Tom Raw* shares many of the features of the Fort William burlesque school, its author was very far from being a frustrated cadet or moping mofussilite. In fact, D'Oyly was approaching the peak of a successful career in the Company Civil Service, having been Collector at Calcutta in 1818, and Opium Agent at Behar in 1821; in 1833 he would be appointed a senior member of the board of Customs, Salt and Opium before retiring to Italy in 1838. D'Oyly had imported a lithographic press to Patna, which he ran with the help of local artists, and founded the no-doubt aptly titled 'United Patna and Gaya Society, or Behar School of Athens, for the promotion of the Arts and Sciences, and for the circulation of fun and merriment of all descriptions'.[51] Adapting the jingling rhyme scheme of *Don Juan* – the pseudonymous 'narrator' admits his dependence upon a rhyming dictionary – and adding an extra line to Byron's octet, *Tom Raw* depicts life in colonial Bengal in scurrilous but scrupulous detail. The poem's plucky but unremarkable hero (based on Byron's ineffectual unheroic Juan) is a 'Griffin' – slang for a new Company Cadet – 'an inexperienced youth':

> A raw, bewildered boy, who seeks his fortune
> In Asiatic climes, unfledged, in truth,
> But told the fickle goddess to importune,
> Lacking the means at home.
>
> The colonies and foreign governments
> Are famous drains for pride and poverty;
> For gentlemen deficient in their rents,
> Always on India turn a longing eye.   (*Tom Raw*: 2)

In the course of his voyage out and his arrival in Calcutta, Tom runs the whole gamut of comic misadventures reserved for the picaresque hero, very much in the vein we have seen in *The Grand-Master*. British life in Bengal is shown to be luxurious in a tawdry, *nouveau-riche* manner, and Anglo-Indians are shown to be desperately anxious to keep up to date with the latest doings of the metropolis. They also apparently suffer from an enormous inferiority complex, a feeling of being disregarded or disliked at home. The popular image of the corrupt Nahob widely disseminated in the Georgian theatre and the logomachia of the Warren Hastings impeachment had cast Anglo-Indians in a distinctively shady light:

> We've heard it traced to envyings and jealousies
> Of our rupees, and characters of Nabobs
> Obtained by acts that richly merit gallowses.
> ... We've heard that folks of ton have gone so far,
> As to place 'gainst all Indian company a bar!   (p. 60)

D'Oyly's urbane satire provides a complete contrast to the romantic image of India we looked at in Medwin's poetry, captured by the account of Tom's visit to the emporium of Taylor & Co, in Calcutta's Lal Bazaar:

> Here rich gilt, bronze, and di'mond cut epergnes,
> And alabaster vases, meet Tom's view,
> With plated dinner sets, and silver urns,
> And strings of pearls, and shawls of splendid hue,
> And diamond necklaces or false or true,
> Boots, shoes and cotton stockings, silks and laces,
> Toys, walking sticks, and vermicelli too,
> Milroy's neat hunting saddles – cues, and maces,
> Preserves, pale ale, and hams, and jocky caps for races.   (p. 92)

For the impoverished Griffin (as for the Fort William collegian), this is all well out of reach:

> He wondered mightily the enormous stretch
> Of speculative purse-strings that could ope
> So widely, and from foreign nations fetch
> Of costly articles so great a scope,
> To purchase, Thomas ne'er indulged a hope,
> But gaz'd intensely on whate'er he saw,
> As Cath'lick pilgrims when they saw the Pope.   (p. 92)

Struggling to keep within his narrow budget, Tom visits the races, unsuccessfully courts the aptly-named Miss Cross at one of Calcutta's most select Ladies Academies, awkwardly presents letters of introduction to powerful members of the Civil and Military establishment in a vain search for patronage, and suffers the tedium of the rainy season when 'One's very blood forgets its circulation, / And days drag listless on, in mis'rable stagnation' (p. 84).

Although Kopf has done valuable service in drawing scholarly attention to anti-orientalist burlesque poetry, his claim that in these poems 'we look in vain for descriptions of British civil servants in contact with the Indian people ... we learn instead of relationships between one European and another' is misleading.[52] Indeed, one of the most interesting (and repellent) aspects of *Tom Raw* is its portrayal of Bengali society. The poem consistently debunks orientalist expectations by its negative portrayal of Indians and their customs, 'If you expect in oriental palaces / What the Arabian Nights so well unfold / ... You will be disappointed, and our story / Seem, in the contrast, very tame and cold' (*Tom Raw*: p. 96). Invited to a nautch, or Hindu dance festival, Tom is disgusted by his host Churbee Doss (Churbee is Hindi for 'blubber') described as a 'hack sircar'. Doss, a cheat and a conman, 'Drinks ghee, which swells him from a bag of bones / To blubber cheeks and paunch enormous!' (p. 100). Indian music and song, the sophistication of which Sir William Jones had admired in his essay on *The Musical Modes of the Hindus*, is dismissed here as 'tones obstrep'rous from convulsive throats' (p. 102). The poem also reflects a reaction against Jones's interest in Hindi mythography, as represented by the *Gods of Greece* ... essay and the *Hindu Hymns*. It is a symptom of Tom's callowness that he wishes to study Hindu mythology: 'Our hero hugely long-ed for Hindoo nonsense, / As children do for cakes and ginger-bread' (p. 168). This despite the fact that his mentor and fellow-cadet Randy warns him that

> Indian mythology is nothing more
> Than cut-glass beads – most miserably strung,
> Fit only to amuse the thoughtless and the young.   (p. 156)

As Randy patiently relates the story of the 'twice 500 armed' Parvati's combat with Doorga, the credulous Tom is so absorbed that he takes fright in the belief that the goddess has materialised before him. Such a sublime visitation is quickly shown to have a farcical resolution. It turns out that all he has seen is:

> A milliner but late arrived from France,
> With brandishing arms and open tongue advanced
> Scolding like mad, because he had returned,
> Some flowery cambric handkerchiefs.   (p. 172)

Nob Kishen's nautch is the occasion for another denunciation of the Indian treatment of women, who have earlier been described as 'untaught, unlettered, in their earliest days, / Fattened, and oiled, and married in their dawn' (p. 99). Although the dancing girls are admired by Tom for their 'wriggling turns' and 'well formed limb', they are clearly no longer prime objects of desire: 'satisfy[ing] if not the English Taste – the whim' (p. 102). The generation gap between Leyden with his Telinga dancing girl and D'Oyly is illustrated by the fact that only the elderly Major Crossbow finds the nautch-girls interesting:

> He'll make you goddesses of all the wretches,
> And roll his goggle eyes, and smack his lips,
> And flirt the whole night with the dusky demi-reps. (p. 176)

Homo-eroticism (or rather homophobia), which Sara Suleri reads as a key signifier of 'colonial intimacy' and hence of 'the rhetoric of English India', is strikingly present in *Tom Raw*. Here is the account of Tom's refusal to embrace the Nabob of Bengal at the latter's durbar:

> Tom was presented – the Nabob advanced,
> To give him – par usage – th'embrace fraternal;
> But, from the hug, he shrank with fearful glance,
> Deeming such salutations most infernal. (p. 205)

Tom's homophobia bears out Suleri's argument that 'while colonised effeminacy ostensibly indicates whatever is rotten in the state of the colony, the hysterical attention that it elicits provides an index for the dynamic of complicity that renders the colonizer a secret sharer of the imputed cultural characteristics of the other race'.[53] A note of caution is necessary here, though, in considering Suleri's claim that homo-eroticism is the key signifier of 'colonial intimacy' rather than the 'alteritist' heterosexual discourse so frequently evoked in recent critiques of orientalism. Homo-eroticism is not particularly evident in the poetry of Leyden and Medwin, which are more ostensibly concerned with a form of 'colonial intimacy'; indeed, in the context of Medwin's 'The Lion Hunt', the theme of male friendship (albeit between Europeans) is something of a false trail which diverts interest from the central romance of Oswald and Seta. It would therefore seem rather perverse to read this clearly homophobic incident in *Tom Raw* – a poem dedicated to establishing a *distance* between coloniser and colonised – as a secret signifier of intimacy. It is more accurate to say that whilst the poetry of Anglo-Indian romanticism is infused with transcultural desire symbolised by a constantly frustrated heterosexual romance, anti-orientalist satire replaces sexuality with a disquieting idiom of racial disgust. It is precisely Tom's fear that the proffered embrace might lead him into a position of colonial intimacy that compels him to court an aggressive distance, by threatening to 'spit in the black rascal's face' (p. 206).

Tom Raw eventually assumes his commission and begins the long journey up the Ganges to join his regiment at Mhow. After narrowly escaping being savaged by a tiger whilst out hunting with a mofussilite dandy called Sprightly (obviously based on the figure of 'Rinaldo'), his boat is wrecked and he narrowly escapes with his life. Stranded in the back of beyond, he is forced to ask the local *ryots* or peasants for assistance, the occasion for a display of the 'griffin jargon' which is Tom's excuse for Hindostani. D'Oyly carefully represents this 'Hobson-Jobson' type of language, anticipating later writers like Meadows Taylor and Kipling and footnoting every word for the benefit of non Anglo-Indian readers:

> He used – most frequently – Hunara now –
> Toom deckho! – hum – God damn me, and Kiswashi
> Sub doop gea, – and nooksaun, – and manjee lou!
> In intonations very cross and hasty,
> And made the Ryutts laugh – and then, at last, he
> Said something of rupees – and surely there's
> A magic in its sound – so great and vasty,
> It tingles, from pure instinct, in the ears,
> And hocus pocus like – all understanding clears.   (p. 253)

When the local native police fail to be cooperative, Tom flaunts his rank and race, with the desired effects:

> A burkendoze [native policeman], now stepping up behind,
> Drew out his tulwar, and our hero pinned,
> Who roaring out – "Hum Comp'ny Ke lupteenant
> Bhote khubberdar!" – as if they all had sinned
> Beyond redemption, they quick lowered their pen'nant,
> And made salaams – as to the landlord does the tenant.   (p. 254)

And so on. To cut a long story short, Tom reaches his regiment, and is welcomed by the choleric and tattered Colonel Kyan, surrounded by his numerous Eurasian children. Tom loses little time in falling in love with Charlotte Kyan 'Of all his dingy squad – his eldest daughter, / A girl of sixteen, pretty too, though brown' (p. 261), and his feelings are quickly reciprocated. It is noteworthy that this mention of Charlotte's 'brownness' is the last reference made to her colour or mixed race; as the Colonel's daughter, brought up as a Christian, she is evidently good enough for an ambitious Griffin. At the wedding, the impossibility of a conventional lily-and-roses description of female beauty is cleverly resolved by D'Oyly in transferring the conventionally white skin colour to Charlotte's glove: 'She pulls off her snow-white left-hand glove, as / Soon as the bridegroom shews the magic ring' (p. 289).

Life is, however, never easy in colonial India, even for newly-weds. The couple run into a series of misfortunes clearly drawn from the narrative of *The Grand-Master*: Tom runs into serious debt, the Colonel marries a Scottish gold-digger called Girsy Macnamara, who inherits his fortune at his death, and Tom has his leg blown off in his first and only military engagement against a refractory zemindar in Awadh. Fortunately, he ends up better off than Qui Hi. The £100 annuity which he receives as compensation permits the Raw family to contemplate financial independence, Tom is mentioned in dispatches for his bravery and finally awarded a Staff Appointment. Although *Tom Raw* reflects many of the anti-orientalist concerns of the Fort William burlesque poems, D'Oyly, with his secure position in the Company's establishment, evidently seeks to moderate the message of *The Grand-Master*. However, despite *Tom Raw*'s conciliatory conclusion, it is evident the anti-orientalist mood to which we saw Medwin becoming a late convert had made a powerful impact even upon D'Oyly's elite circle.

Conclusion

The work of these three 'Company' poets, almost entirely over-looked by literary critics and historians of British India, represents *both* an inflection of European romanticism and a significant episode in the culture of British India. When the engraver Thomas Danniell sent his first set of views of Calcutta back to England in 1788, he wrote to his friend, the painter Ozias Humphry, apologising for the quality of his work, 'It will appear a very poor performance in your land, I fear. You must look upon it as a *Bengalee* work'.[54] Daniell's scruples were no doubt shared by the many amateur poets of early British India, reflecting an anxiety closely linked to the low cultural capital of Anglo-Indians in metropolitan Britain. Moreover, if these poets were amateurs in relation to the mainstream of British literature, they might also be seen as amateurs in relation to the Indian culture in which they resided, in their work expressing, like Sara Suleri's British women writers in India, 'an unofficial fear of cultural ignorance ... converting amateurism into an elaborate allegory through which Anglo-India examines in hiding colonialism's epistemological limits'.[55]

Torn between a desire to keep up with the latest literary models from Europe, and at the same time to express their sense of what it meant to write in the contact zone, Anglo-Indian poets searched for a literary form adequate to their colonial predicament. We saw how John Leyden found a way of literalising the plots and figures of sensibility so that conventional tropes of absence and bereavement might connote the geopolitical realities of colonial service, whilst tropes of heat and cold (as in the 'Telinga Dancing Girl') could be read in terms of the cultural difference which hampered the coming-together of Indian and Briton. The romantic discourse of exile and the visionary quest narrative provided Medwin with the means to represent alienation as a permanent quality of the colonial self, ironically just at the moment in which British power in the subcontinent, after its global triumph in the Napoleonic Wars, assumed a new confidence and sense of purpose. Perhaps for this very reason it became necessary to stigmatise the orientalist mentality as a fatal dalliance with a sublime alterity, which was easily recast in the mode of the ridiculous in D'Oyly's burlesque poetry. Although *Tom Raw* is concerned with many of the same issues of colonial life that preoccupy Leyden and Medwin, its flippant, irreverent satire anticipates the negative attitude towards Indian culture which would shape the reforms of Lord Bentinck and Thomas Babington Macaulay. However, the self-conscious amateurism of D'Oyly's poem suggests that the artistic insecurity which dogged the earlier Anglo-Indian poets was pervasive enough to survive the transformation of colonial ideologies. The distinctiveness of early-nineteenth-century Anglo-Indian poetry can thus be said to lie more in the negative qualities of this cultural instability rather than in any positive sense of identity and unity of purpose.

Notes

1 Raymond Schwab, *The Oriental Renaissance: Europe's Rediscovery of India and the East, 1680–1880* (New York: Columbia University Press, 1984).

2 *The Works of Sir William Jones*, ed. Lady Jones, 6 vols. (London 1799), III, p. 547.

3 Schwab, *op. cit.*, Garland Cannon, 'The Literary Place of Sir William Jones', *Journal of the Asiatic Society*, 2,1 (1960), pp. 47–61: Javed Majeed, *Ungoverned Imaginings: James Mill's 'The History of British India' and Orientalism* (Oxford: Clarendon Press, 1992).

4 Cf. *Memoirs of William Hickey*, ed. Peter Quennell (London: Routledge & Kegan Paul, 1975).

5 Victor Jacquemont, *Letters from India 1828–31*, 2 vols. (London, 1834), I, p. 84.

6 Sara Suleri, *The Rhetoric of English India* (Chicago: University of Chicago Press, 1992), pp. 37–48.

7 Mary Louise Pratt, *Imperial Eyes: Travel Writing and Transculturation* (London & New York: Routledge, 1992). The 'contact zone' is defined as a social space 'where different cultures meet, clash and grapple with each other, often in highly assymetrical relations of domination and subordination', p. 4.

8 Majeed, *Ungoverned Imaginings*, pp. 23–4.

9 *The New Oxford Book of Romantic Period Verse*, ed. Jerome McGann (Oxford: Oxford University Press, 1993), p. 1.

10 G. H. R. Tillotson, 'The Indian Picturesque: Images of India in British Landscape Painting 1780–1880' in C. A. Bayly (ed.), *The Raj: India and the British 1600–1947* (London: The National Portrait Gallery Publications, 1990), pp. 141–51.

11 Pratt, *Imperial Eyes*, p. 87.

12 Suleri, *Rhetoric*, p. 4.

13 J. D. Yohannan, 'The Persian Poetry Fad in England 1770–1825', *Comparative Literature*, 4 (1952), pp. 137–60.

14 *OED* entry under 'Costume'.

15 See the entry on D'Oyly in the *Dictionary of National Biography*.

16 *Ibid.*

17 Jane Rendall, 'Scottish Orientalism: from Robertson to James Mill', *The Historical Journal*, 25, I (1982), pp. 43–69; 45.

18 *Poetical Remains of the Late Dr John Leyden*, ed. Rev. James Morton (London, 1819), p. 399. Subsequently referred to in the text as *PR*.

19 John Reith, *The Life of Dr John Leyden* (Galashiels: A. Walker & Sons, 1908), pp. 229–30.

20 Henry Mackenzie, *The Man of Feeling*, ed. Brian Vickers (Oxford: Oxford University Press, 1970), p. 103.

21 P. Seshadri prefers to find in the poem a reminder of the ' "vers de société" of Matthew Prior'; cf. *An Anglo-Indian Poet: John Leyden* (Madras: Higginbotham, 1912), p. 22.

22 Alexander Pope, *Poetical Works*, ed. H. Davies (Oxford: Oxford University Press, 1966), pp. 117, 11.260–2.

23 Suleri, *Rhetoric*, p. 92. Poems about nautch-girls seemed to have constituted a minor genre. See for example 'Miss Porden's' 'To a Nautch-Girl, imitated from the Hindoostani' in the *Asiatic Journal*, I (Jan.–June 1816), p. 558.

24 H. Rider Haggard, *King Solomon's Mines* (Herts: Wordsworth Eds Ltd, 1993), p. 225. Cf. also Kipling's story 'Beyond the Pale' for an admonitory treatment of transcultural love. *Plain Tales from the Hills*, ed. Andrew Rutherford (Oxford: Oxford University Press, 1988), pp. 127–32.

25 *Asiatick Researches*, X (Calcutta 1808), pp. 158–289.

26 *Life of John Leyden*, p. 363.

27 *Ibid.*, p. 385.

28 *The Angler in Wales*, 2 vols. (London: Richard Bentley, 1834), II, p. 73, Henceforth *Angler* in text.

29 Gayatri Spivak, 'Can the Subaltern Speak? Speculations on Widow Sacrifice' in Cary Nelson and Lawrence Grossberg (eds.), *Marxism and the Interpretation of Culture* (London: Macmillan, 1988), pp. 271–313; 296.

30 Suleri, *Rhetoric*, p. 92.

31 P. B. Shelley, *Collected Letters*, ed. Frederick L. Jones, 2 vols. (Oxford University Press, 1964), II, p. 183.

32 *Ainsworth's Magazine*, II (1842), pp. 57–63.

33 *Sketches in Hindostan with other Poems* (London: C. and J. Ollier, 1821), p. 9 (no line numbers).

34 *Ibid.*, p. 9.

35 *Ibid.*, p. 81.

36 *Ibid.*, p. 81.

37 *Ibid.*, p. 11.

38 C. A. Bayly, *Indian Society and the Making of the British Empire* (Cambridge: Cambridge University Press, 1988), p. 106.

39 *Ibid.*, p. 172.

40 Lata Mani, 'The Production of an Official Discourse on *Sati* in early 19th century Bengal' in Francis Barker *et al.* (eds.), *Europe and Its Others*, 2 vols. (Colchester: University of Essex, 1984), I, pp. 107–27; 117.

41 Suleri, *Rhetoric*, p. 11.

42 David Kopf, *British Orientalism and the Bengal Renaissance: The Dynamics of Indian Modernisation 1773–1835* (Berkeley and Los Angeles: University of California Press, 1969), pp. 215–35.

43 *Ibid.*, p. 221.

44 *Ibid.*, p. 222.

45 Seshadri, *Anglo-Indian Poet*, pp. 98–9.

46 *Asiatic Journal* (Jan.–June 1816), pp. 45–7.

47 *Asiatic Journal* (Nov. 1821), p. 453.

48 Kopf, *British Orientalism*, pp. 222–7. Verse quotations are from Kopf.

49 *Ibid.*, p. 226.

50 *Tom Raw* was published in London in 1828. Subsequent page references in text are from this edition. There are no line numbers.

51 Pheroza Godrej and Pauline Rohatgi, *Scenic Splendours: India through the Printed Image* (London: The British Library, 1989), p. 59.

52 Kopf, *British Orientalism*, p. 226.

53 Suleri, *Rhetoric*, p. 82.

54 Quoted in Godrej and Rohatgi, *Scenic Splendours*, p. 75.

55 Suleri, *Rhetoric*, p. 82.

Bibliography

Ainsworth's Magazine, II (1842).

Asiatick Researches, X (Calcutta 1808).

Bayly, C. A., *Indian Society and the Making of the British Empire* (Cambridge: Cambridge University Press, 1988).

—— (ed.), *The Raj: India and the British 1600–1947* (London: National Portrait Gallery, 1990).

Cannon, Garland, 'The Literary Place of Sir William Jones', *Journal of the Asiatic Society*, 2, I (1960), pp. 47–61.

D'Oyly, Sir Charles, *Tom Raw the Griffin: a burlesque poem in 12 cantos … descriptive of the Adventures of a Cadet in the East India Company's Service from the period of his quitting England to his obtaining a Staff Situation in India* (London, 1828).

Godrej, Pheroza and Pauline Rohatgi, *Scenic Splendours: India through the Printed Image* (London: British Library, 1989).

Hickey, William, *Memoirs*, ed. Peter Quennell (London: Routledge & Kegan Paul, 1975).

Jacquemont, Victor, *Letters from India 1828–31*, 2 vols. (London, 1834).

Jones, Sir William, *Works*, ed. Lady Jones, 6 vols. (London, 1799).

Kopf, David, *British Orientalism and the Bengal Renaissance: The Dynamics of Indian Modernisation 1773–1835* (Berkeley and Los Angeles: University of California Press, 1969).

Leask, Nigel, *British Romantic Writers and the East: Anxieties of Empire* (Cambridge: Cambridge University Press, 1992).

Leyden, John, *Poetical Remains*, ed. Rev. James Morton (London, 1819).

Mackenzie, Henry, *The Man of Feeling*, ed. Brian Vickers (Oxford: Oxford University Press, 1970).

Majeed, Javed, *Ungoverned Imaginings: James Mill's 'The History of British India' and Orientalism* (Oxford: Clarendon Press, 1992).

Mani, Lata, 'The Production of an Official Discourse on *Sati* in early 19th century Bengal' in Francis Barker *et al.* (eds.), *Europe and its Others*, 2 vols. (Colchester: University of Essex, 1984), pp. 107–27.

McGann, Jerome (ed.), *The New Oxford Book of Romantic Period Verse* (Oxford: Oxford University Press, 1993).

Medwin, Thomas, *Sketches in Hindostan with other Poems* (London: C and J Ollier, 1821).

——, *The Angler in Wales*, 2 vols. (London: Richard Bentley, 1834).

Pope, Alexander, *Poetical Works*, ed. H. Davies (Oxford: Oxford University Press, 1966).

Pratt, Mary Louise, *Imperial Eyes: Travel Writing and Transculturation* (London & New York: Routledge, 1992).

Reith, John, *The Life of Dr John Leyden* (Galashiels: A. Walker & Sons, 1908).

Rendall, Jane, 'Scottish Orientalism: from Robertson to James Mill', *The Historical Journal*, 25, I (1982), pp. 43–69.

Rider Haggard, H., *King Solomon's Mines* (Herts: Wordsworth Eds Ltd., 1993).

Schwab, Raymond, *The Oriental Renaissance: Europe's Rediscovery of India and the East 1680–1880* (New York: Columbia University Press, 1984).

Seshadri, P., *An Anglo-Indian Poet: John Leyden* (Madras: Higginbotham, 1912).

Shelley, P. B., *Collected Letters*, ed. Frederick L. Jones, 2 vols. (Oxford: Oxford University Press, 1964).

Spivak, Gayatri, 'Can the Subaltern Speak? Speculations on Widow Sacrifice' in Cary Nelson and Lawrence Grossberg (eds.), *Marxism and the Interpretation of Culture* (London: Macmillan, 1988), pp. 271–313.

Suleri, Sara, *The Rhetoric of English India* (Chicago: University of Chicago Press, 1992).

Tillotson, G. H. R., 'The Indian Picturesque: Images of India in British Painting 1780–1880' in C. A. Bayly (ed.), *The Raj: India and the British 1600–1947* (London: National Portrait Gallery, 1990).

Yohannan, J. D., 'The Persian Poetry Fad in England 1770–1825', *Comparative Literature*, 4 (1952), pp. 137–60.

3

Meadows Taylor's *Confessions of a Thug*: the Anglo-Indian novel as a genre in the making

JAVED MAJEED

In her study of the colonial state in early nineteenth-century India, Radhika Singha has shown how the East India Company's campaign to suppress *Thagi* in the 1830s was a crucial element in the state's changing conception of its role in its territories. The way *Thagi* was perceived by the Company clearly reflected its recent sense of paramountcy, as well as the new role it had defined for itself in its territories.[1] Crucial to this sense of a new role was the systematisation imposed on *Thagi* as an all-India confederacy of murderers dedicated to the goddess of destruction, Kali, whom they had adopted as their patron deity. These bands of murderers apparently saw the strangulation of their victims as a form of sacrifice to the goddess, and had elaborated all sorts of rituals and ceremonies around their activities. However, the extent to which the official British picture of *Thagi* can be relied upon is a moot point. Some of the articles on *Thagi* in this period contain rather extravagant claims and theories. This is the case with R. C. Sherwood's piece in the *Asiatick Researches* of 1820, which appears to push back the origins of *Thagi* to the beginning of the Muslim conquests of India, and even mentions some hints of it in Hindu legends and mythology.[2] The fact that this article appeared in the journal of the Asiatic Society of Bengal shows how seriously such views were taken at the time. It seems likely that the appearance of wandering bands of murderous bandits in the early nineteenth century had much to do with the political and economic dislocation caused by the British defeat of the Maratha confederacy in 1818, which released considerable numbers of disbanded soldiers into the community at large.[3] The earlier defeat of Tipu Sultan in 1799 had already led to the appearance of the freelance soldier on the scene, a figure whose services in the disturbed conditions of this period were very much in demand.[4]

The 'Thug scare' also probably derived from an exaggerated British fear of mendicant groups, which was sharpened by these uncertain conditions of the 1820s and 30s.[5]

However, as far as the Company was concerned, the system of *Thagi* could only be extirpated by the countersystem of British rule itself. This perception mirrored the increasing sense among British officials of the need to place Company rule on a more systematic footing. The anti-*Thagi* legislation of the 1830s was particularly important in this respect. This legislation was part of a general drive by the Company to extend the scope and reach of criminal law in order to control as many sources of authority in Indian society as possible. Singha has pointed to the un-precedented features of Act XXX of 1836, promulgated to deal with *Thagi*.[6] For example, the Act applied with retrospective effect, it extended Company jurisdiction to territories outside its actual dominions, the offence in question could be tried in any Company court irrespective of where the crime had been committed, trials were conducted without any of the forms of Islamic law (this especially applied to laws of evidence pertaining to the testimony of informers),[7] and the term Thugs was used without being defined. This last feature of the anti-*Thagi* legislation was perhaps one of the most important. It allowed for conviction on the basis of membership of a gang of thugs alone, irrespective of whether or not a particular crime had been committed. In other words, certain groups in Indian society were beginning to be seen as inherently criminal. *Thagi* in particular was seen as a hereditary criminal system which was a sort of grotesque parody of a religion, whose very existence was taken to be proof of Indian society's backwardness as a whole.[8]

In addition to the novel features of the legislation surrounding the anti-*Thagi* campaign of the 1830s, the strategies of the cam-paign itself brought to the fore the growing importance of the role of surveillance and information-gathering for the maintenance of imperial authority and legitimacy.[9] The entire campaign rested on captured thugs turning informers or what were called 'approvers', and it used increasingly sophisticated techniques for the control and policing of suspect groups. The official literature surrounding *Thagi* indicates the emergence of some important preoccupations which become increasingly evident in the themes of a number of Anglo-Indian novels. These included a suspicion of peripatetic groups, such as wandering fakirs and mendicants, as a source of subversion and conspiracy,[10] and a fascination with secret languages and mysterious codes.[11] A clear example of this fascination was W. H. Sleeman's *Ramaseena* of 1836, which the author described as a 'Vocabulary [into which is entered] every thing to which Thugs in any part of India have thought it necessary to assign a peculiar term'.[12] Intertwined with this was a preoccupation with accumulating bodies of official knowledge to penetrate and expose the mysteries of cult and language,[13] and an equal fascination with strategies to control the complex cultural, linguistic and communal heterogeneity of the subcontinent, which afforded so many opportunities for disguises and counter-disguises.

It comes as no surprise that many of these preoccupations are evident in Meadows Taylor's first novel, *Confessions of a Thug* (1839). Taylor's subsequent novels were more in a historical mode;[14] his interest in historical narrative was also evident in his popular *A Student's Manual of the History of India* (1870). But *Confessions of a Thug* was Taylor's most popular work; it was republished in 1840, 1858, 1873, 1901, 1916, 1922 (in an abridged version), 1938 (also in an abridged version), and more recently in 1986 (by Oxford University Press). Taylor himself was not personally involved in the anti-*Thagi* campaign of the 1830s. In 1830 he was appointed adjutant to the Nizam of Hyderabad's service and his military duties in Hyderabad prevented him from participating fully in the campaign. None the less, in his autobiography, *Story of My Life* (1878), he writes of his activities in collecting evidence from captured Thugs of the Deccan: 'Day after day I recorded tales of murder, which, though horribly monotonous, possessed an intense interest; and as fast as new approvers came in, new mysteries were unravelled and new crimes confessed'.[15] He also claimed that he would have been 'the first to disclose the horrible crime of Thuggee to the world', had it not been for his transfer to Hyderabad.[16] However, irrespective of the extent to which Taylor himself was involved in the anti-*Thagi* campaign, *Confessions of a Thug* is one of the first novels to display many of the themes which seem to typify the later Anglo-Indian novel as a whole. The aim here is to show how the preoccupations discussed above translate into the text of the novel, and how this in turn helps to suggest some ways in which we can begin to read the Anglo-Indian novel in terms of the structures of some of its devices and the rhetoric of its preoccupations. This might also help to illuminate the Anglo-Indian novel's perception of the context of its own genesis, as well as its engagement with that context.

Thagi as a system

The author's perception of *Thagi* as a 'system' which both necessitated and mirrored the countersystem of East India Company rule is made clear in his introduction to the novel, when he points out that until the 1830s 'no blow was ever aimed at the *system*' of *Thagi* itself.[17] He also paints a picture of *Thagi* as an all-Indian confederation, invoking a wide geographical sweep as he does so, in order to emphasize the sheer physical distances over which this secret network operated. Discussing the gathering of information from the increasing number of thugs turned approvers, he writes of how 'the circle widened till it spread over the whole continent – from the foot of the Himalayas to Cape Comorin, from Cutch to Assam, there was hardly a province in the whole of India where thuggee had not been practised' (*Confessions:* 5–6). Ameer Ali's depiction of *Thagi* as a brotherhood embracing both Hindus and Muslims parallels the author's emphasis on its geographical sweep. Ameer Ali is at pains to describe *Thagi* as 'the only profession and brotherhood in which I hope to find good faith existing', and he goes on to quote his father as saying: 'in it, the Hindoo and the Moslim both unite as brothers: among them bad faith is never known: a sure proof, that our calling is blessed and sanctioned by the divine authority' (*Confessions:* 30). For thugs themselves, then, the fact that *Thagi* included both Muslims and Hindus in its ranks was a sure sign of its divine status. The author's implication, however, is that this grotesque cult is the only way anything approaching a cultural unity in India can be achieved among Indians themselves, which underlines the importance of the civilising and unifying role of the British themselves in India.[18]

In the course of his depiction of *Thagi* as a system, special attention is paid by the author to its operation as a cult with its initiation ceremonies, its hermeneutics of omen divination, and its code of procedures (*Confessions:* 46, 49, 50, 81, 83, 86). The author is also concerned to show how *Thagi* is associated with religious mendicants and fakirs. For example, in his introduction he writes of how the huts of hermits and fakirs outside city walls afford shelter to the thugs; and how fakirs often entice travellers into their hands (*Confessions:* 3). One of Ameer Ali's favourite disguises is that of a fakir; he finds that it ensures he is safe on the roads and that he never goes without a meal (*Confessions:* 528). Meadows Taylor is thus careful to link thugs with peripatetic groups, such as fakirs, who, because they were beyond the reach of policing and taxation, were suspect in British eyes. Colonel Sleeman, whose role in the anti-*Thagi* campaign was central, described such groups as 'floating loosely upon society, without property or character'.[19] But Taylor goes a step further, and shows how mainstream religious priests themselves are connected with *Thagi*. In relating his adventures Ameer Ali often describes meetings with *mullahs* and Brahmin priests who are involved in *Thagi* (*Confessions:* 78, 480, 530). The result is that the cultist aspects of *Thagi* merge into mainstream religious aspects of Indian society; as a result, there is a tendency for Indian society as a whole to stand condemned. This discursive slippage between *Thagi* as an esoteric hereditary criminal group and its status as representative of the rest of Indian society further reinforces the British mission for reforming India.[20]

The heterogeneity of India

The fear of, and fascination with, peripatetic groups and their links with respectable parts of Indian society seem to be closely connected to the text's concern with the heterogeneous nature of Indian society as a whole. The perception of India's heterogeneity was to become central to British official thinking in the later part of the nineteenth century, when it was used as a justification for schemes of political representation supposedly tailor-made for the peculiar conditions and nature of Indian society.[21] India, it was argued, was not one nation, but many nations, and as a result it was unable to sustain European-style democratic institutions.[22] Such a view was evident in the deliberations of the Committee appointed by Lord Dufferin in September 1888 to consider the issue of Indian representation. This Committee saw its task as defining a system of representation which would reflect as accurately as possible the diversity of interests in Indian society, but it perceived these interests as flowing from caste and religious groups which were intrinsic and unalterable parts of Indian society.[23] It is clear, too, that this view of Indian society's heterogeneity in terms of a series of competing and culturally distinct communities also formed the basis for justifying British rule itself.[24]

Meadows Taylor's *Confessions of a Thug* clearly marks the emergence of this important perspective on India's heterogeneity in the earlier part of the nineteenth century. There are many passages describing landscapes in the novel; these frequently evoke intractable jungles and wilds which are difficult to traverse. One such passage occurs in the first part of the novel, where Ameer Ali describes a scene of some murders: 'the creepers and trees were matted overhead, and the sides so thick that it was impossible that anyone could have got down from above. The tangled character of the spot increased as we proceeded, until it became necessary to free our clothes from the thorns which caught us at every step'. Sometimes the density of jungle is exaggerated by moonlight, as described slightly earlier in the same chapter: 'As we approached the small hills, the jungle became pretty thick, and appeared doubly so by the moonlight' (*Confessions:* 84, 82). What is stressed in these descriptions is the tangled nature of the vegetation, combined with a desolation which makes travel difficult and dangerous (*Confessions:* 249). The evocation of these tangled matted textures operates as a metaphor for the density of Indian society with all its complexities, which the British were negotiating in the process of establishing paramountcy in the subcontinent. The emphasis on dark, uncultivated areas with poor roads is a vivid illustration in the novel of those physical and cultural parts of India yet to be penetrated and rendered safe by British hegemony.

So the recurrence of such descriptions, coupled with invocations of the sheer geographical immensity of the subcontinent, can be seen as images of the social and other complexities of India with which the British were brought face to face in their campaign to suppress *Thagi*. Another level on which this fear of and fascination with India's heterogeneity manifests itself is in the depictions of crowds, which are presented as both difficult to control and ephemeral. The clearest example of this are the hordes who join the Pindari chieftain Cheetoo in his rapacious campaigns against the British. Ameer Ali describes how at Cheetoo's place of residence 'were collected men from every part of Hindostan, as various in their tribes as they were in their dreses, arms, and accoutrement' (*Confessions:* 337). Later on, at the beginning of the second campaign, when thousands flock to Nemawur once more, Ameer Ali himself comments: 'it was no easy task to organize this heterogeneous mass, for the men would have preferred acting independently and on their own account' (*Confessions:* 372). Indeed, much of the gruesome description of the pillage and rape by these hordes emphasises

how difficult they are to control. Here there is an obvious contrast
with the discipline shown by the East India Company soldiers.
One of the noblemen of the Deccan stresses this quality when
describing the defeat of *Tipu Sultan*: 'I saw the whole; and if you
had also, you would have wondered to see the battalions scramble
up the breach like cats, headed by their officers, in the face of
a fire of guns and matchlocks which would have scattered the
people we call Sipahees [i.e. soldiers] like chaff' (*Confessions:*
105–6). In contrast to the disciplined East India Company ranks
led by reliable officers, the text emphasises the variety of tribes
from all over India who are held together by the prospect of
plunder alone.

A similar evocation of the chaotic quality of crowds occurs
when Ameer Ali witnesses a *muhurram* procession. Once again,
there is a stress on the variety of costumes, arms, accoutrements,
pennants, priests, and races, culminating in an almost visionary
spectacle with which Ameer Ali is mesmerised (*Confessions:*
176–85). Somewhat inevitably, after the frenzy of procession
reaches its climax, Ameer Ali describes how it dissolves into
exhausted individuals, the implication being that the loose
unity of the procession was short-lived, based as it was on a
mixture of religious frenzy and drug-induced intoxication. The
fear of crowds is also to be found in the writings of a number
of other authors in the early nineteenth century, perhaps most
notably in those of Thomas De Quincey and Robert Southey,
where it plays a role in the construction of a threatening
'Orient'.[25] The chapter on the *muhurram* procession in *Confes-*
sions of a Thug encapsulates the novel's preoccupation with
India's heterogeneity, but the accent is more on a fascination
with that heterogeneity, rather than a fear of it. Here the depiction
of Indian crowds involves stressing how quickly they dissipate
into ineffectual individuals, thus underpinning the suggestion
that it is only the British who can form an effective counterweight to Indian heterogeneity.

Disguise and the polyglot density of India

The hypnotic quality of these signs of India's heterogeneity, be
it in the almost visionary spectacle of the *muharram* procession,
or the evocations of density and intractability in the landscapes
which both thug and British soldier negotiate, raises some

questions about the relationship between the text's fascination with Indian heterogeneity, and the status of the Anglo-Indian novel itself as a cultural artefact. As the author himself states in his introduction, India's heterogeneity affords many possibilities of disguise: 'the greatest facilities of disguise among thieves and Thugs exist in the endless divisions of the people into tribes, castes, and professions' (*Confessions:* 2). The novel is of course full of disguises. Ameer Ali and his cohorts are masters at it, and adopt a variety of disguises in order to entice travellers to their deaths. To a certain extent, this anticipates the preoccupations with disguise which are such an important part of the narratives of spying in *Kim*, as well as *The Raj Quartet*. However, of more interest here is a focus on language itself as an instrument of deception, and as part of the repertoire of disguises in the novel. It is frequently stressed that Ameer Ali is a master at using language for his own purposes; as he says at one point, 'the whole art consists in having a smooth tongue in one's head' (*Confessions:* 429). Ameer Ali's impressive manners and mode of address are also often emphasized; he is referred to by Cheetoo, the Pindari chieftain, as a 'gentleman, [who] knows how a gentleman ought to be received' (*Confessions:* 354), and indeed, on many occasions he is shown to be at ease with the polished Persianised etiquette of the courts of Hindostan (*Confessions:* 103, 244). In other words, Ameer Ali's successful career as a thug depends on his ability to mimic elaborate modes of address and forms of etiquette. This *Thagi* mimicry has the effect of discrediting such modes and forms, and exposes them as hollow and superficial contrivances, easily mastered by the unscrupulous.

This discrediting of indigenous forms of elaboration can be partly seen in terms of the defining of social and cultural hierarchies on the basis of language usage, which took place in both a British domestic and imperial context.[26] What seems to be emerging in the *Confessions of a Thug* is an opposition between English plain speaking and Oriental hyperbole. This must be set against the text's references to the linguistic diversity of India itself. Thus there are references to Persian, Urdu, Hindi, various local patois, and the 'secret' language of the thugs themselves, *Ramasee*. Furthermore, many of the references are to these languages as inscribed with or containing secret and specialised information. For example, there are references to bills of exchange in Gujarati and Hindi, petitions and lists of gifts in Persian, and permits in Marathi (*Confessions:* 182, 213, 63, 356, 418).

There are also broad references to parts of indigenous high literary culture; for example, to Arabic verses, Persian *ghazals*, as well as specific references to the Persian poet Hafiz (*Confessions:* 481, 312, 388, 470). Ameer Ali's sense of importance is attributed by the author to his command of a language of high culture; the author writes: 'His language is pure and fluent, perhaps a little affected from his knowledge of Persian, which, though slight, is sufficient to enable him to introduce words and expressions in that language, often when they are not needed, but still it is pure Oordoo; he prides himself upon it, and holds in supreme contempt those who speak the corrupt patois of the Dukhun, or the still worse one of Hindostan' (*Confessions:* 266). Part of the exotic tone of the novel consists in capturing the flavour of etiquette and elaborate modes of address characterising various regions of India, and sometimes phrases are put into characters' mouths which read as though they are translations of Urdu or Persian idioms. For example, on one occasion one of the characters speaks of 'sitting down on the carpet of patience, smoking the pipe of regret', while another talks of spreading the 'carpet of patience' (*Confessions:* 70, 137). At another point Ameer Ali alludes to a Persian proverb (*Confessions:* 477). Characters also talk picturesquely of throwing dirt on the beards of their enemies, whilst there are instances of colourful and rather quaint torrents of abuse (*Confessions:* 135, 453). Furthermore, the characters in the novel themselves comment on the aesthetic qualities of languages; a favourite reference is to the musical tones of a language, and Ameer Ali's speech is described as 'sweet and mellifluous like a verse of Hafiz' (*Confessions:* 411–12, 470).

The polyglot density of India thus has an important, if uneasy, presence in the text. The weaving together of a patchwork of references to Indian languages and dialects, as well as a mixture of tones which are registers of indigenous styles of speech and the codes of etiquette in which they are embedded, forms part of the novel's evocation of India's heterogeneity.[27] This representation of India's linguistic heterogeneity also has a place in later Anglo-Indian novels, such as *Kim*, where the exotic flavour of the text in part derives from the picturesque ways in which Indian vernaculars are rendered in dialogue. There is, too, an obvious concern with secret codes. Thus, in its depiction of India's polyglossia, and its quaint rendering of vernacular speech, *Confessions of a Thug* can also be seen to anticipate significant strands in later Anglo-Indian novels. Three reasons can be put forward to explain Taylor's concern with the polyglot density of India. First, the novel was published in 1839, soon after Act XXIX of 1837 allowed for the Company to dispense with any provision of any of its Regulations which enjoined 'the use of the Persian language in any judicial proceeding or in any proceeding relating to the Revenue'.[28] Whilst this Act marked a decisive stage in the supplanting of Persian as the language of the courts in the Company's territories, it also serves to remind us how the East India Company in this period sought to legitimise itself through indigenous idioms in the late eighteenth and early nineteenth centuries. As an Indian power, it built itself upon the administrative, judicial, and revenues systems of its predecessors,[29] and in so doing, drew upon their linguistic systems as well.[30] It was partly as a result of these *Indian* legacies that the administrative language of the East India Company was replete with indigenous judicial and revenue terms, or as the Sanskritist H. H. Wilson put it, 'thickly studded with terms adopted from the vernacular languages of the country'.[31] Thus, to a certain extent, the signs of India's polyglossia in *Confessions of a Thug* reflect the overall interaction between the Company's idioms and those of its predecessors. It is also indicative of its engagement with the high textual worlds of Indian learning through such institutions as Fort William College,[32] and through its definition and management of indigenous codes of law.[33]

Secondly, the presence of India's polyglot density in the text, and the references to some of its high literary forms like the *ghazal*, serve to create a sense of the novel's historical and cultural specificity as a literary form in the Indian context. These references also create a distancing effect, an effect which often has a parodic twist to it. This becomes clear in the role which *ghazals* play in the text.[34] Whilst there are references to *ghazals* and their composers by the characters in the novel, and occasions when *ghazals* are sung, there are also cases of the characters actually speaking the sort of idiom which characterises the world of the *ghazal*. This is especially the case where Ameer Ali's amorous escapades are involved. On these occasions Ameer Ali is almost reduced to a cipher, the stock lover of the world of the *ghazal*. Interestingly, the other characters sometimes comment on this. Part of the reason Ameer Ali is seen by his father and Nawab Yar Jung Bahadur as naive in matters of love is that he takes the language of the *ghazal* at face value, and not as the diction of a literary genre which has only a tenuous relation to everyday life (*Confessions:* 107–8, 118–19). This is a lesson he himself learns quickly enough when his beloved's mother not only refuses him entry to her daughter's house, but mocks his naivete.[35]

The result of all this is not just that the novel distances itself from the literary form of the *ghazal*; it also offsets the hyperbolic language of the form as slightly ridiculous. The novel's play with the form of the *ghazal* provides an instance of relations between different literary traditions; in this case a genre new to the Indian scene, the English novel, gives a carefully defined role to an older indigenous form, the *ghazal*, and by so doing, distances and parodies it. The overall effect is to increase the novel's sense of its own historicity and cultural specificity, whilst also pointing to its competition with older, indigenous Indian forms. To a certain extent, the epigraphs drawn from Shakespearean plays at the commencement of many of the chapters can also be seen in this light. Of the forty-eight chapters in the novel, sixteen begin with such epigraphs. For example, Chapter Three contains the comic episode of Dildar Khan, and the epigraph to the chapter frames this episode with an appropriate citation from *Henry IV, Part 2*, on swaggerers (*Confessions:* 32). It is as though parts of the novel play out episodes which are best encapsulated by citations from one of the central figures of the newly emerging canon of English literature. This adds to the sense of a confrontation between literary genres and traditions. Thus, *Confessions of a Thug* bears the imprint not just of the East India Company's engagement with Indian idioms and textual worlds, but also of the increasingly important trend in official thinking which first clearly manifested itself in Macaulay's Education Minute of 1835. This Minute lay behind the shift in government policy towards English medium higher education in India.[36] The sense of competition with indigenous forms and literary traditions points to the beginnings of the important impact that English literature as a canon and discipline of study was to have on the educational policy of the British in India and on the development of modern Indian literatures.[37]

A third reason for these references to the linguistic complexities of India, and to some of its polished literary forms, is also linked to the fear of conspiracy which *Thagi* provoked. The cult-like status of *Thagi* consists in part of the secret language which thugs use. Of central importance here is the depiction of the scene when Ameer Ali first hears *Ramasee*. He describes himself as eavesdropping on a conversation 'in a language I only partially understood; and I thought this strange, as I knew Hindoostanee and the common dialect myself' (*Confessions:* 23). What is particularly interesting here is the feeling of the uncanny which Ameer Ali's description evokes.[38] In this instance *Ramasee* is partly familiar and half understood. This sense of the uncanny surfaces strongly later, when unknown to Ameer Ali, he visits the village where he spent his early childhood with his real parents. Thus, when he sees a fakir's abode outside the village, he relates how 'I almost started when I approached it, for it seemed like the face of a familiar friend one meets after a long, long absence, when one hesitates to accost him by name, though almost assured of its identity'. Similarly, the scene of the village 'seemed unaccountably fresh to me – as though I had but left it yesterday' (*Confessions:* 458). When he meets Futih Mahomed Khan, Ameer Ali exclaims how he 'could have called him too by name, though his features were shrunken and withered' (*Confessions:* 458–9). Even though at some level it dawns on Ameer Ali that he is the boy whose story he is hearing, he dismisses this recognition as some 'wild dream' and 'a foolish thought, such as one harbours sometimes upon the slightest cause, and dismisses after a moment's reflection' (*Confessions:* 459). What makes this sense of the uncanny even more powerful is that it touches upon an intimate sense of personal identity and self-discovery, in this case a narrative of Ameer Ali's early childhood and true parentage. Firdous Azim has argued that the emergence of the Gothic novel in the eighteenth century was centred on the creation of the uncanny. This, in part, was related to the stock theme of the Gothic novel, that of endangered femininity.[39] In *Confessions of a Thug*, however, instances of the uncanny are evocative both of the resonances of the British fascination with eavesdropping and cracking secret codes and languages, and of the implications it had for their own identity as the ruling elite of India. Narratives of self-discovery figure largely in Anglo-Indian novels such as *Kim*, because self-discovery had a part to play in the British definition (or more precisely, lack of definition) of themselves as a community in India.[40] The British in India never became a creolised elite; as Ballhatchet has argued, the maintenance of social and psychological distance between British official society and the indigenous populations of India became a defining feature of British imperial rule in the subcontinent.[41] In some ways, the figure of Ameer Ali as the thug in Meadows Taylor's novel maintains that distance between India and the author's persona. In this way, India can be vicariously experienced without it subverting the author's persona as a British official. Ameer Ali ensures that the author does not become creolised by the experience of India.

Competing narratives

The cultural and linguistic heterogeneity of India, then, is used by Meadows Taylor to emphasise the unifying potential of British rule. Equally interesting, however, is the connection between this narrative of British mastery and the complex attempt to create an omniscient author for and in the text. This attempt is complex because Ameer Ali does virtually all the talking; there is not as much explicit comment from the author as one would expect. At first glance, the author's voice hardly exists, but it is this absence of the author's voice in the main text that paradoxically points to the attempt to create him as omniscient. It is the author who enables Ameer Ali to become a narrator, as a captive who rehearses his narrative in prison (*Confessions*: 521). It is his captivity which affords Ameer Ali the opportunity to yield up his story. So whilst the author's voice is not an intrusive presence, this in itself reinforces the author's role as the enabling presence behind Ameer Ali's narrative.

However, it would be misplaced to see *Confessions of a Thug* solely in terms of the triumph of a narrative which constructs the British in India as a masterful, unifying, and enabling presence. Such a triumph is at best a qualified one. At times there are signs that the author himself is seduced by Ameer Ali's charm; at one point he grudgingly admits that Ameer Ali's swagger does not sit amiss, even in his reduced condition as a captive (*Confessions*: 266). These points in the text where the author succumbs to Ameer Ali begin to lend the latter's narrative a status independent of the author's mediations. This suggestion is reinforced when the author himself is sometimes affected by Ameer Ali's narration, for example, when he is moved by Ameer Ali's grief at the death of his son (*Confessions*: 334). These hints at the independent status of Ameer Ali's narrative are combined with points in the text where, as narrators, the author and Ameer Ali appear to be in collusion. This is borne out when the author actually hands over the manuscript of his novel to Ameer Ali, not just for his comments, but for his approval as well (*Confessions:* 266). The points of identity between the author and Ameer Ali are also reinforced by the general theme of eavesdropping in the novel, mostly in the context of the thugs going about their business, but sometimes also in such circumstances as when Ameer Ali is attempting to decipher the language of *Ramasee*. Given the important role of surveillance and spying in the anti-*Thagi* campaign,[42] it is odd that the only instances of eavesdropping in the novel are those when the thugs are spying. It is as if the thugs become a sort of reverse self-image of the British official turned author, who stands in the shadows attempting to crack the secret codes of the societies over which he administers. This suggestion of reverse self-images in the figures of eavesdropping thugs further undercuts the distance between the British narrative of mastery and the Indian narrative of *Thagi*, suggesting as it does the way opposed positions in the text merge at points into mirror images of each other.[43]

These signs of a narrative which at points is independent of the author's mediation, and at other points colludes with him, hint at its occasional development into a rival narrative which challenges the master narrative of the British official turned author. There is a clear contrast between Ameer Ali's views of himself and his profession, and the author's sometimes moralising comments.[44] For Ameer Ali, *Thagi* is a profession which involves skill and honour, and has its own rules of engagement. For example, he stresses that women are excluded as victims, and he is anxious to die as 'a man or a soldier', not like 'miserable thief' (*Confessions:* 538). He is himself appalled at the pillage and rape perpetrated on the Indian countryside by Cheetoo and his hordes, so much so that he actually takes revenge on one of Cheetoo's lieutenants for the rape of a Brahmin woman. He is often seen to be a family man, who spends long periods at home as a devoted father and husband. The existence of Ameer Ali's counter-narrative points to other instances of rival stories within the text of the novel, or to narratives within narratives. So, for example, Bhudrinath and Ameer Ali construct rival narratives within their respective legendary traditions regarding the origin of some rock formations they come across in Telingana, while Ameer Ali is part of the audience of a satirical play at Nawab Hoosein's court (*Confessions:* 159–61, 108–11). There are also a number of instances where characters relate their stories to other characters; one example of this is Mohamed's story about Brij Lall (*Confessions:* 58–71).

These instances of rival narratives, and of narratives within narratives, sharpen the sense of Ameer Ali's counter-narrative as independent of the author's mediations. Also, since events are plotted into different narratives through the mediation of different story-tellers, the novel also raises the question of the reliability of story-tellers. To a certain extent, this can be seen in terms of the problem facing the British as a whole in the area of surveillance and policing, particularly during the anti-*Thagi* campaign. This problem can be summed up in terms of the British need for reliable information from native sources which, because they were native, were by their very nature unreliable.[45] The anti-*Thagi* campaign rested crucially on the testimony of 'approvers', and it was the possible unreliability of such testimony which posed a grave problem for British officials.[46] The question of the reliability or otherwise of story-tellers and their narratives in the novel thus reflects this dilemma faced by the colonial state in its surveillance and policing of Indian society.

Sublimity and harmony

The sense of competing, overlapping, and colluding narratives in *Confessions of a Thug* is thus yet another indication of the interaction in the novel between imperialist ideologies and the linguistic complexities and literary diversities of its Indian context. Paradoxically, the constrictions of the novel's ideological context are highlighted by those occasions in the text when there are signs of a straining against that context. This is the case with those passages where there is an attempt, through the creation of an almost transcendental aesthetic language, to place the novel itself outside the series of disguises and chains of testimony within which it is enmeshed. These passages are of two kinds. One bears the influence of the category of the sublime, and the other draws upon 'classical' concepts of symmetry and harmony which the category of the sublime in part sets itself off against. The first kind involves depictions of landscape; of these, two representative passages describe Ameer Ali's panoramic views of a lake and the ocean, and his rhapsodic reaction to those views (*Confessions:* 162, 411). These rhapsodic passages signal the novel's attempt to transcend its context and subject-matter. The features of both passages fit in well with Edmund Burke's discussion of the sublime in his *A Philosophical Enquiry into the*

Origin of our Ideas of the Sublime and Beautiful (1757), in which he links the sublime with terror and 'greatness of dimension'.[47] Thus, Ameer Ali describes the lake in the vicinity of Hyderabad as 'illimitable, its edge touching as it were the heavens, and spread out into an expanse which the utmost stretch of my imagination could not compass, – a fit type, I thought, of the God of all people, whom every one thinks on; while the hoarse roar of the waves as they rolled on, mountain after mountain ... seemed to be a voice of Omnipotence which could not fail to awaken emotions of awe and dread in the most callous and unobservant!' (*Confessions*: 162). The references to awe and dread, and the evocation of vastness of size, draw very much on the notion of the sublime as defined by Burke. Also, in both passages Ameer Ali's rhapsodic response to the scenes are caused by his perception of an idea of the 'Infinite'. Burke described 'Infinity' as having 'a tendency to fill the mind with that sort of delightful horror, which is the most genuine effect, and truest test of the sublime'.[48] The depiction of the lake and ocean in Meadows Taylor's novel, and the description of Ameer Ali's response, are thus quite clearly exercises in creating a sense of the sublime. They are also indicative of how the category of the sublime, together with that of the picturesque, had such an influential impact on British perceptions of Indian landscape, art and architecture in the late eighteenth and early nineteenth centuries.[49] These two aesthetic movements of the sublime and picturesque created new maps of Indian architecture for a European audience; this was especially evident in the work of such figures as Thomas and William Daniell, whose *Oriental Scenery* (1795–1808) brought Indian temples to European viewers in a dramatic manner by portraying famous monuments in their actual landscape settings.[50] Descriptions of cave temples such as those of Elephanta and Ellora fulfilled the criteria of vastness and awfulness which Burke had defined for the concept of the sublime.[51]

The second type of passage involves the description of aesthetic objects, such as jewels. One example occurs when Ameer Ali is selling a stone to a nawab, where the latter's reaction is described thus: 'he was evidently much struck with its beauty and the fine water of the precious stones, and after turning it in every position he could to catch the exact light for it, he laid it down with a kind of sigh' (*Confessions*: 115). Sometimes these two types of passages are linked, as above where the waves of the lake are likened to diamonds (*Confessions*: 162). The harmonious symmetry of jewels here is another type of the transcendent aesthetic world which the text attempts to reach towards. This symmetry is evocative of a conception of beauty as harmony which Burke had rejected as inadequate.[52] It could also be argued that the notion of the sublime during this period was, in part at least, a reaction against 'classical' aesthetic values of harmony and symmetry;[53] Burke himself traced the genesis of these values to Plato.[54] The tendency for the diction of the passages to bear the imprint of the language of the sublime in the one case, and of the conception of beauty as harmony and symmetry in the other, is thus indicative of the novel's engagement with another set of strands in its context, namely the diverse aesthetic conceptions which influenced European perceptions of landscape, art, and architecture in colonial India. The tension between the two aesthetic categories of the sublime and the harmonious is perhaps also expressive of the tension between the dazzling and fascinating heterogeneity of India on the one hand, and the British virtues of order and control on the other. That sublimity is associated with India's heterogeneity in some way is clear from some of the passages discussed above, such as the visionary spectacle of the *muhurram* procession. Furthermore, the fact that it is Ameer Ali who is sensitive to the experience of the sublime reinforces this identification between India and the sublime. At the same time, it helps to create a safe distance between the author himself and the potentially subversive experience of the sublime, which is inimical to those virtues of control and order that form such a central part of the ideological context of the novel.

Conclusion

Linda Colley has stressed the many roots of British patriotism in the context of the forging of a British nation in the eighteenth and early nineteenth centuries.[55] If this is combined with the framework of John Barrell's and Firdous Azim's work as well,[56] *Confessions of a Thug* can be read in terms of the defining of a British imperial self in relation to a colonised 'Other'. In part, this process is typified by the antithetical and merging identities of the author's persona and Ameer Ali in the novel. It has been mentioned above that Ameer Ali is also presented as a contented family man, who spends long periods at home as a devoted father and husband. In his study of De Quincey, John Barrell has considered the apparent discrepancy between De Quincey as a happy family man and the psychopathological quality of his imaginative writings. In this regard, he has suggested that the preoccupation with endangered and violated femininity in the violent 'Orient' served to confirm the figure of the English gentleman and his sense of sexual civility at home. Here he has also pointed to the scenes of the murder of beautiful women which run through the *Confessions of a Thug*.[57] This further suggests that the *Confessions of a Thug* can be read not just as the playing out of a drama about the colonial self, but also of its familial space, in the context of the changing nature of British rule in India in the 1830s.

However, by way of conclusion, it might be useful to recapitulate two related features of *Confessions of a Thug* as a prototypical Anglo-Indian novel which this essay has tried to focus on. Both these features emerge from the novel's 'interanimating' relationships with its contexts. The first feature is the interplay between the novel's historical context of British imperial rule in India with its constricting ideologies, and its straining against the limits imposed on it by this context. This interplay is partly evident in those passages which invoke the sublime or harmonious symmetry as the types of a transcendent aesthetic. More importantly, it is also evident in the unravelling and subverting of the narrative of mastery, mainly through the narrative of the thug himself. This narrative at points achieves a status independent of the author's interference, amounting to a challenging rival to the narrative of mastery and control.

The second feature of some importance is the novel's sometimes parodic relationships with the polyglot density of India and some of the genres of its high literary cultures. As Mikhail Bakhtin has suggested, in its struggle for hegemony in an alien environment, the novel as a genre parodies its rival genres and exposes the conventionality of their forms and language. It is in its 'interanimating' relationships with new contexts that the novel is individualised and stylistically shaped.[58] *Confessions of a Thug* is very much the Anglo-Indian novel as a genre in the making; its parodic distancing of other Indian genres, and its treatment of India's polyglot societies, signal its cultural and historical specificity, as well as its struggle to achieve hegemony as a genre. The engagement with the linguistic and literary contexts of India brings into focus the relationships of competition, appropriation, and collaboration between indigenous literatures and their British colonial heritage, which acted in part as a vehicle for the imposition of European genres and aesthetic values.[59] These relationships were central to the processes by which the later modern identities of indigenous non-English literatures were shaped. They also afford us clues as to the limits of the impact of European literary values on the shaping of these modern literatures. To a certain extent, too, they can be seen as running parallel to the development of Indian nationalism and its problematic relationships with the idioms and authority of the colonial state.[60] It may be that significant insights into the shaping of the Anglo-Indian novel as a genre can also be found through an examination of the development of non-English Indian literatures over the past two centuries, which engaged with European novelistic discourse in a variety of ways.[61] The uneasy presence of India's polyglot density in the colonial novel, and its sometimes parodic engagement as a genre with indigenous modes of address and literary styles, needs to be viewed from the perspective of those marginalised and travestied traditions and genres themselves. A fuller and more comprehensive picture of the Anglo-Indian novel would emerge from a comparative perspective, in which British literary constructions of India are measured against indigenous literary constructions in certain key areas. But the exclusive concentration on the latter perpetuates a self-referential world of English studies, in which India appears as a (mis)represented object in British discourse, rather than as an entity in its own right.

Notes

1 Radhika Singha, ' "Providential" Circumstances: The Thuggee Campaign of the 1830s and Legal Innovation', *Modern Asian Studies*, 27, 1 (1993), p. 90.

2 R. C. Sherwood, 'Of the Murderers called Phansigars', *Asiatick Researches*, 13 (1820), pp. 250–83.

3 H. Gupta, 'A Critical Study of the Thugs and their Activities', *Journal of Indian History*, 37, 2 (Aug 1959), pp. 167–77.

4 C. A. Bayly, *Imperial Meridian. The British Empire and the World 1780–1830* (London and New York: Longman, 1989), pp. 172–3.

5 C. A. Bayly, *Indian Society and the Making of the British Empire* (Cambridge: Cambridge University Press, 1988), p. 122.

6 Singha, 'Thuggee Campaign', p. 84.

7 For the Company's engagement with Islamic criminal law, see Jorg Fisch, *Cheap Lives and Dear Limbs: The British Transformation of the Bengal Criminal Law 1769–1817*

(Wiesbaden: Franz Steiner Verlag, 1983); N. J. Coulson, *A History of Islamic Law* (Edinburgh: Edinburgh University Press, 1964), pp. 164–72; Joseph Schacht, *An Introduction to Islamic Law* (Oxford: Oxford University Press, 1964), pp. 94–99 and Michael Anderson, 'Islamic Law and the colonial encounter in British India', in *Institutions and Ideologies. A SOAS South Asia Reader* (London: Curzon Press, 1993), pp. 165–85. For a parallel study of the British engagement with Hindu law, see J. Duncan M. Derrett, *Religion, Law and the State in India* (London: Faber & Faber, 1968), esp. pp. 225–314.

8 Singha, 'Thuggee Campaign', pp. 91, 118–19.

9 For a suggestive overview of the role of surveillance and information-gathering in British India, see C. A. Bayly, 'Knowing the Country: Empire and Information in India', *Modern Asian Studies*, 27, 1 (1993), pp. 3–43.

10 Singha, 'Thuggee Campaign', pp. 94, 102–03, 139.

11 *Ibid.*, pp. 101, 107.

12 W. H. Sleeman, *Ramaseena or a Vocabulary of the Peculiar Language used by the Thugs, with an introduction and appendix, descriptive of the System pursued by that Fraternity and of the Measures which have been adopted by the Supreme Government of India for its Suppression* (Calcutta: G. H. Huttman, 1836), p. 3.

13 Singha, 'Thuggee Campaign', p. 124.

14 These include *Tippo Sultaun, a Tale of the Mysore War* (1840), *Tara, a Mahratta Tale* (1863), *Ralph Darnell* (1865), and *Seeta* (1872).

15 Philip Meadows Taylor, *Story of My Life* (1878; London: Zwan Publications, 1989), p. 72.

16 *Ibid.*, p. 57.

17 Philip Meadows Taylor, *Confessions of a Thug* (1839; Oxford: Oxford University Press, 1986), p. 4; italics are the novelist's. Hereafter *Confessions*; all citations are from this edition.

18 For the rhetoric employed in adumbrating this role, see G. D. Bearce, *British Attitudes towards India 1784–1858* (Oxford: Oxford University Press, 1961), pp. 141–63, 213–33, and Francis G. Hutchins, *The Illusion of Permanence. British Imperialism in India* (Princeton: Princeton University Press, 1967), pp. x–19.

19 Singha, 'Thuggee Campaign', p. 102.

20 *Ibid.*, pp. 104–05, 118–19.

21 For a detailed discussion of this part of official thinking, see Farzana Sheikh, *Community and Consensus in Islam. Muslim Representation in Colonial India, 1860–1947* (Cambridge: Cambridge University Press, 1989), pp. 49–75, where she comments on the political systems of representation which British officials evolved for what they perceived to be the peculiar conditions of India's heterogeneous society.

22 *Ibid.*, pp. 49, 52.

23 *Ibid.*, pp. 70–1.

24 David Washbrook, 'Ethnicity and Racialism in colonial Indian society', in *Racism and Colonialism*, ed. Robert Ross (The Hague: Leiden University Press, 1982), pp. 156–7.

25 John Barrell, *The Infection of Thomas De Quincey. A Psychopathology of Imperialism* (New Haven and London: Yale University Press, 1991), pp. 5, 11; and J. Majeed, *Ungoverned Imaginings. James Mill's 'The History of British India' and Orientalism* (Oxford: Clarendon Press, 1992), pp. 83–4.

26 Olivia Smith, *The Politics of Language 1791–1819* (Oxford: Clarendon Press, 1984) considers in detail these definitions and their political ramifications in the British domestic context; see also Firdous Azim, *The Colonial Rise of the Novel* (London: Routledge, 1993), pp. 16, 19.

27 The work of some European linguists in India also displays an interest in language in conjunction with social groups, modes of address, forms of etiquette, and costume; for example, see J. Gilchrist, *The Anti-Jargonist, or a Short Introduction to the Hindoostanee Language* (Calcutta: Ferris & Co., 1800), pp. xxii, xxv.

28 William Theobald, *The Legislative Acts of the Governor General of India in Council 1834–67 with an Analytical Abstract prefixed to each Act; Table of Contents and Index to each volume; the Letters Patents of the High Courts, and Acts of Parliament authorizing them* (Calcutta: Messrs. Thacker, Spink & Co., 1868), 1, p. 73.

29 Bayly, *Indian Society*, pp. 14–16, 45–78; Bayly, *Imperial Meridian*, p. 60; Majeed, *Ungoverned Imaginings*, pp. 18–25.

30 For a discussion of the interaction between the administrative idiom of the East India Company and the administrative lexicons of its predecessors, see my ' "The jargon of Indostan" – an exploration of jargon in Urdu and East India Company English', in *Languages and Jargons*, eds. Peter Burke and Roy Porter (Cambridge: Polity Press, 1995), pp. 182–205.

31 H. H. Wilson, *A Glossary of Judicial and Revenue Terms, and of Useful Words, occurring in Official Documents relating to the Administration of the Government of British India* (London: W. H. Allen & Co., 1855), p. i.

32 For an important study of Fort William College, see David Kopf, *British Orientalism and the Bengal Renaissance: The Dynamics of Indian Modernization 1773–1835* (Berkeley: University of California Press, 1969).

33 For the Company's concerns with indigenous systems of law, see footnote 7 above.

34 Formally, a *ghazal* may be defined as a love-poem of some four to thirty couplets; each couplet is divided into two half-couplets, each known as a *misra'*. The two *misra's* of the first couplet rhyme with each other and with the second *misra's* of the remaining couplets. For two useful introductions to the *ghazal* as a genre, see D. J. Matthews and C. Shackle, *An Anthology of Classical Urdu Love Lyrics. Text and Translations* (London: Oxford University Press, 1972), pp. 1–16, and R. Russell, *The Pursuit of Urdu Literature. A Select History* (London: Zed Press, 1992), pp. 26–52.

35 The fact that his beloved is a courtesan further reinforces the sense of Ameer Ali's naivete. By far the best evocation of this world of the courtesan and high Perso-Arabic literary culture is Mirzā Rusvā's Urdu novel *Umrāo Jān Adā* (1899; Aligarh: Education Book House, 1986); in relation to the point discussed here, see pp. 144–5 where Umrao and the author discuss the self-conscious play-acting of love that was so central to the relationships between courtesan and client. See also Ch. 9, pp. 144–51 on the jealous (and naive) *maulvi* who is infatuated with Umrao.

36 For a discussion of the issues surrounding this notorious Minute, see, amongst others, K. Ballhatchet, 'The Home Government and Bentinck's Educational Policy', *Cambridge Historical Journal*, 10 (1950–52, pp. 244–9; J. F. Hilliker, 'English Utilitarians and Indian Education', *Journal of General Education*, 27 (April 1975–Jan 1976), pp. 103–10; and G. Sirkin and N. R. Sirkin, 'The Battle of Indian Education: Macaulay's Opening Salvo newly discovered', *Victorian Studies*, 14 (June 1971), pp. 407–28.

37 For a recent study of the impact of English on educational institutions in India, see Gauri Vishwanathan, *Masks of Conquest: Literary Study and British Rule in India* (London: Faber & Faber, 1990). See also Chris Baldick, *The Social Mission of English Criticism 1848–1932* (Oxford: Clarendon Press, 1983), p. 70 for a discussion of the emergence of English language and literature as a discipline for the Indian Civil Service.

38 Here, in general terms, by uncanny is meant experiencing the familiar as unfamiliar; at least, this seems to be how Freud characterises it in a definition of the uncanny as 'nothing new or alien, but something which is familiar and old-established in the mind and which has become alienated from it only through the process of repression', 'The Uncanny', in the *Standard Edition of the Complete Psychological Works of Sigmund*

Freud, ed. James Strachey (London: Hogarth Press and the Institute of Psycho-Analysis, 1955), 17, pp. 226, 241.

39 Azim, *Colonial Rise of the Novel*, p. 184.

40 For a discussion of this aspect of British colonial society in India, see P. J. Marshall, 'British Immigration into India in the Nineteenth Century', in P. C. Emmer and M. Morner, *European Expansion and Migration* (New York: Berg, 1991), pp. 179–96; see also his 'The Whites of British India: A Failed Colonial Society?', paper delivered at the Institute of Commonwealth Studies, University of London, 12 Nov 1987, and *Indian Society*, pp. 202–03 on British India as a 'failed' colonial society.

41 K. Ballhatchet, *Race, Sex and Class under the Raj. Imperial Attitudes and Policies and their Critics, 1793–1905* (London: Weidenfeld & Nicolson, 1980), p. vii.

42 For a suggestive exploration of this aspect of imperial rule, see C. A. Bayly, 'Knowing the Country: Empire and Information in India', *Modern Asian Studies* 27, 1 (1993), pp. 3–43.

43 Firdous Azim discusses this process at work in *Jane Eyre*, see *Colonial Rise of the Novel*, pp. 176–8.

44 For a discussion of the self-perceptions of captured thugs as reflected in their narratives of testimony, see Singha, 'Thuggee Compaign', pp. 96–8.

45 Bayly, 'Knowing the Country', pp. 3–4.

46 Singha, 'Thuggee Campaign', pp. 136–8.

47 Edmund Burke, *A Philosophical Enquiry into the Origins of our Ideas of the Sublime and Beautiful*, ed. James T. Boulton (1757; Oxford: Basil Blackwell, 1987), pp. 39, 72–3.

48 Burke, *A Philosophical Enquiry*, p. 73. On the relationship between the sublime and concepts of the self, see Stephen D. Cox, *'The Stranger Within Thee'. Concepts of the Self in late Eighteenth-Century Literature* (Pittsburgh: Univ. of Pittsburgh Press, 1980), pp. 7–8.

49 Partha Mitter, *Much Maligned Monsters. History of European Reactions to Indian Art* (Oxford: Clarendon Press, 1977), pp. 119–23.

50 *Ibid.*, pp. 126–7.

51 *Ibid.*, p. 123.

52 Burke, *A Philosophical Enquiry*, pp. 91–110.

53 Mitter, *Much Maligned Monsters*, pp. 121–2.

54 Burke, *A Philosophical Enquiry*, p. 101.

55 See her study, *Britons. Forging the Nation 1707–1837* (London: Pimlico, 1992).

56 In *The Infection of Thomas De Quincey* and *The Colonial Rise of the Novel* respectively.

57 Barrell, *The Infection of Thomas De Quincey*, pp. 191–2. It is worth noting that Ameer Ali goes a step further than De Quincey and actually does murder his sister, albeit unknowingly.

58 Mikhail Bakhtin, *The Dialogic Imagination. Four Essays by Mikhail Bakhtin* (Austin: University of Texas Press, 1981), ed. Michael Holquist, translated by Caryl Emerson and Michael Holquist, pp. 5, 276, 345.

59 For a discussion of some of these issues, see Aijaz Ahmad's excellent ' "Indian Literature": Notes towards the Definition of a Category', in his *In Theory. Classes, Nations, Literatures* (London: Verso, 1992), pp. 243–85.

60 For these purposes, some of the more interesting accounts include David Gilmartin, *Empire and Islam. Punjab and the Making of Pakistan* (London: I. B. Tauris & Co. Ltd., 1988), David Page, *Prelude to Partition. All-India Muslim Politics, 1921–1932* (Delhi:

Oxford University Press, 1981), Gyanendra Pandey: *The Construction of Communalism in Colonial North India* (Delhi: Oxford University Press, 1990) and Anil Seal *et al.* (eds.), *The Emergence of Indian Nationalism: Competition and Collaboration in the Later Nineteenth Century* (Cambridge: Cambridge University Press, 1968).

61 This field is of course vast, but some suggestive accounts include C. Coppola (ed.), *Marxist Influences and South Asian Literature* (Asian Studies Center, Michigan State University, 1974), 2 vols.; Amrik Kalsi, 'Pariksaguru (1882): The First Hindi Novel and the Hindu Elite', *Modern Asian Studies* 26, 4 (1992), pp. 763–90; G. C. Narang, 'Tradition and Innovation in Urdu: Poetry', in *Poetry and Renaissance*, ed. M. Govindan (Madras: Kumara Asan birth centenary volume, 1974), pp. 415–34; Tapan Raychaudhuri, *Europe Reconsidered: Perceptions of the West in Nineteenth Century Bengal* (Delhi: Oxford University Press, 1988); Ralph Russell, *The Pursuit of Urdu Literature*, pp. 83–111, on the elements of the oral *dastan* in the modern Urdu novel; C. Shackle, 'A Sikh spiritual epic: Vir Singh's Rana Surat Singh' (unpublished paper).

Bibliography

Ahmad, Aijaz, *In Theory. Classes, Nations, Literatures* (London: Verso, 1992).

Anderson, Michael, 'Islamic Law and the colonial encounter in British India', in Peter Robb (ed.), *Institutions and Ideologies. A SOAS South Asia Reader* (London: Curzon Press, 1993), pp. 165–85.

Azim, Firdous, *The Colonial Rise of the Novel* (London and New York: Routledge, 1993).

Bakhtin, Mikhail, *The Dialogic Imagination. Four Essays by Mikhail Bakhtin*, ed. Michael Holquist (Austin: University of Texas Press, 1981).

Baldick, Chris, *The Social Mission of English Criticism 1848–1932* (Oxford: Clarendon Press, 1983).

Ballhatchet, K., 'The Home Government and Bentinck's Educational Policy', *Cambridge Historical Journal*, 10 (1950–52), pp. 244–9.

Ballhatchet, K., *Race, Sex and Class under the Raj. Imperial Attitudes and Policies and their Critics, 1793–1905* (London: Weidenfeld & Nicolson, 1980), p. vii.

Barrell, John, *The Infection of Thomas De Quincey. A Psychopathology of Imperialism* (New Haven and London: Yale University Press, 1991).

Bayly, C. A., *Indian Society and the Making of the British Empire* (Cambridge: Cambridge University Press, 1988).

—— *Imperial Meridian. The British Empire and the World 1780–1830* (London and New York: Longman, 1989).

—— 'Knowing the Country: Empire and Information in India', *Modern Asian Studies*, 27, 1 (1993), pp. 3–43.

Bearce, G. D., *British Attitudes towards India 1784–1858* (Oxford: Oxford University Press, 1961).

Burke, Edmund, *A Philosophical Enquiry into the Origin of our Ideas of the Sublime and Beautiful*, ed. James T. Boulton (1757; Oxford: Basil Blackwell, 1987).

Colley, Linda, *Britons. Forging the Nation 1707–1837* (London: Pimlico, 1992).

Coppola, C., *Marxist Influences and South Asian Literature* (South Asian Studies Center, Michigan State University, 1974), 2 vols.

Coulson, N. J., *A History of Islamic Law* (Edinburgh: Edinburgh University Press, 1964).

Cox, Stephen, *'The Stranger Within Thee': Concepts of the Self in late Eighteenth-Century Literature* (Pittsburgh: Pittsburgh University Press, 1980).

Derrett, J. Duncan M., *Religion, Law and the State in India* (London: Faber & Faber, 1968).

Fisch, Jorg, *Cheap Lives and Dear Limbs: The British Transformation of the Bengal Criminal Law 1769–1817* (Wiesbaden: Franz Steiner Verlag, 1983).

Freud, Sigmund, 'The Uncanny', in the *Standard Edition of the Complete Psychological Works of Sigmund Freud*, ed. James Strachey (London: Hogarth Press and the Institute of Psycho-Analysis, 1955).

Gilchrist, J., *The Anti-Jargonist, or a Short Introduction to the Hindoostanee Language* (Calcutta: Ferris & Co., 1800).

Gilmartin, David, *Empire and Islam. Punjab and the Making of Pakistan* (London: I. B. Tauris & Co., 1992).

Gupta, H., 'A Critical Study of the Thugs and their Activities', *Journal of Indian History*, 37, 2 (Aug 1959), pp. 167–77.

Hilliker, J. F., 'English Utilitarians and Indian Education', *Journal of General Education*, 27 (April 1975 – Jan 1976).

Hutchins, Francis, *The Illusion of Permanence: British Imperialism in India* (Princeton: Princeton University Press, 1967).

Kalsi, Amrik, 'Pariksaguru (1882): The first Hindi novel and the Hindu Elite', *Modern Asian Studies* 26, 4 (1992), pp. 763–90.

Kopf, David, *British Orientalism and the Bengal Renaissance: The Dynamics of Indian Modernization 1773–1835* (Berkeley: University of California Press, 1969).

Majeed, Javed, *Ungoverned Imaginings. James Mill's 'The History of British India' and Orientaslism* (Oxford: Clarendon Press, 1992).

—— ' "The jargon of Indostan": an exploration of jargon in Urdu and East India Company English', *Languages and Jargons*, eds. Peter Burke and Roy Porter (Cambridge: Polity Press, 1995), pp. 182–205.

Marshall, P. J., 'British Immigration into India', in P. C. Emmer and M. Morner (eds.), *European Expansion and Migration* (New York: Berg, 1991).

—— 'The Whites of British India: A Failed Colonial Society?', unpublished paper.

Matthews, D. J., with Shackle, C., *An Anthology of Classical Urdu Love Lyrics. Text and Translations* (London: Oxford University Press, 1972).

Mitter, Partha, *Much Maligned Monsters. History of European Reactions to Indian Art* (Oxford: Clarendon Press, 1977).

Narang, G. C., 'Tradition and Innovation in Urdu Poetry', in *Poetry and Renaissance*, ed. M. Govindan (Madras: Kumara Asan birth centenary, 1974), pp. 415–34.

Page, David, *Prelude to Partition. All-Indian Muslim Politics, 1921–1932* (Delhi: Oxford University Press, 1981).

Pandey, G., *The Construction of Communalism in Colonial North India* (Delhi: Oxford University Press, 1990).

Raychaudhuri, T., *Europe Reconsidered: Perceptions of the West in Nineteenth Century Bengal* (Delhi: Oxford University Press, 1988).

Russell, Ralph, *The Pursuit of Urdu Literature. A Select History* (London: Zed Press, 1986).

Rūsvā, Mirzā, *Umrāo Jān Ādā* (1899; Aligarh: Education Book House, 1986).

Schacht, Joseph, *An Introduction to Islamic Law* (Oxford: Oxford University Press, 1964).

Seal, Anil (ed.), *The Emergence of Indian Nationalism: Competition and Collaboration in the Later Nineteenth Century* (Cambridge: Cambridge University Press, 1968).

Shackle, C. *see* Matthews, D.J. above.

—— 'A Sikh spiritual epic: Vir Singh's Rana Surat Singh', unpublished paper.

Sheikh, Farzana, *Community and Consensus in Islam. Muslim Representation in Colonial India, 1860–1947* (Cambridge: Cambridge University Press, 1989).

Sherwood, R. C., 'Of the Murderers called Phansigars', *Asiatick Researches*, 13 (1820), pp. 250–83.

Singha, Radhika, ' "Providential" Circumstances: The Thuggee Campaign of the 1830s and Legal Innovation', *Modern Asian Studies*, 27, 1 (1993), pp. 83–146.

Sirkin, G. and N. R., 'The Battle of Indian Education: Macaulay's Opening Salvo newly discovered', *Victorian Studies*, 14 (June 1971), pp. 407–28.

Sleeman, W. H., *Ramaseena or a Vocabulary of the Peculiar Language used by the Thugs, with an introduction and appendix, descriptive of the System pursued by that Fraternity and of the Measures which have been adopted by the Supreme Government of India for its Suppression* (Calcutta: G. H. Huttman, 1836).

Smith, Olivia, *The Politics of Language 1791–1819* (Oxford: Clarendon Press, 1984).

Taylor, Philip Meadows, *Confessions of a Thug* (1839; Oxford: Oxford University Press, 1986).

—— *A Student's Manual of the History of India* (London: 1870).

—— *Story of My Life* (1878; London: Zwan Publications, 1989).

Theobald, William, *The Legislative Acts of the Governor General of India in Council 1834–67 with an Analytical Abstract prefixed to each Act; Table of Contents and Index to each volume; the Letters Patents of the High Courts, and Acts of Parliament authorizing them* (Calcutta: Messrs. Thacker, Spink, & Co., 1868).

Vishwanathan, G., *Masks of Conquest: Literary Study and British Rule in India* (London: Faber & Faber, 1990).

Washbrook, David, 'Ethnicity and Racialism in colonial Indian society', in Robert Ross (ed.), *Racism and Colonialism* (The Hague: Leiden University Press, 1982), pp. 143–81.

Wilson, H. H., *A Glossary of Judicial and Revenue Terms, and of Useful Words, occurring in Official Documents relating to the Administration of the Government of British India* (London: W. H. Allen & Co., 1855).

4

'The Bhabhal of Tongues': reading Kipling, reading Bhabha

BART MOORE-GILBERT

As suggested in the introduction to this volume, Homi Bhabha's essays constitute an important reformulation of the model of colonial discourse analysis developed in Said's *Orientalism* (1978). In this chapter, I intend to consider in more detail how Bhabha's use of psychoanalytic theory invites reconsideration of Said's ideas about the intentionality and unity of colonial discourse. My principal contention is that Bhabha's critique allows new ways of looking at certain areas of Kipling's representation of colonial relations which have come in for particularly severe treatment, especially from literary critics adopting the premises and methodology of *Orientalism*.

A much older tradition of Kipling criticism insists that one of his major weaknesses lies in a failure to register real criticism of, or opposition to, colonial rule. This charge is often tied up with another, which is that Kipling's narratives are transparent and monologic in large measure because they are unable to register a challenge to their own, and colonial, authority. Such complaints go back at least as early as Francis Adams in 1891 and recur throughout the twentieth century, for example in the work of Edmund Wilson and Allen Greenberger. Criticism elaborated in the wake of *Orientalism* has taken a slightly different line, giving limited recognition to Kipling's sense of unease about various aspects of imperial policy, particularly in his stories dating from the 1880s. But on the question of the representation of nationalist opposition, such critics tend to follow precedent. John McClure sets the tone, arguing that 'Kipling simply wipes out, erases from his picture of India, all those groups and forces that were making life there in his time difficult for any imperialist, country-born or not'.[1]

It may be as well, then, to begin this reconsideration of Kipling's political vision with analysis of 'On the City Wall' (1888), a tale which critics like McClure grudgingly admit does demonstrate some engagement with subaltern resistance. Despite this, McClure and his followers usually conclude that 'On the City Wall' is, in fact, evidence of Kipling's desire to neutralise the oppositional voices to which he gives brief discursive space. Thus Benita Parry concludes that the tale fails to penetrate in any meaningful way into the subordinate culture and that a confident reaffirmation of 'the positioning master/native' is its principal thematic concern; meanwhile Mark Paffard sees 'the generalities' of the narrator's opening paragraphs of political reflection in 'On the City Wall' as an example of Kipling at his most 'knowing and superficial'.[2]

As the introduction to this volume also argued, the problem with the 'ideological' model of colonial discourse analysis derived from Said is that it is generally insensitive to questions of form and, in particular, the way form complicates the ostensible thematic meanings of literary versions of colonial discourse. 'On the City Wall' bears comparison with 'Beyond the Pale' from the point of view of narrative technique; it is narrated by another unnamed figure who – in contrast to the narrator of 'Beyond the Pale' – is also a principal protagonist in the embedded tale. The critics mentioned above take no account of possible tensions in the tale, assuming an overall coherence of meaning and perspective because frame narrator and protagonist are one and the same. This section of the chapter argues that no such coherence can be presumed; rather the narrative instabilities of 'On the City Wall' reveal a complex structure of ideological contradiction and psychic ambivalence which point to disabling resistances in the unconscious of imperial discourse.

This conflictual structure of psychic affect reflects on, and is partly determined by, two particular developments in Anglo-Indian politics in the 1880s. Firstly, there was a significant change of imperial policy on the arrival as Viceroy of Lord Ripon, who in some ways seemed a throw-back to the aggressively modernising Anglicists represented by figures like Macaulay and Lord Bentinck, who dominated Indian policy for more than a generation prior to the uprisings of 1857. Secondly, the story is framed in the context of the inauguration of the Indian National Congress in 1885, the first major movement of organised political opposition to Anglo-Indian rule. Its formation can be understood in part as a reaction to the failure of important elements of Ripon's programme of reforms, most notoriously the Ilbert Bill, which proposed to allow Indian judges to try whites in certain tightly defined circumstances.

Ripon's policy was distinguished by a renewed emphasis on attempting to secure control of India by encouraging Indians to identify with, and internalise, British values and cultural forms. In contrast to the policy adopted in the wake of the 'Mutiny', which relied largely on coercion and repression, Ripon sought to secure the consent of the native subject by means of acculturation and limited devolution of imperial power. This changed political climate is immediately apparent to the guerrilla leader Khem Singh, veteran of three different phases of armed resistance to British rule, on his release from prison. As he comments to his jailer, ' "you [now] do great honour to all men of our country and by your own hands are destroying the Terror of your Name which is your rock and your defence. This is a foolish thing. Will oil and water mix?" '[3]

The narrator corroborates this perception of a change of strategy in imperial policy in the fifteen or so years that Khem Singh has been exiled in Burma, for his part in the Kuka uprising of 1871. The tale opens with the narrator surveying the still tranquil city from his vantage point in Lalun's salon; the panorama includes the significant detail of young Indians playing cricket in the grounds of the Government College. The process of acculturation this scene implies is even more obvious in the depiction of Wali Dad, the young Muslim intellectual, the degree of whose identification with imperial culture is evident in his vision of the future: ' "I might wear an English coat and trousers. I might be a leading Mohammedan pleader. I might be received even at the Commissioner's tennis-parties where the English stand on one side and the natives on the other, in order to promote social intercourse throughout the Empire" ' ('City Wall': 233). The political success of this policy of acculturation is apparently confirmed by Khem Singh's inability to instigate a new revolt along the lines of the 'Mutiny' or the Kuka uprising of 1871. The young men to whom he appeals are disdainful, preferring incorporation within the imperial system to the uncertain rewards of insurgency; they 'were entering native regiments or Government offices, and Khem Singh could give them neither pension, decorations, nor influence' (p. 242). Khem Singh's failure explains the collected tone with which the narrator recounts his hair-raising experience on the night of the riot. There could be no more certain statement of the security and legitimacy of imperial rule than the narrator's description of the Indian Civil Service at work 'in order that the land may be protected from death and sickness, famine and war, and may eventually become capable of standing alone. It will never stand alone' (p. 223).

The confident tone of the opening paragraphs might also be read as evidence that the split between himself as narrating and narrated personae – a division to which he alludes at the end of the story – has been resolved: 'When the news went abroad that Khem Singh had escaped, I did not, since I was then living this story, not writing it, connect myself ... with his disappearance' ('City Wall': 242). Restored to unity of being as he believes himself to be, the narrator can now, seemingly, assume the role of reader's guide, in full command of the meaning of his experience. While this might well seem to confirm the legitimacy of the readings provided by McClure, Paffard and Parry, closer attention suggests that the narrator's identity – and the tale itself – remain riven by contradictions, preventing either from attaining the kind of unity necessary for colonial authority to operate with full effect. This suggests the degree to which the psychic economy of the coloniser, as well as of the colonised, was being destabilised by the new political strategy inaugurated by Lord Ripon. In this sense, the tale appears to corroborate Bhabha's argument that in attempting to secure colonial rule more effectively through the production of mimic and hybrid subjects, rather than relying on simple repression, imperialism also induced radical fractures in its own ways of feeling, knowing and representation: 'Mimicry is thus the sign of a double articulation; a complex strategy of reform, regulation and discipline, which "appropriates" the Other'; mimicry also, however, 'poses an immanent threat to both "normalized" knowledges and disciplinary powers'.[4]

Affective and discursive disturbance are evident in the first place in the narrator's confused regime of representation. As Bhabha points out, one symptom of fracturing in colonial discourse is its highly conflictual vision of the colonised subject. This is borne out in the way that the narrator employs mutually cancelling stereotypes to portray the native Indian, as the example of Khem Singh illustrates. On the one hand, like Wali Dad and Lalun, he is an example of the wiliness and untrustworthiness of the subaltern. He breaks his word that he will not attempt to escape from the Fort, in exchange for which he has been offered a relatively liberal regime of incarceration. On the other hand, the narrator is at pains to point out that Khem Singh only reneges on the return of the Senior Captain, an uncomplicated 'racist', who shows him none of the respect that his junior does. Paradoxically, moreover, the generally positive light in which Khem Singh is seen derives from the fact that he is presented as a model of fidelity to his traditionalist cause – albeit that the aim of this is to eject the British from India. This division in the way Khem Singh is represented persists at the end of the story, where he is an object of both pity and admiration on the narrator's side, and at once harmless and a continuing source of real danger.

Furthermore, the narrator simultaneously relies on stereotype yet undermines it as the ground on which colonial representation rests as a form of 'knowledge', by fixing identities which can then be generalised and repeated for the purposes of imperial control. This is suggested by his critical attitude towards the Senior Captain of Fort Amara, where Khem Singh is imprisoned: 'He called all natives "niggers", which, besides being extreme bad form, shows gross ignorance' ('City Wall': 231). Above all, the narrator takes the Captain to task for his inability to recognise the native subject as differentiated: ' "Sikhs, Pathans, Dogras – they're all alike, these black people" ' (p. 232). The political dangers of this regime of knowledge are suggested by the fact that the Senior Captain consequently allows two members of Khem Singh's own ethnic group, the Sikhs, to guard him. In due course they are suborned and aid in his escape.

Affective and discursive disturbance are also apparent in the narrator's formulation of the imperial mission. The opening paragraph of the story suggests the degree to which the narrator has absorbed the point of view of the subject culture. Far from condemning the institution of hereditary prostitution, a practice which, like *sati* and polygamy, had traditionally been invoked to demonstrate the degraded nature of native culture, and thus to legitimise the redemptive mission of empire, the narrator recognises the cultural integrity of the practice and the society which it exemplifies. The narrator's defence of traditional India thus contradicts the narrative of empire as modernisation and progress, which is implied in his loan to Wali Dad of books on Athenian democracy.

The narrator's own sympathy for Indian society thus becomes an unforeseen source of resistance from *within* to hybridisation as imperial strategy.[5] The paradox is intensified by Wali Dad's return to his Muslim roots at the time of the riot, an act of 'reversion' which brings into question the success of the policy of acculturation. In place of a rationale for empire articulated in terms of the 'civilising mission', then, the narrator at first offers Britain in the role of peace-keeper. His premise for this legitimising narrative rests ultimately on the inter-ethnic and religious hostility which in his view proves that India can 'never stand alone' ('City Wall': 223) as one nation. This is immediately gainsaid, however, by the narrator's description of Lalun's salon, where all castes and ethnic groups meet and, like the Athenians, enact a model of democratic political debate which provides a striking image of unity in India's multiplicity. More obviously, the combination of Hindu (Lalun), Muslim (Wali Dad) and Sikh (Khem Singh) to outwit the narrator suggests Kipling's anxious recognition of the real potential, as well as ambition, of organised nationalist politics to create a common front between India's varied cultures to oppose the British.

The narrator's reduced version of the imperial mission is then in turn brought into question. The ironic description of *Pax Britannica* as an 'idol' suggests some scepticism about its status as imperial master-narrative, which is reinforced by evidence of the violence by which this peace is, contradictorily, enforced. The destructive power of the peace-keepers is represented not only by 'the line of guns which could blow the City to powder in half an hour' ('City Wall': 203), but by the casualty left behind after the riot: 'The skull had been smashed in by *gun-butt* or bamboo-stave' (p.242, my emphasis). The fact that the per-petrator of this death cannot be readily identified, but may indeed be one of the British themselves, together with Pettit's cynically expedient attitude to the victim, sets up an ironic parallel between the violence of local religious 'fundamentalism' and the attitude of the English 'peace-keepers': 'The Garrison Artillery ... to the last cherished a wild hope that they might be allowed to bombard the city at a hundred yards' range' (p.238).

Perhaps most damagingly, even at the moment when the narrator is eulogising the self-sacrifice of the Indian Civil Service, an obvious conflict is registered in his conception of India as ontologically incapable of independence and the simultaneous assertion of that goal as Anglo-India's *raison d'être*, for the former proposition renders Anglo-India's presence in the subcontinent literally absurd. This suggests a fundamental fracture in the discursive constitution of imperial identity, as well as the limited nature of the (self-) understanding the narrator has acquired as a result of his experience. Ambivalence continues to be evident across the whole range of his feelings, opinions and actions.

As suggested, this fracturing in the narrator's authority as spokesman of empire is largely generated by his unstable positioning *between* Indian cultures – represented at one extreme by the 'fundamentalist' Khem Singh – and British officialdom, represented at another extreme by the equally 'fundamentalist' Captain of Fort Amara. On the one hand the narrator has the ear of the military authorities at the Fort and of the Deputy-Commissioner. On the other, his relationship with Lalun and Wali Dad has provided a deep immersion in native life, with which he comes to identify closely. Thus he can interpret for Lalun when Wali Dad speaks in English, and is able not simply to understand the ostensible meaning of the praise song dedicated to Lalun, but also its deeper symbolic significance, which depends on a capacity to decode Wali Dad's vernacular puns. He is also able to identify particular varieties of Indian and Persian verse forms and uses Indian diction at many points in his story. And, of course, it is native contacts as much as British sources which inform him of Khem Singh's changing state of mind in the course of his incarceration.

The intimacy with native life which the narrator enjoys in fact makes him as much of a 'hybrid' as Wali Dad and, in crucial senses, his double or 'secret sharer'. Thus the irony of the narrator's condescension towards Wali Dad on the grounds of the latter's cultural syncretism and unreliability – which are, of course, mirrored in the narrator as the tale unfolds. Indeed, the narrator's complex, if finally limited, understanding of native life is precisely what makes him such an apposite instrument for the conspirators' use. This suggests that the very forms of knowledge which imperialism generates and on which it relies depend on a dialogue with native culture, which allows the native subject to turn those discourses back against the dominant power. While the narrator complains that Wali Dad spends his time 'reading books which are of no use to anybody' ('City Wall': 222), access to such knowledge comes, of course, principally through the narrator himself. This reinforces the irony of the narrator's earlier observation that at Mission-school, the young Muslim 'absorbed more than ever ... the Missionaries intended he should' (p. 222). It is therefore apposite that in the crucial scene of the story, when the fugitive Khem Singh is hauled to safety up the city wall and into Lalun's salon, the narrator takes the place of (and exchanges subject positions with) Wali Dad. Mistaken at first for Wali Dad by Lalun, he is easily seduced into securing a safe conduct for Khem Singh out of the city to the safety of his co-conspirators.

This motif of 'doubling', then, supports Bhabha's argument that hybridisation not only destabilises colonial authority from within, but opens up new and unforeseen spaces of subaltern resistance to the dominant power.[6] By the end of the story the narrator has been made an accessory in the plot to free Khem Singh, so that – as he acknowledges – he becomes 'Lalun's vizier after all' ('City Wall': 243). Not only does Kipling reverse the hierarchically-ordered binary opposition organised along the axis of active white male/passive subaltern female traditionally apparent in colonial discourse (in a more pointed manner than in 'Beyond the Pale'), but, crucially, he implies that the narrator remains compromised by events. Despite his access to the authorities, and his evident duty to report on dissidents (compare the narrator of 'The Man Who Would Be King' who immediately reports the movements of the loafers to higher authority), the narrator allows the former regime at Lalun's house to resume.

This suggests that the narrator's loyalty and identity as colonising subject has been, and continues to be, fatally split by a relationship with Lalun and Wali Dad which ultimately dissolves him as imperial agent. Thus 'On the City Wall', arguably, is plotted round a process whereby the possessing sovereign subject of imperial discourse (the narrating persona as reader's guide) becomes the dispossessed subject (the narrated persona as Lalun's vizier) of the 'plot' of empire – which the tale presents as the process by which power will, with historical inevitability, be transferred from ruler to ruled. That this transfer is already underway – an unexpected consequence of the strategy of imperial control that created hybridity and ambivalence in the native subject – is indicated in Wali Dad's expectations for the future alluded to earlier.

The dissolving imperial agent: the case of *Kim*

I want now to argue that similarly disabling structures of contradiction and ambivalence attend Kipling's vision in *Kim*, despite its use of providential romance genre and an apparently omniscient third person narrative voice. To suggest such links between an early tale like 'On the City Wall' and *Kim* is once more to contradict important elements of much recent Kipling criticism. The currently accepted interpretation of the writer's ideological development is that Kipling retreated progressively from occasional early willingness to express critical and subversive insights about the conduct of the Indian empire. Thus Parry sees *Kim* as politically regressive compared with certain early stories: 'If "To be Filed for reference" both intimates and averts a challenge to British knowledge, then *Kim* (1901) confidently reaffirms its validity'.[7] Similarly, Zohreh Sullivan, who is much more alert to the narrative instabilities of *Kim*, concludes that they offer 'only an apparent subversion' of imperial ideology, which she, too, suggests was subjected to more rigorous critique earlier in Kipling's career.[8]

Much of the evidence for seeing *Kim* as confidently reaffirming imperial certainties rests on a particular reading of the ending of the text. Recent analysis of *Kim* generally repeats the argument of earlier critics like Boris Ford that Kipling reaches thematic and aesthetic closures through making an unambiguous choice for Kim to continue in the Secret Service. McClure suggests that Kim, 'in choosing to manipulate the old man [the lama], expose him to danger, and use him as an instrument, has made an important personal choice for cold exclusiveness. This choice is further confirmed at the book's end, when Kim decides to continue his work as a spy'.[9] Said reaches an identical conclusion. The lama is ultimately betrayed and Kim becomes 'an enforcement officer for British Imperialism'.[10]

Three corollaries of such analysis deserve particular emphasis. The first is that the threat to imperial security is contained and neutralised, and that it is precisely Kipling's confidence in colonial power which allows him to produce such an apparently beneficent vision of empire. Secondly, in supposedly making a free choice to remain in the Secret Service, such critics assume that Kim also attains a fixed and coherent identity as a member of Anglo-Indian society. (This alleged resolution to his existential and moral crisis at the end of the text also, of course, marks his transition from uncertain adolescence into stable adult identity.) To Sullivan, the political meaning of this resolution is clear: the emergence of 'the essentially unified Kim' is Kipling's 'demonstration of power through knowledge and [the] subsequent triumph of the colonizer over his deepest anxiety – loss of self in India'.[11]

The third corollary is that the interest in cultural syncretism and relativism which Kipling demonstrates throughout *Kim* is actually evidence of political and artistic bad faith. McClure, for instance, argues that 'the generous inclusiveness of *Kim* is in the spirit of wish-fulfilment, not of hard-won victory or compromise'.[12] Gail Ching-Liang Low, similarly, proposes that 'a *syncretism* is offered in *Kim* which writes out conflict in an all-encompassing vision'.[13] Meanwhile Parry argues that Kim's 'recovery is effected without any engagement with the competing commitments and it acts to abolish conflict'[14] – presumably within Kipling's political vision as well as within Kim himself. Said's introduction to *Kim* argues that India's multiplicity is presented only to demonstrate that no aspect of it escapes colonial knowledge and classification by the all-seeing eye of the Secret Service. This all implies that in attaining full identity as an Anglo-Indian at the end of the text, Kim writes off his ties to his Indian past.

In order to contest such readings, it may be useful first to indicate the thematic continuities between 'On the City Wall' and *Kim* in respect of Kipling's recognition of resistance to British rule. It is clear that *Kim* presents concerted opposition, which, if not nationalist in the sense that the INC was to prove to be, is certainly national in scope. Apart from one moment of apparent complacency about the ease with which dissent can be contained,[15] *Kim* generally rebuts those who see Kipling creating a conflict-free India in the text. First of all, in keeping with its setting in the time of the second Afghan War,[16] there is reference to the mobilisation of 8000 British troops. As one character comments, '"there is always war along the Border"' (p. 94), which suggests the degree to which the hegemony of British India still, in Kipling's time, required force to be maintained.

More importantly, *Kim* corroborates the central perception of 'On the City Wall' that dissidents 'must exist among two hundred million people, and, if they are not attended to, may cause trouble and even break the great idol *Pax Britannica*, which, as the newspapers say, lives between Peshawur and Cape Comorin' ('City Wall': 223). And while Khem Singh surrenders, there is no evidence that the leaders of the conspiracy, represented by the man in the gold pince-nez to whom the narrator unwittingly delivers Khem Singh, are captured and incarcerated. The implication that anti-British agitation is, in fact, endemic is reiterated in *Kim*, where the conspiracy has not simply a national, but an international, dimension, involving 'five confederated [border] Kings, the sympathetic Northern power [Russia], a Hindu banker in Peshawur [representing the nationalist bourgeoisie], a firm of gun-makers in Belgium, and an important, semi-independent Mohammedan ruler to the south [representing traditional feudal India]' (*Kim:* 70). In due course these conspirators are joined by a French spy, who provides further evidence of European rivals eager to exploit internal dissension with British rule in India. While the most visible source of threat – in the form of the foreign spies – is dispatched, there is again no assurance that this means an end to conspiracy. The increasing scale of resistance to British rule in *Kim* is suggested in other ways. Whereas in the stories from the 1880s, surveillance is a matter for local police officers like Strickland, *Kim* attests to the existence of a vast and complex underground system of counter-insurgency. As Mahbub Ali suggests: ' "The Game is so large that one sees but a little at a time" ' (p. 217), and Kim learns that it 'never ceases day and night, throughout India' (p. 224). Occasional references to the 'Mutiny', moreover, clearly indicate the anxiety which organises this elaborate web of operations.

Anxiety is also evident in the text's admission of the Service's shortcomings. As Hurree's comments on Creighton's complacency in allowing the conspiracy to develop suggest (*Kim:* 271), when vigilance is slackened, serious consequences may ensue. The Secret Service seems curiously prone to infiltration. Kim is able to spy on Creighton quite undisturbed, and consequently learns the plans for the military expedition to the north. The implications of this are clear in the later description of Simla as a place where, as in Lalun's salon, courtesans discuss 'the things which are supposed to be the profoundest secrets of the India Council' (p. 194). Most troubling of all to the conventional account of *Kim* is Creighton's clear admission of his limited insight into native ways of thinking (pp. 159–60). Coming as they do from the head of Counter-Intelligence, and an ethnological scholar, his comments suggest Kipling's deep scepticism about any easy assumption of the extent of colonial knowledge and power.

There are also grounds for reconsideration of the current critical orthodoxy that Kipling reaches formal and thematic closure in *Kim* by offering Kim a secure identity as enforcement officer for the Raj. Robert Moss opens the way to a very different reading, by his stress on 'Kim's recurrent states of psychological tension over the alternatives of East and West ... Powerfully ambivalent, he vacillates back and forth between his two identities, or semi-identities, until at last the split results in a severe emotional crisis'.[17] Moss is alluding here to the trauma Kim experiences at the end of the novel, which he sees as provoked in the first place by Kim's guilt at using the lama as a front in his spying enterprise. But for Moss this is simply a more acute manifestation of the 'schizophrenia [which] is only imperfectly suppressed during Kim's "Indian" and "British" periods'.[18] Enabling as Moss's argument is, however, his principal focus is on the existential implications of the still unresolved 'split in [Kim's] personality'[19] at the end of the text for the protagonist's transition from adolescence to adulthood. What remains to be done is to show how this lack of resolution has political implications which problematise the line of interpretation developed through the ideological critique of McClure and his followers.

Over the whole novel hangs the crucial question ' "Who is Kim?" ' (Kim: 166), a question which is reiterated at the climax (p. 331). There, as before, it is not definitively answered. There is simply no sure way of knowing whether Kim will become a true Briton in the Secret Service, pursue another career or even abscond and 'go native' once again – as he has done recurrently throughout the text (and, indeed as his father, a one time soldier/ imperial agent also did). Certainly, the ending contradicts the triumphalist conclusions to imperial boys' adventure stories characteristic of writers such as Henty – and, it must be noted, Kim's own earlier expectations of a glorious future (p. 210).

The question cannot be answered in the simple way that Gail Low proposes, which is that at the end of the novel Kim resumes his 'original' identity.[20] As Robert Moss acutely observes, Kim's first task as an apprentice spy involves the very question of pedigree which becomes the focus of his own personal quest. From the beginning, Kim oscillates between altogether distinct versions of selfhood and cultural identity. With his early playmates he is both similar and equal, as befits a boy raised by a native foster-mother and who sees India as his 'mother'; yet he is also superior and different, as suggested by the eviction of his playmates off the gun outside the museum. He is both a colonising subject and (as an Irish boy) himself a colonised subject. Such contradictions underlie his increasing sense of isolation as the novel progresses and provoke his recurrent psychic crises (at least five in all, each of which centres on the question of his identity). At times, one cultural affiliation predominates, so that he can successively fool Creighton, the Sahiba, the Woman of Shamlegh and even Mahbub Ali into taking him for an Indian. At others, he is a Sahib and is seen as such by the lama, Father Victor, Mahbub Ali and Rev. Bennett, all of whom insist in their different ways that Sahibdom is Kim's inescapable estate. At times Kim can indeed act like the stereotypical young Sahib, as in his early condescension towards Hurree Chunder, his treatment of Lurgan's Hindu boy, or his occasionally professed distaste for those of mixed-race – a distaste which is strongly marked, however, by the contradictory affective structure of disavowal.

The extent of Kim's problems are indicated by the fact that when he most desires or needs to identify with a particular culture, he can never be fully part of it. He may still be thinking and even dreaming in Indian vernacular at the end of the text (*Kim*: 303–6), but Hurree tartly reminds him after his last crisis that this does not make him fully Indian: ' "[When] next you are under thee [sic] emotions please do not use the Mohammedan terms with the Tibetan dress" ' (p. 330). The reverse is also true. In the contexts where it is most important for Kim to be a Sahib, something fails him – for instance, he is never fully himself at St Xavier's. Indeed, Sahibdom is in some ways a positive danger to him in the Great Game. Thus Hurree's perceptive comment that Kim must spend six months becoming 'de-Englishized' (p. 232) in order to be an effective part of the Secret Service. Hybridity, it seems, is the key to continuing British control of India; yet hybridity, of course, undermines any claim to authority on the grounds of an essentialist notion of the innate nature of British identity, let alone its intrinsic superiority.

Indeed, *Kim* insists throughout not only that Britishness is something which is constructed and learned, but also that imperial identity depends upon subaltern culture for its self-constitution. It can therefore never be either originary or complete. This is suggested principally through the novel's engagement with the theme of education. Here, in ironic fashion, Kipling invokes another traditional narrative of imperialism, which legitimised empire by insisting on the duty of the coloniser to transfer western knowledge to the colonised. Not only is the lama the most important source of Kim's moral education, but the crucial period in which Kim's Sahib identity is developed at St Xavier's is paid for by the lama as an act of charity. Equally, when Hurree recommends to Kim knowledge of the British literary tradition (*Kim:* 210–11) as a suitable preparation for the Great Game, Kipling subversively reverses the terms and logic of the Anglicist policy of using such classics as the central plank of an educational system designed to seduce Indians into identification with the aims of British imperialism.[21]

In this sense, Kim's hybrid subject position mirrors that of Hurree Chunder, the educated Hindu who represents the class of 'interpreters' that Anglicists from Macaulay to Ripon hoped would form an acculturated intermediary class between British rulers and the mass of native subjects. In an alignment which reminds one of the narrator's 'doubling' with Wali Dad in 'On the City Wall', Kim's initial half-contemptuous reaction to Hurree constitutes a disavowal, which he is still too immature to realise masks the common ground which subsequently makes them so suitable as partners in their enterprise. While Said is undoubtedly right that Hurree is represented as willingly incorporated into the project of empire, he nonetheless misses important nuances in Kipling's construction of this Indian hybrid. Whereas an earlier tale like 'The Head of the District' (1891) is an unambiguous statement of the unfitness of such figures to rule, Hurree Chunder marks a crucial shift of perception in Kipling's vision, as the text itself quite self-consciously implies (*Kim:* 208). In the same frontier setting where Grish Chunder De fails, plunging the district into chaos, Hurree triumphs.

Hurree Chunder is not in any simple way the grimacing stereotype that Said imagines, if only because 'the Babu' is a persona he self-consciously uses as a disguise for his work (*Kim:* 231 and 317). On his first entrance in the novel he immediately establishes himself as Lurgan's equal, and elicits a formidable testimonial from the jeweller. Moreover Hurree is the key to the success against the spies, not only by virtue of his strategic planning, but by his quick wits when the spies attack the lama and his physical courage in exposing himself to their retribution. Kim himself acknowledges that Hurree's bravery surpasses his and in doing so punctures stereotypes about the intrinsic superiority of the British youth, particularly in comparison to the allegedly craven Bengalis of Anglo-Indian stereotype (p. 317). His relationship with Creighton, whom Said sees as expressing Kipling's viewpoint within the text, is particularly interesting. Creighton accords him the respect due to a fellow-scholar, but it is clear that in certain respects Hurree is Creighton's superior. Thus the text is at pains to suggest that it is Creighton's complacency which allowed the conspiracy to develop as far as it has done, despite Hurree's warnings about the unreliability of the Five Kings (p. 271). Kipling does not, of course, suggest that Hurree represents the future leadership of India. But the text registers Hurree as a full actor in the management of the empire and endows him with an authority and agency which contrast sharply with the dissolving agency of Kim, the alleged epitome of colonial power, at the end of the text.

If Hurree is indeed a loyal servant of the British (and one upon whom its rule is, at the historical moment of the novel's writing, already dependent, with all that implies for the myth of British self-sufficiency and superiority), he is also acutely aware of the disabling paradoxes of Kim's position as would-be representative of colonial power. It seems no accident that it is Hurree who expresses the impossibility of Kim's predicament in his observation that ' "you cannot occupy two places ... simultaneously. That is axiomatic" ' (Kim: 299). It is Kim's misfortune that this is precisely what colonial power is coming increasingly to demand of its servants. As with 'On the City Wall', the lesson of Kim is that without the intimacy with native culture which Kim's hybridity embodies, security is impossible. Yet hybridity chronically destabilises the foundational identity upon which colonialism relies for its authority. It is this fracturing of imperial identity and power that is symbolised when Kim dissolves in tears under the stress of his inner conflict, tears which portend the dissolution of imperial agency itself.

The politics of narrative hybridity

The importance attached by Kipling to the question of hybridity is marked at a moment of the text which has attracted little or no critical comment. In undermining the pretensions of Russia to take over from Britain in India, Kipling puts the following description of Hurree into the mouth of the Czarist spy: ' "He represents in little India in transition – the monstrous hybridism of East and West ... It is *we* who can deal with Orientals" ' (Kim: 288). The clear implication of this is that Britain's authority as an imperial power is closely related to its capacity for sympathy and identification with its subject peoples, as against a master/slave model built upon policies of absolute separation between ruler and ruled.

Kipling's narrative technique in *Kim* suggests the degree to which hybridity is registered not only at the level of theme, as such passages suggest, but within its form, thus marking the very modes of its knowledge and regime of representation. In Kipling criticism since *Orientalism*, the Indian elements in the narrative discourse of *Kim* are often understood as both politically and aesthetically dubious. Said deplores Kipling's articulation of native voices, which he sees as designed to produce an impression of widespread support for imperialism among the ordinary people of India.[22] Meanwhile Gayatri Spivak argues that Kipling's use of vernacular produces a demeaning kind of pidgin which violates and appropriates the subordinate culture.[23] Parry synthesises these accounts: 'On those occasions when the Indians do appear to speak, they are the mouthpieces of a ventriloquist who, using a facile idiom that alternates between the artless and the ornate, projects his own account of grateful native dependency'.[24]

While these critics deplore Kipling's Indianisation of his discourse, others have been less hostile. For example, Zohreh Sullivan's response is mixed. On the one hand she views it, following Spivak, as 'a strategy that necessarily reminds us of the larger appropriations of European imperialism';[25] on the other she also sees Kipling as at times exemplifying a Bakhtinian model of the dialogic, whereby his narrative not only engages with the Other, but allows genuinely oppositional and marginal voices to be expressed. Such a reading is perhaps confirmed by 'On the City Wall' in which Khem Singh and Wali Dad are allowed to voice direct and damaging criticism of the conduct of imperial affairs. Thus Wali Dad reminds the narrator that ' "you are here today instead of starving in your own country" ' ('City Wall': 226). Sullivan explains this investment in the dialogic mode with reference to Lacanian theory, arguing that the Other is never seen by Kipling as simple alterity; 'he also sees the West from the vantage point of the internalized Other, the underground Indian child who is always and unavoidably within him'.[26]

While Sullivan conducts her argument about Kipling's engagement with Indian culture at a strategic level, Afzar Husain provides a detailed attempt 'to determine the impact of Indian languages and culture on Kipling's prose style'.[27] Perhaps the most surprising conclusion Husain draws is that the Indian elements in Kipling's narrative discourse steadily increase as his career develops, despite the widening time-gap between later work and the writer's residence in India. Thus the frequency of

Indian elements is highest in *Kim*. Though recognising Kipling's propensity to denigrate certain aspects of Indian society, particularly the figure of the educated nationalist, Husain accuses him of neither appropriation nor ventriloquism. He argues instead that Kipling was in fact a 'brilliant translator. His genius lies in his ability to transfer successfully contextual features of Indian linguistic terms'.[28] Husain shows that Kipling uses a number of devices, from collocation and hybridisation to phonological transfer, to produce a narrative discourse which is often 'significantly different from Standard British English'.[29] This deviation is apparent not just in tales with native narrators, or in the speech of native protagonists, or even in the discourse of Kipling's white narrators and protagonists, but – in certain instances – in Kipling's own authorial voice, *Kim* being a particularly good example in this respect. Husain's conclusion about the cultural/political meanings of Kipling's 'Indianness' is unambiguous: 'Kipling knows the idioms and the situations in which they are used very well indeed ... [they] show his deep understanding of the emotions of Indian characters and the language used to express them'.[30]

Whether one agrees with this judgement or not, Husain is undoubtedly right about *Kim*'s experiments with non-Standard English. The unstable identity of the narrative discourse is marked in the very first paragraph of the text. While the first sentence presents no challenge to the English reader's expectations, the second does so quite markedly. Linguistic and stylistic norm is, then, immediately followed by deviation, which may be understood as an example of Anglo-India's propensity to 'quaint reflections, borrowed unconsciously from native foster-mothers, and turns of phrase that showed they had been that instant translated from the vernacular' (*Kim*: 172). The mixed character of the narrative discourse in much of *Kim* is evidence of an uncertain cultural politics and positioning which mirrors Kim's own divided cultural loyalties throughout the novel. The text's thematic failure to reaffirm any foundational notion of pure English identity is complemented, then, in its own form, principally in the mixed English, Anglo-Indian and Indian vernacular of its narrative discourse. (The extent of these borrowings is indicated by the fact that Said's edition of the text requires roughly 25 pages of explanatory footnotes.)

The important implications of Husain's argument for *Kim* need to be extended, however, by reconsideration of the text's

larger discursive structures. In his autobiography Kipling commented that *Kim* was 'nakedly picaresque and plotless',[31] and it
is also somewhat lacking in the sequential pattern of developing
dramatic climaxes one might expect in the western novel, particularly of the spy thriller genre, an inconclusiveness which is
reinforced if one accepts the proposition that Kipling leaves the
novel unresolved in the crucial respects outlined in the last
section.

There is strong evidence to suggest that these features of *Kim*
derive in part from Kipling's recourse to non-British narrative
modes. This may seem a perverse claim to those persuaded by
Parry's argument that Kipling polemicised against the indigenous
forms of Indian culture: 'Kipling's journalism made a major
contribution to the text of the Raj ... by ... ridiculing its ancient
literary heritages'.[32] As evidence, Parry cites a scathing review
of a translation of the *Mahabharata* which appeared in 1886.
While Parry's argument may seem incontrovertible, Thomas
Pinney, from whose collection of Kipling's journalism Parry takes
this piece, reminds one of the considerable range and contradiction in Kipling's journalistic opinions,[33] an argument reinforced
by Kipling's positive consideration in *Letters of Marque* (1891)
of the attempt of 'independent' native princes like the ruler of
Jaipur to preserve local cultural traditions. (Pinney's argument,
moreover, serves to remind of the dangers of conflating literary
and non-literary forms of colonial discourse.) More pertinently
still, perhaps, Bhabha reminds one that overt disavowal often con-
ceals profound unconscious attraction for the object in question.

Whatever the reason, there seems clear evidence in *Kim* of
Kipling's borrowings from indigenous sources, most particularly
the *Mahabharata*. Both texts can be understood in a general sense
as epics, sharing the genre's primary concern for both spiritual
truths and questions of national and cultural identity. Each has
a large range of characters and an emphasis on action and colourful adventure. Each lacks psychological realism, relying on
character typing instead; each has a strongly episodic nature
and an ambition to provide a synoptic and apparently deliberately
anti-historicist vision of Indian life. (The objection of Said and
others that Kipling makes an obfuscating political choice in
portraying India as 'permanent and essential'[34] needs reconsideration in the light of Raja Rao's description of traditional
Indian narrative, which Rao sees as characterised by 'the
deliberate timelessness of its historical reportage'.)[35]

More particularly, Kim seems in many ways comparable to the young God Krishna, one of the three principal Hindu deities celebrated in the *Mahabharata*. Both Kim and Krishna are of humble birth. Each is initially believed to be an orphan. Like the young Kim, the boy Krishna is full of pranks and intrigue. As the 'black god', Krishna resembles Kim, who is 'burned black as any native' (*Kim:* 49). Exegesis suggests that Krishna was of mixed race, while Kim is also, symbolically if not literally, hybrid. Kim, too, is a shape-changer, going through different incarnations – metaphorically at least – as is suggested by both his recurrent existential crises and his assumption of new disguises. Like Kim, Krishna spends part of his youth as the pupil of a sage, the lama in the former case, Ghora Angirasa in the latter. Like Krishna, Kim has fantastic adventures in which he usually triumphs. Kim, too, is very attractive to diverse female figures. The analogies between Krishna's sport with the cowherds and Kim's dalliance in Huneefa's house seems particularly pointed. Like Krishna, Kim seems to inhabit two spheres, those of the material world and the spiritual world. As the lama comments, his protege seems at times to have come ' "from the other world" ' (p. 96). Equally both figures have very varied social roles, from beng warriors at one extreme to obedient and peace-loving disciples at the other.

Kim draws on other non-western narratives, too. Most conventional, perhaps, is the allusion to *The Arabian Nights* (*Kim:* 51), which serves to emphasise again the epic and episodic quality of Kipling's text, as well as its elements of orality and fantasy. More interesting, perhaps, is the use Kipling makes of Buddhist texts like the *Jataka*. The narrative voice alludes to the 'beautiful story' of the Buddha (p. 56), and presents sympathetically the lama's fantastic religious narratives (p. 307), which seem little different in kind to those to which Kipling apparently objected so violently in his review of the *Mahabharata*. Kim's relationship with the lama is certainly modelled to some extent on that between the Buddha and Ananda (pp. 213–15). The novel also resembles the Wheel of Life which the lama draws (pp. 260–1), not least in its strongly visual or 'painterly' qualities, its crowded panoramas and mixed focus on spiritual and secular realities. Both favour cyclical rather than linear temporalities and each mixes elements of realism and fantasy in equal parts.

The hybrid cultural/political vision which such narrative elements suggest is also evident in the authorial persona's contradictory pronominal positioning. Early in the novel, it alludes to 'the Magic House, as we name the Masonic Lodge' (*Kim*, p. 50). The 'we' here appears to be aligned with Anglo-Indians such as Kim's father, whose indirect discourse the comment interrupts. Shortly afterwards, however, the narrative persona alludes to the cloisters of the Kashmir Serai, which are rented out 'as we rent the arches of a viaduct' (p. 66). This appears to share the viewpoint of a metropolitan British audience. Elsewhere, references such as that to 'almond-curd sweet-meats [*balushai* we call it]' (p. 179), or the use of untranslated words like *murasla*, *khud* and *kilta* (p. 303) inscribe the perspective of the subordinate culture to which Kim initially belongs. It is these varied loyalties, moreover, which in part explain the fluctuations in the narrative perspective, at times omniscient and detached, at others subjective and involved.

In producing this mixed and multi-coded narrative form, drawing as much on the traditions of eastern religious epic as the western forms of the spy thriller and *Bildungsroman*, Kipling produces a discourse which, ironically enough, looks forward to postcolonial narrative. As Richard Cronin has already established, *Kim* provides one model for the generically and culturally mixed narratives of postcoloniality's most celebrated contemporary writer, Salman Rushdie, the Indo-British writer whose *Midnight's Children* (1981) was recently voted the overall winner of the first twenty-five years of the Booker prize's history.[36] Thematically, too, Kipling's interest in cultural difference and syncretism anticipates what is perhaps the key theme of postcolonial writing. Rushdie's *Satanic Verses*, for example, explores not only the contradictions in the identity of the often multiply-positioned postcolonial citizen, but also insists on the degree to which English identity continues to be shaped by a long imperial history of contact with the Other. Its key insight in this respect is voiced by Whisky Sisodia: ' "The trouble with the EngEnglish is that their hisshishistory happened overseas, so they don't know what it means" '.[37] Kipling put it rather more pointedly, perhaps, than Sisodia: 'And what should they know of England who only England know?'[38]

Precedent for a detailed reconsideration of Kipling in this light – a task which space does not permit here – now exists in the wake of Shelley Fisher Fishkin's recent work on Mark Twain, which presents the case for a new understanding of *Huckleberry Finn* (itself a major precedent for *Kim*) on the basis of Twain's recourse to important elements of black American culture, especially its oral narrative character and conventions. Fishkin produces evidence that the model for the voice of Huck was a black child and not the white one whom Twain himself claimed as inspiration. Fishkin recuperates Twain to a large extent, if not completely, from recent criticism of his racial politics (which is comparable in kind to the treatment received by Kipling in the last fifteen years),[39] by emphasising the degree to which Twain's text admitted African-American experience into the literary mainstream. More than this, she stresses how it enabled the emergent tradition of twentieth-century African-American writing, including Langston Hughes, Ralph Ellison and David Bradley. Most interestingly, perhaps, from the point of view of this reconsideration of Kipling, Fishkin rejects the proposition that relations between dominant and subordinate cultures are always appropriative and advantageous to the former. In Twain's incorporation of black oral narrative, she finds the source of the 'multicultural polyphony' which is now such a central part of the American literary tradition. This reinforces her salutary point that 'cultural exchange takes place within parameters that are less predictable than those that shape a society's economic and political structures'.[40] Perhaps only now, as questions of imperialism, ethnicity and representation become less constrained by essentialist notions of cultural identity, can Kipling's partially enabling, rather than simply conflictual, relationship to post-colonial literature be broached.

Conclusion

This chapter has sought to challenge several current critical orthodoxies about Kipling as both artist and political thinker. The first is that Kipling fails to take sufficient account of opposition to British rule. I suggest both that this is in itself a mistaken notion and that the definition of political resistance needs to be rethought in the light of Bhabha's critical interventions. Put somewhat bluntly, many contemporary critics of Kipling have too narrow a conception of resistance both to, and within, imperial discourse. In the latter sense, indeed, Kipling has anticipated Bhabha in his exploration of the political implications of hybridity and ambivalence. The second orthodoxy in need of revision is closely related to the first: that Kipling's narrative technique in his Indian work is generally confidently monologic, transparent and secure in its articulation of the official version of imperialism. (Or as Parry puts it: 'Since the language of European ascendancy and Anglo-Indian conceit remain uncontradicted, the narrating structure of such tales is sealed against any interrogation of the Raj's self-presentation'.)[41] Finally, I question the perception that a distinct discontinuity exists between Kipling's treatment of imperial rule in the 1880s – which is supposed to allow some degree of criticism of the conduct of Indian affairs, albeit only to then neutralise and suppress it – and that of his later work, particularly *Kim*, which is deemed to resolutely reaffirm Kipling's faith in empire.

These received ways of understanding Kipling now seem limited after the kind of close, detailed and patient analysis, exemplified by Zohreh Sullivan, of the narrative techniques employed by early Kipling in his effort to register disquiet about aspects of imperial policy. Indeed, it may not be too much to claim that such work sets up the possibility of a major reappraisal of Kipling, not only in his perceived role as 'laureate of empire' but as narrative technician. Particularly useful in this respect is Homi Bhabha's attention to how questions of psychic affect complicate colonial discourse in the areas of narrative and discursive form. For it is there, as least as much as at the level of manifest content, that the destabilising fractures in imperial ideology are registered. It may now be possible to apply David Lodge's recent argument about the narrative sophistication evident in Kipling's middle period to his Indian narratives. In so doing, one may claim a much larger proportion of Kipling's *oeuvre* as genuinely proto-modernist.[42]

Despite their fruitfulness, certain problems remain in these approaches. As suggested, Sullivan pulls back unnecessarily from the radical potential of her insights, restoring Kipling to the ideological position usually ascribed to him, and in the process suggesting that his narrative experimentation is aborted by a desire to reaffirm the received 'truths' of colonial knowledge. In the context of *Kim*, particularly, this closes off important ambiguities and instabilities of meaning, particularly at the level of the novel's style.

Detailed analysis of a small but representative selection from the work of Kipling also reveals certain limitations in Bhabha's model of colonial discourse analysis. First of all, it confirms Abdul JanMohamed's objection to Bhabha's conflation of coloniser and colonised subject into a homogenous 'colonial subject'.[43]

While colonial relations construct an affective sphere common to both sides, his model of hybridity tends to discount the important differences both in the quality and degree of that affect and in the subject positions of coloniser and colonised.

Equally, Bhabha's unitary conception of the 'colonial subject' imposes a uniformity of affective response on both coloniser and colonised which again does not do justice to historical realities. To take the coloniser's side first. The narrator of 'On the City Wall' places himself firmly in opposition to metropolitan discourse in his tolerance of local customs such as hereditary prostitution, and, equally importantly, he rejects metropolitan modes of knowledge and representation of India. But at the same time he is no died-in-the-wool conservative who fetishises traditional culture. He is complicit in the process of acculturation – symbolised most obviously in his loan to Wali Dad of books on Athenian democracy – and distances himself from the uncomplicated racism of the Captain of Fort Amara. Such evidence suggests that colonial power was never as unified at the point of enunciation as Bhabha indicates. In other words, there were competing definitions of imperialism on the coloniser's side and, consequently, struggles for control of the hegemonic discourse.

The case of the colonised is equally problematic for Bhabha's thesis. Clearly, Lalun and Wali Dad do not relate to the narrator in precisely the same way, because of material differences between them as subaltern agents; issues of ethnic origin, gender, class and religious difference, in other words, need to be brought to bear on the question of psychic affect. It is not the case, as Bhabha implies, that affective ambivalence operates in the same way and to the same degree for the western-educated intellectual and the illiterate female subaltern.

Moreover, Kipling demonstrates that ambivalence was not the only psychic response to empire on either side of the colonial relationship. The Senior Captain of Fort Amara and those who write tracts in the West against traditional Indian culture show no ambivalence of attitude towards their Indian subjects, and Khem Singh's conversation with his jailer suggests that outright rejection of the Other could be a characteristic of the subaltern side as well. There could hardly be a less ambivalent expression of this than his proud confession to the junior officer: ' "But from the beginning to to-day I would cut the throats of all the Sahibs in the land if I could" ' ('City Wall': 230).

Bhabha's lack of attention to the material and historical realities of the colonial context is also evident in his claim that: 'It is not possible to see how power functions productively as incitement and interdiction'.[44] While accepting the point that colonial power could never rest solely on force to be effective, especially in a vast country like India, there is a real danger in discounting the degree to which colonial power was able – and willing – to resort to force to impose and defend its rule. 'On the City Wall' demonstrates how far colonial power rested on the production of mimic and hybrid subjects; but Kipling also reminds us that its promotion of sporting activities, colleges and local legislatures was complemented by the prison and, in the last resort, the barracks. The rioters avoid attacking whites only because they know that 'the death of a European would not mean one hanging but many, and possibly the appearance of the thrice-dreaded Artillery' ('City Wall': 237). And Khem Singh fails to incite a popular uprising because he can only offer potential rebels the fate which befell many Indian 'mutineers' in the aftermath of 1857, 'a glorious death with their back to the mouth of a gun' ('City Wall': 242).

The question remains, however, of how commensurable the approaches taken by critics like Bhabha and Sullivan really are, or whether contemporary colonial discourse analysis is in fact fragmenting into a variety of mutually incompatible methodologies and techniques. The key question posed by Kipling's work in this respect is the degree to which he is conscious of the destabilisation of the imperial unconscious by ambivalence and hybridity. This chapter and the introduction to this volume argue that Kipling deliberately uses faulty narrators to demonstrate such affective and discursive instability – a position shared by Sullivan, although she reaches somewhat different conclusions about the uses to which Kipling puts that awareness. Equally, the comment by the narrative voice in *Kim* about 'unconscious' borrowings from subaltern culture (*Kim:* 172) seems to suggest a conscious interest in the unconscious of imperial discourse. If this approach is right, then imperial discourse is a good deal more self-aware than Bhabha's perspective recognises. If, however, Kipling is unconscious – or only partly conscious – of the degree to which ambivalence destabilises his narratives (and McClure and his followers would argue that Kipling shows no such self-awareness), this generates a quite different problem for Bhabha's analysis. In this case, it is hard to see how the authority of imperial discourse is undermined from within by epistemological and affective fractures. After all, misogyny and homophobia, for example, are none the less effective for the often radical contradictions in the discourse in which they are expressed, contradictions which derive more often than not from the complex workings of dis-avowal. The fact is that, irrespective of the affective ambivalence and disturbance evident in its discursive constitution, imperial-ism proved an immensely effective and long-lasting system of domination. It was undone not so much by inner contradiction in its discourse, nor by increasing awareness of those contradic-tions within the imperial formation, important as this process undoubtedly was, but by material considerations such as war, subaltern resistance and changing modes of capitalist production.

Notes

1 John McClure, *Kipling and Conrad: The Colonial Fiction* (London: Harvard University Press, 1981), p. 78; see also Edward Said, 'Introduction' to *Kim* (Harmondsworth: Penguin, 1987), pp. 43–5 and Benita Parry, 'The Content and Discontents of Kipling's Imperialism', *New Formations*, 6 (Winter 1988), p. 59.

2 Parry, 'Content and Discontents of Kipling's Imperialism', p. 59; Mark Paffard, *Kipling's Indian Fiction* (London: Macmillan, 1989), p. 129.

3 Rudyard Kipling, 'On the City Wall' in *The Man who Would Be King and Other Stories*, ed. Louis Cornell (Oxford: Oxford University Press, 1987), p. 231. Hereafter cited as 'City Wall' with page references given in the text.

4 Homi Bhabha, *The Location of Culture* (London: Routledge, 1994), p. 86.

5 Bhabha, 'The Other Question' in *The Location of Culture*, *passim*.

6 Bhabha, *The Location of Culture*, p. 112.

7 Parry, 'Content and Discontents of Kipling's Imperialism', p. 54.

8 Zohreh Sullivan, *Narratives of Empire: The Fictions of Rudyard Kipling* (Cambridge: Cambridge University Press, 1993), p. 149.

9 McClure, *Kipling and Conrad*, p. 77.

10 Said, 'Introduction', to *Kim*, p. 23. See also Sullivan, *Narratives of Empire*, p. 176.

11 Sullivan, *Narratives of Empire*, pp. 55 and 169.

12 McClure, *Kipling and Conrad*, p. 78.

13 Gail Ching-Liang Low, 'White Skins/Black Masks: the Pleasures and Politics of Imperialism', *New Formations*, 9 (Winter 1989), p. 91.

14 Parry, 'Content and Discontents of Kipling's Imperialism', p. 59.

15 Rudyard Kipling, *Kim*, ed. Edward Said (1901; Harmondsworth: Penguin, 1987), p. 297. Hereafter page references are given in the text. There is a similar moment of com-placency about the threat posed by 'mere men of the flesh' in 'On the City Wall' (p. 224).

16 According to Said's own notes, the beginning of the novel can be dated by the reference
to the action at Pirzai Kotal to 1877 (*Kim*: 346). Accordingly, it may be assumed to end
around 1882–83. This renders his complaint that Kipling fails to represent organised
opposition to imperial rule rather less forceful, given that the Indian National Congress
was not constituted until 1885. It makes Patrick Williams' similar complaint that
Kipling ignores political developments in the 1890s strictly irrelevant. See Patrick
Williams, '*Kim* and Orientalism', reprinted in Patrick Williams and Laura Chrisman
(eds.), *Colonial Discourse and Postcolonial Theory* (1989; Hemel Hempstead: Harvester
Wheatsheaf, 1993), pp. 496–7. It is ironic that criticisms of Kipling's failure to attend
to real history should themselves rest on such anachronistic readings.

17 Robert Moss, *Rudyard Kipling and the Fiction of Adolescence* (London: Macmillan,
1982), p. 134.

18 Moss, *Rudyard Kipling*, p. 134.

19 Moss, *Rudyard Kipling*, p. 138.

20 Low, 'White Skins/Black Masks', p. 93.

21 For more on this topic, see Gauri Viswanathan, *Masks of Conquest: Literary Study and
British Rule in India* (Columbia: Columbia University Press, 1989).

22 Said, 'Introduction' to *Kim*, pp. 25–6. Again Said anachronistically imposes a concept
of Indian nationality in his argument. Given that the veteran is a Sikh, and the Punjab
remained largely loyal to the British in the 1857 rebellion, the old man's sentiments
are not necessarily a mark of his (or Kipling's) bad faith.

23 Gayatri Spivak, 'Imperialism and Sexual Difference', *Oxford Literary Review*, 8, 1–2
(1986), p. 234, cited in Gail Low, 'White Skins/Black Masks', p. 93.

24 Parry, 'Content and Discontents of Kipling's Imperialism', p. 53.

25 Sullivan, *Narratives of Empire*, p. 48.

26 Sullivan, *Narratives of Empire*, p. 49.

27 S. S. Afzar Husain, *The Indianness of Rudyard Kipling: A Study in Stylistics* (London:
Cosmic Press, 1983), p. 1.

28 Husain, *The Indianness of Rudyard Kipling*, p. 125.

29 Husain, *The Indianness of Rudyard Kipling*, p. 118.

30 Husain, *The Indianness of Rudyard Kipling*, p. 14. This comment reminds one of Nirad
Chaudhuri's description of *Kim* in *Encounter* in 1957, in which he described Kipling's
vision as one 'whose profundity we Indians would be hard put ... to match' (cited in
Moss, *Rudyard Kipling*, p. 131).

31 Rudyard Kipling, *Something of Myself* (1937; Harmondsworth: Penguin, 1977), p. 170.

32 Parry, 'Content and Discontents of Kipling's Imperialism', p. 55.

33 Thomas Pinney, *Kipling's India: Uncollected Sketches 1884–88* (London: Macmillan,
1986), pp. 18–22.

34 Said, 'Introduction' to *Kim*, p. 43; see also Sullivan, *Narratives of Empire*, p. 160. However, Said overlooks abundant evidence of India's transition to modernity, to which the
lama's startled reaction to trains, for example, attests.

35 Cited in Timothy Brennan, *Salman Rushdie and the Third World: Myths of the Nation*
(Basingstoke: Macmillan, 1989), p. 83.

36 Richard Cronin, 'The Indian English Novel: *Kim* and *Midnight's Children*', *Commonwealth Essays and Studies*, 8, 1 (1985), pp. 57–73. Sara Suleri makes similar points
vis-à-vis the relationship between *Kim* and Rushdie's *Shame* in *The Rhetoric of English
India* (Chicago: University of Chicago Press, 1992), p. 174. *Kim*'s influence on Indian
post-colonial writing extends to Rushdie via Tagore's *Gora* (1924) and Desani's *All
About H. Haters* (1948).

37 Salman Rushdie, *The Satanic Verses* (Harmondsworth: Viking Penguin, 1988), p. 343.

38 Rudyard Kipling, 'The English Flag' in *The Definitive Edition of Rudyard Kipling's Verse* (London: Hodder and Stoughton, 1977), p. 223.

39 Twain's representation of Jim has generated very similar criticism to that received by Kipling for his depiction of Hurree Chunder. While there are undoubtedly elements of condescension in both characterisations of the subaltern, they cannot be seen only or simply as examples of negative stereotyping.

40 Shelley Fisher Fishkin, *Was Huck Black? Mark Twain and African-American Voices* (Oxford: Oxford University Press, 1993), pp. 5 and 108.

41 Parry, 'Content and Discontents of Kipling's Imperialism', p. 53.

42 David Lodge, *After Bakhtin: Essays on Fiction and Criticism* (London: Routledge, 1990), pp. 143–53.

43 Abdul JanMohamed, 'The Economy of Manichean Allegory: The Function of Racial Difference in Colonialist Literature' in H. L. Gates (ed.), *'Race', Writing and Difference* (London: Chicago University Press, 1986), p. 78.

44 Bhabha, *Location of Culture*, p. 72.

Bibliography

Bhabha, Homi, *The Location of Culture* (London: Routledge, 1994).

Brennan, Timothy, *Salman Rushdie and the Third World: Myths of the Nation* (Basingstoke: Macmillan, 1989).

Cronin, Richard, 'The Indian English Novel: *Kim* and *Midnight's Children'*, *Commonwealth Essays and Studies*, 8, 1 (1985), pp. 57–73.

Fishkin, Shelley Fisher, *Was Huck Black? Mark Twain and African-American Voices* (Oxford: Oxford University Press, 1993).

Husain, Afzar S. S., *The Indianness of Rudyard Kipling: A Study in Stylistics* (London: Cosmic Press, 1983).

JanMohamed, Abdul, 'The Economy of Manichean Allegory: The Function of Racial Difference in Colonialist Literature' in H. L. Gates (ed.), *'Race', Writing and Difference* (London: Chicago University Press, 1986), pp. 78–106.

Kipling, Rudyard, *The Definitive Edition of Rudyard Kipling's Verse* (London: Hodder and Stoughton, 1977).

Kipling, Rudyard, *Kim*, ed. Edward Said (1901; Harmondsworth: Penguin, 1987).

Kipling, Rudyard, *The Man who Would Be King and Other Tales*, ed. Louis Cornell (Oxford: Oxford University Press, 1987).

Kipling, Rudyard, *Something of Myself* (1937; Harmondsworth: Penguin, 1977).

Lodge, David, *After Bakhtin: Essays on Fiction and Criticism* (London: Routledge, 1990).

Low, Gail Ching-Liang, 'White Skins/Black Masks: the Pleasures and Politics of Imperialism', *New Formations*, 9 (Winter 1989), pp. 83–104.

McClure, John, *Kipling and Conrad: The Colonial Fiction* (London: Harvard University Press, 1981).

Moss, Robert, *Rudyard Kipling and the Fiction of Adolescence* (London: Macmillan, 1982).

Paffard, Mark, *Kipling's Indian Fiction* (London: Macmillan, 1989).

Parry, Benita, 'The Content and Discontents of Kipling's Imperialism', *New Formations*, 6 (Winter 1988), pp. 49–64.

Pinney, Thomas, *Kipling's India: Uncollected Sketches 1884–88* (London: Macmillan, 1986).

Rushdie, Salman, *The Satanic Verses* (Harmondsworth: Viking Penguin, 1988).

Said, Edward, 'Introduction' to Rudyard Kipling, *Kim*, ed. Edward Said (Harmondsworth: Penguin, 1987), pp. 7–46.

Said, Edward, *Orientalism* (1978; Harmondsworth: Penguin, 1991).

Suleri, Sara, *The Rhetoric of English India* (Chicago: University of Chicago Press, 1992).

Sullivan, Zohreh, *Narratives of Empire: The Fictions of Rudyard Kipling* (Cambridge: Cambridge University Press, 1993).

Viswanathan, Gauri, *Masks of Conquest: Literary Study and British Rule in India* (Columbia: Columbia University Press, 1989).

Williams, Patrick, '*Kim* and Orientalism' in Patrick Williams and Laura Chrisman (eds.), *Colonial Discourse and Postcolonial Theory* (Hemel Hempstead: Harvester Wheatsheaf, 1993), pp. 480–97.

5

Secrets of the colonial harem: gender, sexuality, and the law in Kipling's novels

NANCY L. PAXTON

> Arrayed in the brilliant colors of exoticism and exuding a full-blown yet uncertain sensuality, the Orient, where unfathomable mysteries dwell and cruel barbaric scenes are staged, has fascinated and disturbed Europe for a long time. It has been its glittering imaginary but also its mirage. ... There is no phantasm, though, without sex, and in this Orientalism, a confection of the best and of the worst – a central figure emerges, the very embodiment of the obsession: the harem.
>
> Malek Alloula, *The Colonial Harem*[1]

Siting the harem

In *Letters of Marque* (1891), Rudyard Kipling assumes the voice of a strangely impersonal 'Englishman' in relating his own travels in Rajasthan. Throughout this narrative, when he approaches subjects related to what Malek Alloula calls the 'colonial harem', Kipling repeatedly reports dread rather than the aesthetic appreciation or sexual titillation that, according to Alloula, is more typical of the western response. Kipling's impressions of his visit to the deserted women's quarters at Chitor in this text provide a particularly telling case in point.

Kipling focuses on a moment of hubris when his narrator penetrates the harem: 'the Englishman wandered so far in one palace that he came to an almost black-dark room, high up in a wall, and said proudly to himself: "I must be the first man who has been here"' (*Letters:* 121).[2] Yet the Englishman's pride anticipates his fall, for immediately after this remark he trips and, putting out his hands to break his fall, is repulsed by the feel of stairs worn 'smooth by the tread of innumerable naked feet' (*Letters:* 121).

Having inspected and meditated 'on the beauties of kingship, and the unholiness of Hindu art', the Englishman finds himself in a 'perverted' state of mind, which is, he says, 'eminently fitted for a descent into the Gau-Mukh, which is nothing more terrible than a little spring falling into a reservoir' (*Letters:* 125). In his descent, he sees a lingam, that 'loathsome emblem of creation', wreathed in flowers and rice, and then imagines the zenana as a site of mass suicide rather than erotic play. Nearing the 'sub-terranean chambers', he recalls how 'the fair Pudmini and her handmaids had slain themselves' (*Letters:* 126) in order to escape from rape at the hands of their conquerors. Haunted by this 'place of years and blood', and distressed by the gurgle of water from the Gau-Mukh which sounds to him like 'a man in his death throe' (*Letters:* 127), the Englishman flees from the scene but cannot escape the guilty sensation that the worn stone he walks upon felt 'as though he were treading on the soft, oiled skin of a Hindu' (*Letters:* 127). When he returns later that night to the 'unspeakable Gau-Mukh' (*Letters:* 127), he startles a 'living, breathing woman' who has been worshipping at the temple. When she screams, the Englishman flees again, declaring 'he will never try to describe what he has seen – but will keep it as a love letter' (*Letters:* 132).

This passage from *Letters of Marque* is certainly not an anomaly in Kipling's writing about India, for he repeatedly imagines the Indian zenana, the nearest equivalent of the harem, as a place of danger, violence, and guilt rather than erotic pleasure. When young Indian women appear in the short fiction that Kipling wrote in the 1880s, they are much more often associated with violence, loss, and death than with pleasure, love, and desire. From the barred windows of the colonial harem in Kipling's 'Beyond the Pale', Bisesa stretches out her cruelly mangled arms. From the barred gate of Holden's and Ameera's secret dwelling in 'Without Benefit of Clergy', comes the cry of mourning rather than the lovesongs of a devoted mistress.

Ella Shohat, Lisa Lowe, and other critics have called for a more nuanced analysis of the 'colonial harem' than Malek Alloula outlines, one which registers how this orientalist trope is re-shaped by the dynamics of history, geography, culture, and the exigencies of nationalist and imperialist projects. Shohat has demonstrated that the harem becomes a particular 'site of con-tradictions' when a western woman who 'exists in a relation of subordination to Western man and in a relation of domination toward "non-Western" men and women' is inserted into harem narratives. In colonial texts 'the intersection of colonial and gender discourses involves a shifting, contradictory subject positioning, whereby Western woman can simultaneously constitute "center" and "periphery", identity and alterity' (Shohat, p. 63).

These new postcolonial readings of the 'colonial harem' help illuminate Kipling's troubled representation of the zenana as a reflection of actual, historical, ideological, and symbolic tensions of life in British India in the 1880s and 1890s. By examining Kipling's treatment of the zenana in his least known, and perhaps most scandalous novel, *The Naulahka: A Story of West and East* (1892),[3] we can begin to better understand the conflictual position assigned to both colonised and colonising women in Kipling's Indian fiction.

Many of Kipling's most distinguished critics have apparently wished to omit *The Naulahka* from the canon of his works.[4] Certainly one reason for this novel's marginality can be found in the conditions of its authorship. Following the example of many male authors of the 1880s and 1890s, including Joseph Conrad and Ford Madox Ford, Rider Haggard and Andrew Lang, Robert Louis Stevenson and Lloyd Osborne, Kipling collaborated in writing *The Naulahka* (see Koestenbaum, pp. 143–71). His co-author was Wolcott Balestier, the charming young American whose sister Kipling was later to marry. In a letter written in February of 1891, Balestier describes this collaboration: ' "Kipling and I have been wading deep into our story lately, and have written rather more than two thirds of it. It begins in the West where I have a free hand for several chapters. Then we lock arms and march upon India. The process of collaboration is much easier than one could have supposed. We hit it off together most smoothly. ... [Henry] James has been reading the first part of it, and professes himself delighted with the Western atmosphere" ' (Carrington, p. 181). Most critics have not agreed with Henry James' reported assessment.

The Naulahka has invited critical censure not only because it shows the marks of Kipling's disconcerting surrender of authorial sovereignty but also because its plot is often regarded as incoherent or melodramatic. Philip Mason, for example, fulminates: 'That Kipling should have allowed his name to be associated with this dime novel, still more to have allowed it to be included in his collected works, can only be because he was obsessed by Balestier's charm and drive and sales talk' (Mason, p. 96). Mason's judgement here suggests further grounds for embarrassment, for, as Kipling's recent biographer, Martin Seymour-Smith, has argued, *The Naulahka* can be read to reveal how Kipling came to 'trade' his deep, full love for Wolcott for a less enthusiastic embrace of heterosexuality and fatherhood when he married Carrie Balestier so shortly and unexpectedly after her brother's untimely death (Seymour-Smith, pp. 59–61).

Moreover, *The Naulahka* is hard to decipher not only because it is double-authored but also because it uneasily combines the formal features of American romance with those of the British adventure novel, which assign quite different positions to colonised and colonising women and men. Unlike most British novels about India, *The Naulahka* includes two sites of colonial contact rather than one, since it compares life in a boom town in Colorado on the American frontier with life on the 'frontier' in an imaginary Indian town in a small princely state in Rajasthan. By doubling the colonial sites in this novel, Kipling/Balestier were able to have it both ways. In the American chapters, they parody the mindlessness, audacity, and ruthless competition engendered in American men by monopoly capitalism and cast doubt on the naive missionary zeal of American women, without indicting similar values in representing the British imperial project in India.

Second, Kipling/Balestier subvert the usual epistemological premises of orientalist discourse by including two cultures, rather than one, that could be construed as 'western'. While India remains assigned to what Benita Parry characterises as 'the negative pole in that ubiquitous structure of oppositions' that define orientalist discourse, whereby the East represents body, passion, chaos, and incoherence (Parry, 'Contents and discontents', p. 51), *The Naulahka* ostensibly presents two competing loci for the western 'positive pole' of values in this text. This triangulation of values unsettles the neat orientalist polarities that usually identify mind, reason, order, and intelligibility with the 'West'.

Finally, the underlying ideological structure of the colonial discourse about America that Kipling/Balestier employ in *The Naulahka* differs in profound ways from that about India. One index of these differences can be found in the positioning of the colonised and colonising women in these texts. As Peter Hulme argues in *Colonial Encounters: Europe and the Native Caribbean*,

1492–1797, since colonisation in the Americas was based on the usurpation of land and the annihilation or enslavement of its peoples, while in India it was based on 'control of trade', the national narratives produced in these different colonial contexts required different symbolic resolutions. In the literature of the early contact period that Hulme surveys, America was allegorised as a beautiful, nearly naked Native American woman who welcomed, and often married, the colonising European man. By the nineteenth century, however, the benevolent figure of the Native American woman was erased, especially in literature about the American West, and replaced by references to the 'virgin land' (Shohat, p. 46).

The indigenous woman in English colonial discourse about India in the eighteenth century appears much more consistently as the pampered and bored inmate of the 'colonial harem'.[5] In the nineteenth century, however, colonial narratives involving colonising British men and Indian women increasingly defined her as victim and focused on her rescue from the zenana. Many of these narratives also included scenes of *sati* which, as Gayatri Spivak has argued, legitimised British intervention in India by repeating this scenario of 'white men saving brown women from brown men' (Spivak, p. 297). After the Indian Rebellion of 1857, colonised women in colonial narratives were increasingly demonised along with their men, so that Anglo-Indian novels from this period typically presented European women who were captured and imprisoned in the zenanas of Asiatic despots and released by the daring exploits of young British men (see Paxton, 'Mobilizing chivalry', pp. 5–30).

This progressive displacement of the Indian woman from the centre of the Anglo-Indian novel can be read as revealing what Laurie Langbauer has called an effort to 'break with a feminine origin' of the novel as romance (Langbauer, p. 29). By the 1880s, the term 'romance' had been appropriated to describe popular boys' adventure novels. These novels reassert 'the privileged position of the male, and all it represents', by arranging 'the expulsion of woman' from her central place in the plot of the heterosexual romance (Langbauer, p. 29). Rider Haggard, G. A. Henty, Robert Louis Stevenson and a host of imitators presented their novels as offering 'refreshment' by a return to a 'pure' form of romance. Though they claimed their stories conformed to Sir Walter Scott's definition of romance as a 'tale of wild adventures in love and chivalry', they typically emphasised boys' preparation for maturity and the performance of rituals of male identification and affiliation, rather than their erotic awakening to the delights of heterosexual love and its sexual consummation in marriage. Boys' adventure stories shaded into 'romances' written presumably for more adult readers, as Rider Haggard indicated by initially dedicating his *King Solomon's Mines* to 'all the big and little boys who read it' (Koestenbaum, p. 152). These novels were recommended for male readers who wanted an 'escape' from the 'more complicated kind of novel', written, for example, by a growing number of feminists and 'New Women' in America, England, and British India.[6]

Kipling's *Jungle Books* (1894–95) and *Kim* (1901) generally conform to the ideological and symbolic conventions of popular boys' adventure novels, rather than to British or Anglo-Indian romances, since they feature an adolescent protagonist and conclude before the hero might be expected to act on the promptings of heterosexual desire. Eve Sedgewick has invented the neologism, 'homosociality', to describe the paradoxical psychosocial pressures at work in British culture which promote male bonding while at the same time prohibiting any expression of homosexual desire (Sedgewick, pp. 1–3). In discussing Kipling's fiction, she has argued that 'subject territories' like Kim's India, or the school in *Stalky and Co*, 'are male places in which it is relatively safe for men to explore the crucial terrain of homosociality' (Sedgewick, p. 198). The narrative stakes are higher, however, in two of Kipling's works that Sedgwick does not discuss, *The Light that Failed* (1890–91) and *The Naulahka*, because in both works the hero has achieved the age when he is expected to 'route his passionate attachments to older men through a desire for women' (Sedgewick, p. 198). Both these novels display a crisis in gender and sexual relations that occurs when the heroine refuses the part assigned to her in this 'triangulation' of homosocial desire.

In *The Light that Failed*, Kipling hints at the possibilities of alternate sexualities by describing two sexual triangles that fail to end with marriage or to reproduce the usual triangulation of desire that Sedgewick identifies. The ardent friendship of Dick Heldar and Gilbert Torpenhow is disturbed by sexual jealousy when Dick intrudes on his friend's sexual dalliance with the working-class barmaid, Bessie Broke, but Dick later fails, apparently, to refocus his erotic desires on her after he has won her away from his friend. Kipling identifies Bessie Broke's class

origins and vindictive destruction of Dick's painting of 'Melan-
cholia' as the ostensible causes for his failure to unite with her.
Kipling provides even less explanation as to why Maisie remains
immune to Dick's persistent erotic advances. Maisie's relationship with the passionately jealous red-haired girl, mirroring
not only Dick's bond with Torpenhow but also, perhaps, Flo
Garrard's lifelong alliance with Mabel Price, remains only an
enigmatic shadow of the alternate sexual possibilities that began
to find more public expression in the 1890s. Maisie's artistic
ambitions and avowed feminism thus provide a highly politicised
cover for her implicit sexual insubordination.[7]

In *The Naulahka*, Kate Sheriff similarly resists Nick Tarvin's
repeated marriage proposals, but Kipling amplifies the ideological
and symbolic significance of her insubordination by moving this
couple from America to India, where her resistance appears to
threaten not only the hero's happiness but the stability of the
Raj itself. In short, *The Naulahka* reveals the heterosexual im-
peratives of life under the Raj in the 1890s, which enforce, by
violence if necessary, the prohibitions not only against cross-
racial and cross-class erotic alliances but against homosexuality
as well.

The American hero goes East

The early chapters of *The Naulahka* describe the American
hero's and heroine's life on the frontier in Topaz, Colorado, a
virtually lawless world where *laissez-faire* capitalism produces
extreme individualists who recognise very few 'laws' or
restraints. The early chapters of this novel are typical of nineteenth-century American colonial narratives which depend upon
the absence of colonised people. The hero, Nick Tarvin, is a brash,
energetic, ill-educated, rough-riding junior version of Teddy
Roosevelt, who fails to even see the Native American people who
share this land with him. The only 'enemies' Tarvin recognises
are those generated by American competition: they are the rival
town, conveniently named Rustler, the men who have jumped his
mining claims, and his political rivals, the 'democrats', whose
local contingent is headed by the father of the woman he loves.
Marriage is one of the only 'laws' that Tarvin respects, and, as he
sees it, this 'law' assigns to women the task of morally domesti-
cating their partners. Nick acts on this 'law' as he repeatedly

proposes to Kate Sheriff, even after she repeatedly refuses him. Having 'lived with her face to the West and with her smouldering eyes fixed upon the wilderness since she could walk' (*Naulahka*: 2), Kate seems, by contrast, to stare at the virgin land as if trying to recognise the absence this metaphor hides.

The *Naulahka* shows its double-dealing deployment of colonial discourse by representing what happens when Nick Tarvin follows Kate Sheriff to India, bringing his American ideological baggage with him. Tarvin justifies his trip to India, and his undignified inability to take no for an answer, by concocting an alibi drawn from the fantastic world of British adventure novels, though Tarvin's motives are hardly as high-minded as those, for example, of G. A. Henty's heroes. Tarvin tells himself he will save Topaz from economic ruin (and coincidentally protect his own investments) by acquiring the fabulous jewelled necklace, called the naulahka, which is rumoured to be among the court jewels in the princely state of Gokral Seetarun. Tarvin has promised to acquire this necklace for the wife of an American railroad tycoon as a 'trade' (*Naulahka*: 61), in exchange for her efforts to persuade her husband to route his railroad through Topaz. Kipling makes it clear, however, that the 'trades' Tarvin has in mind are euphemisms for theft.

Thus, America, the centre of one 'western' value system in this novel, fails to provide the same normalizing moral standards that England represents in Kipling's other Indian fiction. Nonetheless, it still offers a standard of dynamic economic and technological development against which indigenous Indian culture is judged and found wanting. Tarvin is disoriented when he travels to an India which is characterised, as it is in nearly all of the English adventure fiction of the period, as a 'timeless' and changeless world (David, p. 134). Throughout the novel, Gokral Seetarun appears as a backward little kingdom desperately in need of western technology; the railroad station is poorly run by an overeducated and oversensitive Bengali, the makeshift telegraph office is located in a desecrated tomb, and the journey from the railroad depot to the princely capital of Rhatore takes a maddening four days by bullock cart. Tarvin regards Rhatore as a world which 'doubled desolateness' (*Naulahka*: 64), a verdict that repeats Kipling's similar impressions of Rajasthan recorded in *Letters of Marque*.

He sees himself as bringing technical know-how and 'git up and git' (*Naulahka*: 122) to this princely state, but Kipling demonstrates that Nick produces nothing but waste in Gokral Seetarun. Fearing that he will be 'engulfed' (*Naulahka:* 99) by the 'monumental sloth' (*Naulahka:* 87) that has infected all the Indian men, and some of the Englishmen, he meets, Tarvin keeps himself frantically busy. But Nick shows his American 'lawlessness' by doing what good British heroes, by definition, cannot do: he lies audaciously and continuously to the Maharajah. Since Nick cannot acknowledge either the romantic or the economic motives for his visit, he persuades the gullible prince to bankroll an elaborate plan to extract gold from a local river, though Tarvin knows that this scheme cannot possibly provide an adequate return on the investment.

Ultimately, Kipling shows that Tarvin's energy is completely unproductive, for before he leaves the city, Nick gratuitously blows up the dam he has built with the Maharajah's money and the labour of thousands of his men. Yet the narrator reinscribes orientalist dualities by passing the blame for the waste to the Indians, claiming that Nick stages this spectacle, knowing that the Maharajah will regard it as a huge 'joke'. As the narrator concludes, destruction is 'the one thing that the Oriental fully comprehends' (*Naulahka:* 372). In describing Tarvin's self-serving motives, his obsession with time, his lack of introspection about the consequences of his plans, and his careless wastefulness, Kipling/Balestier criticise the monopoly capitalism that makes imperialism so profitable on both these frontiers, an aspect of colonial life that is concealed in most American and Anglo-Indian fiction.

Entering the colonial harem

The most significant ideological and symbolic contradictions produced by Kipling/Balestier's attempt to combine American romance with British adventure novel become evident in Tarvin's troubled relation to all that the colonial harem represents. The 'colonial harem' in *The Naulahka* is not a site of libidinal pleasures but rather the site of dissipation and the breeding ground for rebellion and violence. Like stereotypical Indian princelings in many British adventure novels, the Maharajah of Gokral Seetarun is described as a 'large and amiable despot, brown and bush-bearded' (*Naulahka:* 103). He is a fiscally irresponsible consumer, an incompetent statesman, a woman-dominated ruler, and an opium addict. Early on, Tarvin learns that the king 'ordered by the ton and paid by the scruple': 'He had purchased guns, dressing-cases, mirrors, mantlepiece ornaments, crochet-work, the iridescent Christmas-tree glass balls, saddlery, mail-phaetons, four-in-hands, scent bottles, surgical instruments, and chinaware by the dozen, gross, or score as his royal fancy prompted. When he lost interest in his purchases, he lost interest in paying for them' (*Naulahka:* 78).

While the Maharajah practises polygamy and supports a large zenana, his second wife, Sitabhai, holds him in a state of credulous infatuation. Sitabhai is beautiful, unscrupulous, and ambitious, and her reported history defines her as the harem's *femme fatale*, similar to many who appear in British adventure novels. The Maharajah first saw Sitabhai 'crouching in an iron cage awaiting execution' for poisoning her first husband. When he 'demanded whether she would poison him if he married her', she is reported to have replied, 'Assuredly ... if he treated her as her late husband had treated her. Thereupon the King had married her, partly to please his fancy, mainly through sheer delight in her brutal answer' (*Naulahka:* 81). Kipling/Balestier, however, undermine the usual orientalist dualities which assign mind and reason to the West and body and passion to the East by describing Nick as similarly captivated by his desire to please the women in his life and similarly unscrupulous in his plans to steal the naulahka.

Because Tarvin is an American, he lives outside the status hierarchy of the Raj, and he feels free to resist the British ethics of race and class affiliation and the homosocial logic that usually organises the code of honour in British adventure novels. Unlike British adventure heroes, Tarvin seeks recognition and protection not from British military or bureaucratic authorities in Gokral Seetarun, but from the Maharajah himself. Nick ignores the censure of the local representative of the British crown as well as of Mr Estes, the American missionary who sponsors Kate. The Maharajah is at first delighted by Tarvin's impudence, his skilful horsemanship, and his sharpshooting, which he displays on more than one occasion by tossing a quarter into the air and putting a bullet-hole in its centre.

Nick's most obvious violation of the unspoken homosocial code occurs when he fails to censor his indiscreet disclosure of Sitabhai's plot to kill the Maharajah's first-born son and heir. The Maharajah acknowledges Nick's betrayal of the rules of homosociality, and the class and gender affiliations they cement, when he thunders, ' "Am I a king or a potter that I must have the affairs of my zenana dragged into the sunlight by any white dog that chooses to howl at me" ' (Naulahka: 189). Like other decadent rulers in Anglo-Indian fiction, however, the Maharajah sinks into an opium-induced sleep before he can plan any retaliation against Nick. Sitabhai, however, is prompted to immediate action.

Tarvin's subsequent exchanges with Sitabhai characterise him as a sexual as well as a moral renegade. Unlike the sexually pure heroes in most British adventure novels of the 1880s, Nick agrees to meet Sitabhai privately, but only because he plans to extort the naulahka from her. Hoping to seduce and silence him, Sitabhai first tries flattery by acknowledging his bravery, then declares her love for him, and finally offers him the role of prime minister: ' "Is it a little thing ... if I ask you to be my king? In the old days, before the English came, Englishmen of no birth stole the hearts of begums, and led their armies. They were kings in all but the name. We do not know when the old days may return, and we might lead our armies together" ' (Naulahka: 282). Though Tarvin is mildly titillated by the proximity of her voluptuous body and by the promise of limitless power that Sitabhai offers, his lovemaking is arrested when he feels the necklace around her hips. Refusing all her sexual offers, then, Tarvin threatens to turn her over to the British authorities for the attempted murder of the Maharajah's son unless she gives him the necklace, saying ' "Is it a trade?" It was his question to Mrs. Mutrie' (Naulahka: 284). Tarvin's immunity to Sitabhai's sexual allure apparently needs little explanation, for sexual surrender to any Indian woman appears throughout Kipling's fiction to jeopardise the coloniser's racial and class status and compromise his authority.

Having seen the Maharajah's son wearing the naulahka, Tarvin has recognised it as the real locus of his desires for material reward, for fame, and, perhaps, for a child of his own. The sight of the jewels, 'the dull red of the ruby, the angry green of the emerald, the cold blue of the sapphire, and the white, hot glory of the diamond', and most of all 'the black diamond — black as the pitch of the infernal lake, and lighted from below with the fires of hell' (239), prompts him to imagine himself as 'the saviour of his town' after having presented the jewels to Mrs Mutrie (Naulahka: 240). Having carefully calculated his interests and decided he will settle for nothing less than the jewels, Tarvin is ready to take the treasure and run. In this calculus, and in his total exemption from the moral codes that otherwise discipline British heroes, Tarvin shows himself to be incorrigibly American.[8]

Colonising women and the terms of romance

Kate Sheriff's part in the American chapters of *The Naulahka* reveal the disordering potential of an emergent international feminism that created new, and often conflictual, subject positions for colonising women in the 1890s. Kate hopes that her career will allow her to escape from the symbolic economy that prevails in American romances where men produce and women reproduce. She has just completed her nursing training and is expected to remain celibate and unmarried in order to practise her profession.

Like many American and Anglo-Indian heroines of the period, Kate invokes the rhetoric of evangelical Christianity to legitimise her resistance to marriage. Believing that God has elected her to work as a medical missionary, Kate embraces her career 'joyfully' (*Naulahka:* 4). Tarvin, predictably, objects to such idealising: ' "You can call it duty, or you can call it woman's sphere ... I've no doubt you've got a halo to put to it. ... But for me, what I say is, it's a freeze-out" ' (*Naulahka:* 4). When Kate corrects him gently, saying, ' "It's a call" ', he counters sacrilegiously, ' "You've got a call to stay at home" ' (*Naulahka:* 5). When Tarvin's bluster fails to deter Kate, he appeals to her sympathy, saying, ' "I can't live without you and I won't" ' (*Naulahka:* 6).

One feature that distinguishes *The Naulakha* from other American romances, however, is Kipling/Balestier's handling of the imaginative vacuum created by the 'absence' of the colonised Native American woman in the American chapters and the void it creates which allows Kate to imagine the needs of her [East] Indian 'sisters' (*Naulahka:* 3). Unlike most Anglo-Indian romances, the feminist appeal that fires Kate's imagination comes from the East rather than the West; she is inspired by a lecture by the Indian feminist Pundita Ramabai, who toured America in 1889, speaking on the conditions of Indian women. According to A.B. Shah, Ramabai was the 'greatest woman produced by modern India' and 'one who lay the foundations for a movement for women's liberation in India' (Tharu and Lalita, p. 243).

Kate does not settle easily into the place her gender would assign to her in the Indian colonial context either, for, in spite of her naive missionary zeal, she is caught in the contradictions created by the intersection of 'colonial and gender discourses' (Shohat, p. 63). Kate expects her work in organising a medical clinic to provide a kind of 'freedom' from the conventional constraints of a western woman's life. In one respect, her work expresses her 'alterity' because it is not directed by the phallic economy that propels Tarvin's frantic projects, but rather by the sympathetic beneficence that Kipling elsewhere identified as the best justification for the Raj.

Yet Kate's work also reveals her implication in the imperial project. When she is challenged, for example, by the passive resistance of an 'idle' 'native' male doctor at the clinic, Kate assumes the memsahib's patronising habit of command, dramatised over and over in Anglo-Indian fiction. In other words, Kate's high-minded feminism does not exempt her from displaying the insidious racism of both American and British cultures. Moreover, like Lady Dufferin, who organised similar clinics during her husband's term as Viceroy (1884–88), Kate hopes to provide a hygenic and efficient hospital where, among other things, Indian women can safely give birth and where suffering children are restored to health. But Kate's choice of this medical work also reveals her unexamined complicity with British imperialism at a time when western medicine became one of the most powerful forces deployed to enforce rearrangements in sexual relationships between the colonisers and the colonised (see Levine, Arnold).

Perhaps in spite of itself, though, *The Naulahka* still shows that international feminism had the potential to crack open some of the most resistant stereotypes about Indian women in orientalist discourse. On her first day at the hospital, for example, Kate shows her desire to establish alliances with Indian women that are outside the reach of colonial surveillance when she enlists the help of 'a woman of the desert, very tall, golden-colored, and scarlet-lipped' (*Naulahka*: 145). Kipling hints at the sexual threats that underlie such feminist solidarity when the woman agrees to help, and Kate responds to 'an impulse of compassion which knows no race' by kissing her 'quietly upon the forehead' (*Naulahka*: 146). Later the widow, who has defended Kate throughout her hospital work, expresses her loyalty, by echoing the rhetoric of Christian marriage vows with her ' "where thou goest I will go" ' (*Naulahka*: 325). Kate's kiss thus eloquently displays one way that international feminism could potentially subvert the sex/gender system and undermine the heterosexual order of the Raj.

Kate's experiences in the colonial harem dramatise the deepest contradictions in the 'colonial and gender discourses' at work in this text, though they also show Kipling's desire to defeat the revolutionary potential of the international feminism represented in this novel. As Billie Melman has shown, when Victorian women entered the closed female world of the harem, which had been the domain of male erotic fantasy in western literature for at least two centuries, they often countered male fantasies by asserting 'new knowledge' about harem life and by turning these critiques of sexual practices back on western men. They often observed, for example, that eastern women enjoyed some legal rights denied to European women concerning marriage, divorce, and inheritance (see Melman, p. 108; Shohat, p. 72). In describing Kate's first visit to the zenana, Kipling illustrates the threat that such exercises of female authority posed and the male anxiety that was consequently generated by the spectacle of a colonising woman moving into a domain ostensibly beyond the reach of the colonial male gaze. Kipling/Balestier display some of the uncanny fear of intercultural female solidarity when Tarvin watches Kate enter the zenana: 'Kate could go where he was forbidden to venture ... on the first day she disappeared, untroubled and un-questioning, behind the darkness of the veiled door leading to the apartments of the women of the palace, he found his hand going instinctively to the butt of his revolver' (Naulahka: 135).

Kipling shows that Tarvin had no need for fear, for Kate's difficulties in understanding differences in the gender roles and sexualities she encounters in the 'colonial harem' illustrate the extent of her own sexual colonisation by western patriarchal culture. She is so overcome by the spectacle of 'monstrous and obscene pictures' and 'shameless gods' (Naulahka: 133), that she loses the assurance of the colonial 'I': 'It seemed impossible that she should ever know the smallest part of the vast warren, or distinguish one pale face from another in the gloom. ... there were many women, – how many she did not know, – worked upon by intrigues she could not comprehend' (Naulahka: 132–3). Later, when she meets Sitabhai, 'a lithe, black-haired young girl', Kate realises that this powerful woman, though her same age, recog-nises none of the fears of sexuality or male domination that Kate herself experiences. Instead, when she looks into 'eyes that had no shadow of fear in them' (*Naulahka*: 218), Kate is confronted by a difference unmapped by the patriarchal language of colonialism, and she responds with competition and indignation rather than sisterly compassion.

After her first visit, Tarvin prompts Kate to tell the stories about the female competition and power struggles behind the curtain that had become standard in Anglo-Indian fiction of this period. In fact, Kate must be schooled by Tarvin to discover the proper meaning of her subsequent experiences in the harem. When the Maharajah's first wife sends Kate a cryptic message, it is repeated by her son and translated by him into English: ' "Protect this work of mine that comes from me – a cloth nine years upon the loom" ' (*Naulahka*: 137). At first, the literal-minded Kate cannot decipher it, so Tarvin interprets it for her, telling her that the young rajah is in danger of being poisoned by Sitabhai so her son will inherit the throne. Tarvin's and the young rajah's translations thus indicate the distance between Kate's actual experience in the harem and the colonial discourse that would encode it. These two male translators serve to remind us of the endless opportunities for 'colonial ventriloquism' that Kipling exploits so masterfully in his Indian fiction (Bhabha, pp. 162–3).

Like most of his contemporaries, Kipling counters long-standing stereotypes of the harem as a realm of lesbian eroticism, and uses Kate's testimony to confirm, instead, Indian women's suffering because of the ruthless sexual rivalries created by heterosexual desire under the conditions of polygamy. Yet something of Kate's experience in this veiled world escapes translation, as she confronts alternatives not only to western bourgeois marriage but also to heterosexuality itself and to the spectrum of desire that she has internalised. Like Lady Wortley Montagu's narrative about harem life, Kate's censored account reveals her confusion over becoming the object of the gaze of the Other, as the women of the zenana threaten to undress her as they 'examined her dress, her helmet, and her gloves' (*Naulahka*: 132).

Ultimately, in spite of the censorship, the zenana represented in *The Naulahka* provides a glimpse of a sensuous realm beyond the male gaze, and a place where Kate is recognised as a beloved 'sister'. When Kate and the Kulu widow meet the Queen Mother in the harem, she asserts their kinship, noting: ' "We be all three women here, Sahiba – dead leaf, flowering tree, and the blossom unopened" ' (*Naulahka*: 341). Holding Kate's hands and caressing her hair, the Queen tells Kate with 'infinite tenderness': ' "Forget that thou art white, and I am black, and remember only that we three be sisters" ' (*Naulahka:* 342). Kipling/Balestier insist, though, that the basis of this solidarity rests on biological function rather than political subjectivity, when she continues, ' "Little sister, with us women 'tis thus, and no other way. From all, except such as have borne a child, the world is hid" ' (*Naulahka:* 344).

Reproducing the colonial harem

Having imagined the zenana as the site of erotic possibilities beyond the constraints of monogamy and heterosexuality, this text attempts to go straight by putting the harem to work in the interests of compulsory heterosexuality and parenthood. Paradoxically, because of her discussions with the Queen Mother, Kate learns to see monogamy as the 'natural' solution to the chaos caused by polygamy and unbridled passion. The Queen explains that Kate's work at the hospital has failed because she was unmarried and did not possess the magical authority of the mother: ' "There was no child in thy arms. The mother look was not in thy eyes. By what magic, then, wouldst thou speak to women?" ' (*Naulahka:* 344). Disarmed by this argument, Kate not only abandons her post at the medical clinic but renounces her work in the zenana as well.

As Malek Alloula observes, what is 'remembered about the harem are the sexual excesses to which it gives rise and which it promotes. A universe of generalized perversion and of the absolute limitlessness of pleasure, the seraglio does appear as the ideal locus of the phantasm in all its contagious splendour' (95). While Alloula focuses on the forbidden pleasures that he labels 'oriental sapphism' (49), he ignores other obvious sexual alternatives, which, by the 1880s, were in more public circulation. Sir Richard Burton's terminal essay to his translation of the *Thousand Nights and a Night* (1886) is, perhaps, the most notorious example of the ways in which male homosexuality was identified as an erotic possibility available on the continuum of 'limitlessness of pleasure' located in the Orient.

These homosexual possibilities threaten to rupture the text in what is certainly the strangest episode in the novel when, in a mood of sportiveness, the Maharajah sends Nick on a pointless excursion to the deserted women's quarters in a ruined city nearby to search for the naulahka. In describing Nick's visit to the temple of the Gau-Mukh, Kipling/Balestier rework Kipling's earlier descriptions of his visit to Chitor in *Letters of Marque* (1891), and the changes they make reveal the deepest wells of anxiety in the novel. In this episode, Nick confronts the terrifying abyss of a world without the conventional ordering polarities defining sexuality and gender roles, and glimpses, for a moment, his own deeply repressed homosexual desires.

Nick Tarvin's descent to the grass-fringed lip of the tank filled with water 'corrupted past corruption' (*Naulahka:* 191), has often been read as disclosing primal fears aroused by the vagina dentata (see Pafford, pp. 48–9; Parry, *Delusions*, pp. 226–7). I would argue, though, that this episode reveals the workings of an imagination so overburdened by the guilty bad faith of the coloniser that it resists containment by such Freudian paradigms which presume heterosexuality. In Kipling/Balestier's revision of this scene, the phallic lingam is submerged and the marble like the 'soft, oiled skin of a Hindu' (*Letters:* 127) is erased. Though Nick also has heard stories about the zenana women who immolated themselves near the Gau-Mukh, the authors provide a more objective correlative for his sense of dread when he steps on human bones, observes malovent 'pale emerald eyes' staring at him out of the darkness, and sees alligators with 'horny eyelids, heavy with green slime' (*Naulahka:* 195) appearing suddenly beneath his feet.

Kipling/Balestier also comply with the colonial taboos of the 1880s, which discourage cross-racial sex, by removing the Indian woman whose scream prompts the Englishman to flee during his midnight visit to the Cow's Mouth (*Letters:* 132). But in replacing her with a Hindu priest, a 'man, old, crippled, and all but naked', who cries ' "Ao, Bhai! Ao!" ', the homosexual possibilities that Kipling would repress find expression nonetheless in his translation of the priest's words: ' "Come, Brother! Come" ' (*Naulahka:* 195). While the words are ostensibly addressed to the 'kid' that the priest prepares as a sacrifice to feed to the alligators in the tank, these words also sound an unspeakable sexual invitation, underscored by the priest's nakedness. Moreover, by adding the 'kid' to this scene, Kipling repeats the strange image of sexual desire that he used in the first chapter of *The Light that Failed* when Maisie and Dick exchange their first kiss in the presence of her pet goat.

In short, all these substitutions indicate the shape of Tarvin's (and Kipling's) fears, suggesting that both lesbianism and male homosexuality are no longer securely contained within the colonial harem. In short, this novel shows that neither alternative is distanced by the dualities of Otherness; both were close at hand. The only remedy Kipling apparently could imagine for the 'fear and aversion' inspired by these visits to the colonial harem was a metaphysical one, imaged in *Letters of Marque* by the Tower of Victory, where the Englishman glimpsed 'one calm face, the God enthroned, holding the Wheel of the Law' (*Letters:* 123). Only an authority of such magnitude could restore a moral order that ensures heterosexuality, marriage, and reproduction. As Martin Seymour-Smith has shown, Kipling's first references to the 'law' preface the chapter of *The Naulahka* where Kate finally accepts Tarvin's marriage proposal and submits to the demands of compulsory heterosexuality (Seymour-Smith, p. 206).

Both Kate's and Nick's experiences in the 'colonial harem' teach them to obey this heterosexual 'law' that will release them from their hopeless adventure quests and lead them back into the marriage plot. Once Tarvin has obtained the necklace, he is ready to submit to the conventional gender arrangements in American and Anglo-Indian romances, expressed in the epigraph Kipling added to *The Naulahka* on his honeymoon: 'The Law whereby my Lady moves / Was never Law to me, / But 'tis enough that she approves / Whatever Law it be' (*Naulahka:* 346). This law is conjured up to obscure the sexual alternatives to heterosexuality and to hide all of the improbabilities that prompt critics to label this text as a cheap romance.

The scandal that Kipling/Balestier attempt to veil by this invocation of the 'law', is that Tarvin and Kate have been represented throughout the novel as people uncompelled by heterosexual desire, for whom marriage necessarily entails a profound sacrifice of self. When Tarvin begins to tell Kate the truth about his adventures with Sitabhai, he suddenly realises she will be so offended by the immoral 'trades' he has conducted that she will forever refuse to marry him. In short, Nick realises that he cannot confess either his plan to bribe the wife of the railway tycoon or the conditions under which he extorted the jewels from Sitabhai, and so must return the necklace to its owner. In this 'luminous moment', Kipling/Balestier write, Tarvin 'knew himself for lost' (*Naulahka:* 364). Tarvin's losses are more than financial, too, for he has come to see himself as a man entirely without morals or conscience: '[Kate] could not know, and probably could not have imagined, how little his own sense of the square thing had to do with any system of morality, and how entirely he must always define morality as what pleased Kate' (*Naulahka:* 362).

Kate's capitulation to Nick's marriage proposal expresses a similarly profound loss of self. Keenly aware that Tarvin regards marriage as a relationship defined by status more than by sexual desire, Kate observes, ' "You want me to round out your life; you want me to complete your other ambitions" ', but she warns him, ' "A woman gives the whole of herself in marriage – in all happy marriages. I haven't the whole of myself to give. It belongs to something else" ' (*Naulahka:* 298). While critics who see heterosexuality as the only alternative may doubt the authenticity of Kate's declaration, I would argue that Kipling succeeds in this novel, as in *The Light that Failed*, in convincingly representing a woman who recognises the lesbian potential in herself.

Finally, by a strategic ellipsis that omits the expected spectacle of the clinch and the kiss, Kipling/Balestier avoid the fundamental narrative keystone of romance. Rather than confess her love for Nick, Kate simply admits defeat: ' "I have failed. Everything I meant to do has fallen about me in a heap. I feel burnt out, Nick – burnt out ... Take me home" ' (*Naulahka:* 359). While Tarvin has finally achieved the goal that has driven him throughout the novel, he is strangely subdued when Kate agrees to marry him. Before they leave India, Kate makes one last visit to the harem, and returns a box to Sitabhai into which Tarvin has secretly deposited the necklace that he had stolen from her. In contracting this marriage, then, Nick and Kate agree to shut the door on all the erotic possibilities they have so fearfully discovered in the colonial harem. In short, Kipling's 'love letter' (*Letters:* 132) remains unwritten.

After their implausible marriage, the Tarvins begin their journey home to Topaz, Colorado, and the transit they make suggests the peculiar ideological problems that this text tries unsuccessfully to solve. As international capitalism, like international travel, became less restricted in the last two decades of the nineteenth century, the opportunities for the exposure of such inconsistencies were multiplied. In *The Naulahka*, Kipling/Balestier chart the collision of an emergent international feminism with a social Darwinism deployed to reduce colonial relations to the dualities of white and black. But Kipling/Balestier must create a 'law' that guarantees that social Darwinism will continue to prevail, by normalising heterosexuality and compelling racially 'pure' fathers and mothers to reproduce the colonial order. These conflicts cannot be fully recognised if *The Naulahka* is compared only with boys' adventure novels, for the doubleness of this hybrid text reveals contradictions in the colonial ideologies that boys' adventure books also try to evade, contradictions that underlie both the American and Indian chapters of Kipling/Balestier's strange romance.

So effective is Kipling in his mystifying references to the 'law' in *The Naulahka* that none of the recent commentators on Kipling's subsequent works have noted his unaccountable omission of any element of sexual selection in his notion of the 'law' in texts otherwise so obviously influenced by social Darwinism. John Murray, for example, follows Shamsul Islam's argument in *Kipling's 'Law': A Study of his Philosophy of Life*, that the 'law' is a 'master idea' in Kipling's more mature fiction. While he convincingly shows that the 'law of command' in *The Jungle Books* is based on a code of 'self-preservation' that echoes the exigencies of British Conservative colonial strategies of control, he fails to note that 'self-preservation' also requires, in its most basic sense, some strategy which provides for the literal reproduction of the colonisers, by authorising gender arrangements which normalise heterosexuality and promote and police legal gender arrangements and legitimise reproduction. In the 'Outsong' at the end of the second *Jungle Book*, Kipling insists that if Mowgli is to return to the human family, he must uncritically submit to the 'Law the man pack make / ... Clean or tainted, hot or stale, / Hold it as it were the trail, / Through the day and through the night, / Questing neither left nor right' (*Jungle Books:* 343). But in defining a developmental law that prevents Mowgli from returning to his brothers in the wolf pack, as Kaa explains, 'Having cast the skin ... we may not creep into it afresh. It is the Law' (*Jungle Books:* 341), Kipling inexplicably returns Mowgli to the arms of the mother rather than the embrace of a wife.

Likewise, because European women are virtually absent in Kipling's *Kim*, his hero, like Mowgli, evades the disciplining norms of heterosexuality which work so tragically in *The Light that Failed* and *The Naulahka* to inhibit the growth and fulfilment of the protagonists. When the hillwoman from Shamlegh approaches Kim, she can be easily rejected, according to the dictates of the imperial organisation of desire, because of her racial and ethnic differences. Kim's teasing kiss, and parting English words to her, 'Thank you verree much, my dear' (Kim: 239), show that he still regards the erotic contest that Dick Heldar plays with Maisie or that Nick Tarvin performs with Kate Sheriff as masquerade. In the end, like Mowgli, Kim returns to the embrace of the mother, when he collapses in the Sahiba's compound.[9]

Given the construction of Indian womanhood in his writing, Kipling could hardly imagine the colonial harem as anything more than a realm of danger and fear, but to focus only on the divide separating colonising men from colonised or colonising women is to miss all the other threats posed by life in the 'colonial harem'. As I hope this reading of Kipling's Indian fiction demonstrates, there were other ideological pressures at work in British colonial culture which find urgent, though ambiguous, expression in Kipling's Indian novels. While Martin Seymour-Smith insists that the emphasis on the 'law' reflects Kipling's painful personal renunciation of a lawless homosexual passion for Wolcott Balestier, we need not reduce the textual possibilities of Kipling's later fiction to this single biographical script, even though we recognise the excessive and pervasive disciplinary power that Kipling evokes in his articulation of the 'law' in *The Naulahka* and subsequent works. Certainly, Kipling's mature fiction is indelibly marked by his efforts, conscious and otherwise, to devise a 'law' that foreclosed alternatives to heterosexuality. And while we recognise that the 'sexual and political semiotic' at work in Kipling's fiction depends upon the restoration of the authority of 'the Father/male heir as Law-giver and Law-provider' (97), as Gail Ching-Liang Low has eloquently shown, we must also recognise that by the 1890s, for Kipling and other writers like him, heterosexuality itself had been called into question. As a consequence, the heterosexual order, as well as the more familiar colonial hierarchies of gender, class, and race required a vigorous, though covert, defence.

Notes

1 Malek Alloula, *The Colonial Harem*, p. 3. See especially studies of the harem by Janaki Nair, Billie Melman, Lisa Lowe and Ella Shohat.

2 *Letters of Marque* (1891; New York: Collier), p. 121. All quotations cited parenthetically in the text are taken from this edition.

3 Rudyard Kipling and Wolcott Balestier, *The Naulahka: A Story of West and East* (1892).
   All quotations cited parenthetically in the text refer to this edition. Critics apparently
   unfamiliar with American geography and history have incorrectly located the opening
   scenes of this novel in the 'Midwest' (Parry, *Delusions*: 225) or in California (Seymour-
   Smith, p. 149), but it is crucial to its ideological structure that this romance begins and
   ends in Topaz, Colorado, an imaginary mining town on the American frontier of the
   1880s.

4 Nearly all Kipling's biographers and critics mention *The Naulahka* only to dismiss it.
   Kipling himself fails to identify it (and many other details of this period of his life,
   including his friendship with Henry James) in his autobiography, *Something of Myself:
   For My Friends, Known and Unknown*.

5 Emily Eden's *Up the Country* is a good case in point. For details, see Paxton, 'Disembodied subjects', p. 393.

6 See Ardis, pp. 29–58. By contrast, Frederic Jameson does not investigate this appropriation of the language of 'romance' in his brilliant study, *The Political Unconscious*.

7 John Lyon handles this issue astutely in his fine preface to *The Light that Failed*
   (Penguin, 1988).

8 Peter Hulme, in *Colonial Encounters*, discusses the thematic importance of a parallel
   story in colonial discourse about the Americas in describing Ikle's careful calculation
   of the benefits of selling Yariko, the native woman who has been his lover; see
   especially p. 236.

9 Nora Crook argues in *Kipling's Myths of Love and Death* that this episode displays
   Kim's recognition of the power of 'women' (p. 2). By identifying the Sahiba as a representative of all 'women', Crook ignores the class dynamics at work in this colonial scene.
   Kipling makes clear Sahiba's deliberate condescension in providing such personal service
   to Kim since she has many male or female servants who could perform this work. Second,
   it overlooks the political significance of Kim's denial of his part in the Great Game in
   his claim of sentimental kinship with Sahiba, a claim that parallels his assertion of
   kinship with the lama. Finally, it ignores the profound divisions that British colonialism
   created to separate unequivocally sexually available from unavailable Indian women and
   both from marriageable colonial European women.

Bibliography

Alloula, M., *The Colonial Harem* (Minneapolis: University of Minnesota Press, 1986).

Ardis, A., *New Women, New Novels: Feminism and Early Modernism* (New Brunswick:
   Rutgers University Press, 1990).

Arnold, D., *Imperial Medicine and Indigenous Societies* (Manchester: Manchester
   University Press, 1988).

Bhabha, H. K., 'The other question: difference, discrimination, and the discourse of
   colonialism', in Francis Barker *et al.* (eds.), *Literature, Politics, and Theory: Papers
   from the Essex Conference, 1976–84* (London, 1986), pp. 148–72.

Carrington, C. E., *Rudyard Kipling: His Life and Work* (Garden City: Doubleday, 1955).

Crook, N., *Kipling's Myths of Love and Death* (New York: St Martin's Press, 1989).

David, D., 'Children of empire: Victorian imperialism and sexual politics in Dickens
   and Kipling', in Anthony H. Harrison and Beverly Taylor (eds.), *Gender and Discourse
   in Victorian Literature and Art* (DeKalb: Northern Illinois University Press, 1992),
   pp. 124–42.

Green, M., *Seven Types of Adventure Tales: An Etiology of a Major Genre* (University
   Park: Penn State University Press, 1991).

Hulme, P., *Colonial Encounters: Europe and the Native Caribbean, 1492–1797* (London: Methuen, 1986).

Islam, S., *Kipling's 'Law': A Study of his Philosophy of Life* (London: Macmillan, 1975).

Jameson, F., *The Political Unconscious: Narrative as Socially Symbolic Act* (Ithaca: Cornell University Press, 1981).

Kipling, R., *The Light that Failed*, ed. J. M. Lyon (1890; London: Penguin, 1988).

—— *Letters of Marque* (1891; New York: Collier, nd).

—— and Wolcott Balestier, *The Naulahka: A Story of West and East* (New York: Macmillan, 1892).

—— *The Jungle Books*, ed. Daniel Karlin (London: Penguin, 1987).

—— *Kim*, ed. Edward Said (London: Penguin, 1989).

—— *Something of Myself: For My Friends, Known and Unknown* (Garden City: Doubleday, 1937).

Koestenbaum, W., *Double Talk: The Erotics of Male Literary Collaboration* (New York: Routledge, 1989).

Langbauer, L., *Women and Romance: The Consolations of Gender in the English Novel* (Ithaca: Cornell University Press, 1990).

Levine, P., 'Venereal disease, prostitution, and the politics of empire: the case of British India', *Journal of the History of Sexuality*, 4, 4 (1994), pp. 579–602.

Low, G. Ching-Liang, 'White skins/black masks: the pleasures and politics of imperialism', *New Formations*, 9 (Winter 1989), pp. 83–103.

Lowe, L., *Critical Terrains: French and British Orientalisms* (Ithaca: Cornell University Press, 1991).

Mason, P., *The Glass, the Shadow, and the Fire* (New York: Harper and Row, 1975).

McBratney, J., 'Imperial subjects, imperial space in Kipling's *Jungle Books*', *Victorian Studies*, 35, 3 (1992), pp. 277–93.

Melman, B., *Women's Orients: English Women and the Middle East, 1718–1918, Sexuality, Religion, and Work* (Ann Arbor: University of Michigan Press, 1992).

Moore-Gilbert, B. J., *Kipling and 'Orientalism'* (New York: St Martin's Press, 1986).

Murray, J., 'The Law of *The Jungle Books*', *Children's Literature*, 20 (1992), pp. 1–14.

Nair, J., 'Uncovering the zenana: visions of Indian womanhood in Englishwomen's writings, 1813–1940', *Journal of Women's History*, 2, 1 (1990), pp. 8–33.

Pafford, M., *Kipling's Indian Fiction* (New York: St Martin's Press, 1989).

Parry, B., *Delusions and Discoveries: Studies on India in the British Imagination, 1880–1930* (Berkeley: University of California Press, 1972).

—— 'The content and discontents of Kipling's imperialism', *New Formations*, 6 (Winter 1988), pp. 49–63.

Paxton, N. L., 'Disembodied subjects: English women's autobiography under the Raj', in Sidonie Smith and Julia Watson (eds.), *De/colonizing the Subject: The Politics of Gender in Women's Autobiography* (Minneapolis: University of Minnesota Press, 1992), pp. 387–409.

—— 'Mobilizing chivalry: rape in British novels about the Indian Uprising of 1857', *Victorian Studies*, 36, 1 (1992), pp. 5–30.

Sedgewick, E. K., *Between Men: English Literature and Male Homosocial Desire* (New York: Columbia University Press, 1985).

Seymour-Smith, M., *Rudyard Kipling* (New York: St Martin's Press, 1989).

Shohat, E., 'Gender and culture of empire: toward a feminist ethnography of the cinema', *Quarterly Review of Film and Video*, 13, 1–3 (1991), pp. 45–84.

Spivak, G. C., 'Can the subaltern speak?' in Cary Nelson and Lawrence Grossberg (eds.), *Marxism and the Interpretation of Culture* (Chicago: University of Chicago Press, 1988), pp. 271–313.

Tharu, S. and K. Lalita (eds.), *Women Writing in India: 600 B.C. to the Present* (New York: Feminist Press, 1991).

6

Married to the empire: the Anglo-Indian domestic novel

ALISON SAINSBURY

Katharine Helen Maud Diver, Flora Annie Steel, Bithia Mary Croker: together these three writers produced over one hundred novels on Anglo-Indian domestic life, yet their work, and that of their numerous if less prolific sisters, is today little studied or remembered.[1] In their time, however, these novels of Anglo-Indian domestic life were popular novels, in both senses of the word, written mostly, but not exclusively, by women of the Anglo-Indian community, official, civilian, or military. Novels of Anglo-Indian domestic life began to appear in the 1880s, made a strong showing through the 1920s, began to die out in the 1930s, and had mostly disappeared by the 1940s, along with direct British rule of India.

The genre rose and fell in the context of a number of historical coincidences and pressures: the wound in the English national psyche produced by the 1857 uprising; the unprecedented investment in India that followed the uprising; changing technology – and the opening of the Suez Canal – that meant less onerous and more frequent travel to India; the new imperialism of the late nineteenth century; and the growing success of both the Indian nationalist movement and the women's suffrage movement in England. These last two are particularly important in understanding the genre, for the novels engage exactly the issues of the very public fight over the status of woman as imperial citizen in many of the same terms.

The literary descent of the genre can be traced to two lines, one English and the other Anglo-Indian. Its English heritage can be found in the 'domestic novel', focused on women's activities in the home, the sentimental novel, with its defence of virginity, and the gothic novel, whose 'exotic' settings betoken threat. Although a detailed study of the development of the Anglo-Indian novel has yet to be written, one can say with some confidence, even in the absence of such a study, that the Anglo-Indian domestic novel follows and eventually supplants travel narratives and more generic adventure stories based loosely on historical events. The naive chronicler of wonder in such travel narratives as Fanny Park's *Wanderings of a Pilgrim in Search of the Picturesque* (1836), and the sensationalism of Meadows Taylor's *Confessions of a Thug* (1839) both give way to the Anglo-Indian domestic novel.[2] The two lines may themselves have crossed, as well: the genre's focus on miscegenation, or the threat of it, may carry elements from the gothic novel and from the fictional rape narratives that Jenny Sharpe has argued appear in Anglo-Indian fiction only after the 1857 uprising.[3]

The complexities of married life in India

As a group, these novels have been variously characterised as 'novels of Anglo-Indian life', 'romances' or 'romantic novelettes', or, more recently, 'Romances'.[4] The definitions offered for these labels, however, are not always explained, well-supported, or internally consistent. Bhupal Singh, the first to undertake an inclusive study of Anglo-Indian fiction, organises his study in three ways: around schools of authors leading to or following from one major figure, such as Kipling or Forster; by theme, including such sub-themes as 'mixed marriages' or 'Indian politics'; and by types or proto-genres, such as 'Novels of Anglo-Indian Life' or 'Anglo-Indian Mystery Novels'. Singh periodises as well, seeing shifts in subject-matter over broad historical periods, and noting major and minor practitioners in each period. His analytical scheme, however, is inconsistent: there is tremendous overlap of authors and texts from one group to another, and although the rubric 'Novels of Anglo-Indian Life' constitutes at one point in his analysis a sub-category, at another these 'Novels of Anglo-Indian Life' define for him Anglo-Indian fiction in its entirety: 'Strictly speaking, [Anglo-Indian fiction] means fiction describing the life of Englishmen in India'.[5] Singh notes that '[a] common theme of these novels [of Anglo-Indian life] is the unhappiness, misunderstanding, and complexities of married life in India'.[6]

Later studies by Margaret Stieg and Benita Parry identify 'the romance' as a distinct genre. For Benita Parry, these novels were 'romantic novelettes', 'tales of love and improbable adventures'.[7]

Parry offers no explanation for either her dating scheme (1890–1930) or her definition of the genre, although her choice of 'romance' is apparently derived from a notion of 'romance' taken from an anonymous review of Anglo-Indian literature, in which a 'romance' is defined as a reflection of how 'the Englishman feels himself to be moving in a mysterious, unrealized world [that] is of the essence of romance'.[8] Stieg derives her definition of 'the Indian Romance' from Singh's 'Novels of Anglo-Indian life', but what to Singh is the 'Novel of Anglo-Indian life' Stieg re-names 'the Indian Romance'. In her rather extreme formulation, the genre is distinguished for, and defined by, what she asserts is its single-minded preoccupation 'with Love, with a capital letter'.[9] Stieg offers a truncated version of Bhupal Singh's plot outline to support her claim:

> A typical novel generally begins with a voyage, bringing the hero, more often the heroine, to the shores of India. On her arrival in a Presidency town or a mofussil 'station' she is welcomed by a father, aunt, or some distant relation, and invariably causes a flutter in the small Anglo-Indian colony there. She becomes the belle of the season, is much sought after, and goes through the usual round of Anglo-Indian gaieties. There follow accounts of *burra-khana*, shooting parties (generally tiger hunts), picnics, visits to places of historical interest, balls and dances with their *kala-juggas*, and race-meetings. There are scandals and gossips at the club regarding her 'doings', interlaced with love-rivalries and misunderstandings, and finally everything ends in a happy marriage.[10]

Later in her article, however, Stieg admits that such novels do not end with marriage, but continue on to chronicle the often difficult course of the marriage, including the birth of children. These 'Romances' don't, that is, cleave only to the conventional marriage plot she initially suggests for them; nor do they confine their attention wholly to the courtship of the hero or heroine.

What we can say about these novels is that they are concerned with domestic life: with courtship and marriage, with the ordering of Anglo-Indian households, with the relations between family members and among households in the Anglo-Indian community, with the status of the Anglo-Indian household in India. Many of the novels, but by no means all of them, do adhere to the plot structure laid out by Singh and repeated by Stieg. The tales do often feature love and marriage; it is that focus, I suspect, that has led to their characterisation – one that is meant as a denigration – as 'romance novels'. In literary analyses, that is, the ideology of separate spheres has been carried out in considerations of form: the Anglo-Indian 'romance' or 'the Indian Romance' is judged a kind of woman's genre, with romance and marriage its chief, indeed, its only business. The critical consequences of this characterisation have been that the genre has been read as fiction 'of little or no literary qualities',[11] as subliterature, monolithic and narrow: judged, that is, as minor and uninteresting, or, if interesting, interesting only in the offensiveness of the Anglo-Indian sensations, attitudes or psychology, which the novels are said 'unselfconsciously' or 'innocently' to reflect.[12]

Recently, however, critics have begun to read Anglo-Indian literary production for particular narrative strategies, locating these strategies in relation to specific historical and ideological currents in colonial discourse. Hennessey and Mohan's reading of three nineteenth-century texts of colonial discourse – Arthur Conan Doyle's 1892 story 'The Adventure of the Speckled Band', Flora Annie Steel's 1894 story 'Mussumat Kirpo's Doll' and an 1895 cartoon from Punch, 'A divided duty', featuring a paternalistic John Bull calming two women, one English and one Indian, who personify the nation's respective textile industries – illuminates the way in which the constitution of subjectivity in the texts serves to 'resecure existing social arrangements' both colonial and patriarchal.[13] They read the 'codes of class, race and gender alterity' that constitute the privileged 'subject' against particular historical events: colonial and women's education; tariffs; and property and consent laws, including the Married Woman's Property Act of 1882, the Criminal Law Amendment Act (1885), and the Indian Age of Consent Law (1891).[14]

Jenny Sharpe also analyses what Hennessey and Mohan describe as 'the complex interconnections between the various axes along which exploitation and oppression takes place'.[15] The figure of woman, argues Sharpe, is a crucial integer in the discourse of colonialism; that figure, she says, 'is instrumental in shifting a colonial system of meaning from self-interest and moral superiority to self-sacrifice and racial superiority'.[16] In examining the emergence of 'the topos of rape' in Anglo-Indian fiction, Sharpe finds that it appears as a response to rebellion; it is, she argues, 'a highly charged trope that is implicated in the management of rebellion',[17] for scenes of the rape of Englishwomen by Indian men begin to surface in colonial discourse only after the 1857 revolt, and do not appear 'so long as there is a belief that colonial structures of power are firmly in place'.[18] For Sharpe, these representations of rape are both symptomatic of colonial discourse and, as part of the complex of colonial discourse, help to produce what she names 'a grand narrative ... of social progress'.[19]

If we set the Anglo-Indian domestic novel, with all of its preoccupation with courtship, marriage, and domestic social arrangements, in its own historical context, we see that the genre emerged after the transfer of power from the East India Company to the Crown following the revolt of 1857, after the consolidation of the Raj, at the beginning of the period of new imperialism. Indeed, the Anti-Woman Suffrage League (a rather unfortunate name, later changed to National League Opposed to Women's Suffrage) was founded in England in 1910 by Lords Cromer and Curzon, respectively the former Governor of Egypt and Viceroy of India. For Cromer and Curzon women's suffrage in England was primarily to be opposed as a grave danger to the empire: to grant the vote to women, they argued, would be nothing less than imperial suicide. In a 1912 speech to the Scottish Chapter of the League, Curzon explicitly invoked the twin pillars of Empire and Separate Spheres: grant the vote to women, he thundered, and the loss of Empire will surely follow. His strategy in that speech was to reinscribe what were commonly thought of and referred to as 'the peculiar offices' of women in the 'interests of the state which overshadow those of any group in it'.[20] In thus defining the state as a third party, Curzon rearticulates the relation between women's private concerns and men's public ones, and between the public and private sphere: women's interests and those of the state can overlap, although Curzon hastens to add that women's 'natural' limitations, specifically woman's inability to wage war, prevent them from acting to preserve the overriding interests of the state. Empire is for Curzon both the foundation and proof of England's greatness as a nation, and in the end it is also for him an exclusively male pursuit, one from which women are excluded and ought to be excluded, as repetitions in his speech make clear: '*By men* was India won, *by men alone* can it be retained'; 'That war ... can be won *only by men. It is man alone* who can save women ... women can take no part ... *By man* the battle has been fought, *by man* it will be won. *It is a man's business, not a woman's*' (emphasis mine).[21] Women, that is, must be public-minded, but to exercise their concern for public issues they must exclude themselves from participating in the resolution of those public issues, because the interests of the state women wish to serve demand it. The loss or retention of the empire, for Curzon, is not just the fulcrum by which the debate over suffrage could be leveraged: it is the crucial point.

Curzon's views that women's suffrage and Empire were antithetical, but that the fate of the empire and the fate of womanhood were one, were also those of the Anglo-Indian official community in India. Mrs Grace Walton of Mussoorie, India, contacted the National League Opposed to Women's Suffrage (NLOWS), asking about the possibility of forming a chapter of the NLOWS in India.[22] In her initial letter to the League Mrs Walton asserts that suffrage is 'an evil', 'a peril' that 'would mean disaster for this part of the Empire'.[23] She repeats this conviction in a second letter reporting the success of the first meeting of the All-India League Opposed to Woman Suffrage, at which 'no less than three hundred and forty attended': 'I know we may count on your sympathy with our fight in this portion of the Empire against an evil which we consider is a peril to the British Empire'.[24] Maintaining the colonial status quo, then, apparently required woman's continued exclusion from the public sphere. The colonial system required the dual management of both women and Indians, and if we follow Curzon, women are to be managed by directing their attention to the danger posed to empire if they refuse to be so managed. For the bulk of the genre's life, there was underway both a growing threat to British rule of India and a rearticulation of Englishwomen's place in the political, a rearticulation in which women were admitted to be political actors, although the ideological distinction between public and private spheres was upheld.

In colonial discourse we can see, that is, the management of dual rebellions, and we can see not only a shift in the 'colonial system of meaning', but also the ways in which Englishwomen were represented as agents in that shift, because the discourse emphasises woman's power to choose. For women to see themselves as public actors and as imperial citizens required a rearticulation of their subjectivity, and the Anglo-Indian domestic novel, I would argue, reinvents the place of the private, domestic establishment in the public, political sphere, an enterprise that concomitantly reconstitutes an Englishwoman's subjectivity in relation to both. In the Anglo-Indian domestic novel we find a new conception of the domestic woman, one who is governed not by familial structures but by imperial service. And as we shall see, one's choice of a husband has everything to do with the management of Indian rebellion and the maintenance of British rule.

When these novels began to appear, the ideological separation of public and private, predicated on naturalised gender differences, had already produced two separate, gendered discourses: that of domesticity and that of Empire.[25] Industrial capitalism, colonisation, and the rise of the middle class were simultaneous, related phenomena; by the late nineteenth century, the interests of the middle class predominated in the social sphere, and the real conflicts between classes were partly elided in a notion of domestic order, attainable by all women regardless of material condition, and partly in a notion of imperial service.[26] Service to Empire could both rescue the English gentleman from the weakness and deterioration into which he was widely held to have fallen and enfranchise the working man. It would, in fact, be difficult to overestimate the extent to which notions of 'The Empire' pervaded English consciousness. The future of the nation was thought to be contingent upon the continuation and expansion of the empire. But while England clearly needed the raw materials and markets supplied by the colonies, England needed an empire in other less visible but equally important ways. Empire was a field for the exercise of Englishness; Englishness required such a field to define itself. To this end boy scouting and organised sports were instituted for males of all classes as preludes to imperial service.

Nancy Armstrong has argued that in this period 'domestic fiction actively sought to disentangle the language of sexual relations from the language of politics and, in so doing, to introduce a new form of political power'; the 'customary way of understanding social experience' she argues, was 'domesticated' and located in the individual.[27] This repositioning of power required, of course, the pretence of separate spheres, but separate spheres in the colonial context was a contradictory construct: in Anglo-India, what was private was public, and Anglo-Indian women's lives were organised and ruled by the fact that they lived as part of the ruling British enclave in India.

It should not surprise, then, that the Anglo-Indian domestic novel does exactly the opposite of what Armstrong argues about the domestic novel: it re-entangles the language of sexual relations with the language of politics in response to the public nature of the colonial domestic space. Even though 'the customary way of understanding social experience' was 'domesticated', the 'new form of political power' was still very much entangled with the 'language of politics'. These novels were still concerned with 'politics', still 'seized the authority' to say 'what was female' in 'narratives which seemed to be concerned solely with matters of courtship and marriage', but did so to argue that 'what was female' was not merely courtship and marriage – while at the same time insisting that matters of courtship and marriage were matters of the greatest import for the maintenance and extension of British power.[28] Accompanying the 'topos of rape' in colonial discourse, then, are these narratives of married life, and these narratives are accompanied, in turn, by a trope of their own: mixed marriage and miscegenation. The overpowering of English-women by Indian men – rape – is matched by Englishwomen's power to choose. Written from the point of view of and about the ruling British community, Anglo-Indian domestic novels marry the ideology of patriarchy to the ideology of imperialism. These novels, I would argue, merge the 'story' of love and marriage and the 'story' of European civilisation, subsuming all relations to an identity rooted in imperialism.

This national identity – and the interests it represents – almost invariably defines itself against its colonial subjects, hence the racist images and attitudes so prevalent and so studied by literary critics in the texts. Romance and nationalism dovetail in an economy of race, and woman's reproductive capacity becomes a figure for the reproduction and extension of state power. The threat of miscegenation elevates the female as 'the figure ... on whom depended the outcome of the struggle betwen competing ideologies' (as Armstrong argues happens in domestic novels),[29] but in order to define and position 'what was female' in the colonial context, these novels, unlike those Armstrong reads, re-centre erotic desire in the body rather than, as Armstrong asserts, transferring erotic desire from body to word, from 'those forms of pleasure that derive from mastering [the] body' to 'the pleasure of the text'.[30] We need, however, to consider the degree to which the transfer of desire from body to text is itself ideo-logical. Foucault argues that the proliferation of discourse about the body is a way to manage it, suggesting that the actual, physical body remains the object to be contained.[31] The same may be applicable to Armstrong's configuration as well: textual pleasure – and its mastery – does not so much replace mastery of the body, but may rather enable it, because the disposition of that body is still very much at issue. Certainly, in the Anglo-Indian domestic novel any such transfer of desire from woman's body to woman as text is accompanied by the transfer of eroticism to the colonial body. In Bithia Mary Croker's *Babes in the Wood*, a novel we will turn to in greater detail, Stieg's concept of 'Love above All', presumably accompanied by, if not founded on, sexual desire, is roundly condemned as a threat to the empire because the object of attraction can be Indian as well as English. Nor is this one instance of an Englishwoman's love for her Indian husband unique: Anglo-Indian romances are filled with English women and men who marry Indians. Mastering the body does come quite clearly back into focus in Anglo-Indian romances, although desire is usually displaced onto Indians: the Indian man callously 'uses', 'desires' and 'masters' women's bodies, but his appeal – and apparently also the appeal of such behaviour – is just as clear.

The prevalence of threats by Indian males (sometimes abetted by India herself) to the Englishwoman's sexual 'purity' are to be read as threats to the purity and health – moral and economic – of England, and hence to British rule over India. Tales of miscegenation, then, are not just the result of the 'febrile imaginings' of authors penning tales drawing on the conventions of the gothic romance.[32] Instead, these sexual threats function as tests of imperial citizenship, and in plot structures, a successful disarming of the threat by the girl is rewarded by marriage to a young Englishman who has undergone his own test of bravery and loyalty to the empire. For example, contrary to Bhupal Singh's claim that the 'realm of romance' tends to lead Maud Diver in *Lilamani* (1910) to smooth the course of the romance between her 'inter-racial' couple, she does so not, I would suggest, because she is incurably romantic but because she wants to pose the question of whether or not an Indian woman can ever take up the duties and interests required of English citizens. When Mrs Penny, in contrast to Diver, prevents a marriage between an Indian and an Englishwoman, she is not, as Singh puts it, 'shirk[ing] the logical development of her plot'.[33] Her plot, the story her reader already knows, and whose conventions she follows, is the story of English superiority, and in arguing for such superiority, she is also denying Indian men access to the basis for it. The threat of mixed marriage or miscegenation and any threat to the romance of a young English couple, then, is simultaneously a threat to the empire, and in this way the novels recast marriage as dedication to an object beyond one domestic union – the ideal of imperial citizenship.

The big matrimonial stake

Bithia Mary Croker's *Babes in the Wood* typifies the Anglo-Indian domestic novel. Published in 1910, mid-way through the life of the genre, it follows closely the genre's most conventional plot structure, that outlined by Singh and modified by Stieg: the arrival in India of two young English people, Philip Trafford, a newly-commissioned assistant forest conservator, and his younger sister Milly, who journeys out to India to keep house for him; it ends with their engagements to, respectively, Joan Hampton and Eliot Scruby, both old Anglo-India hands. Although this bare-bones plot structure suggests that romance and marriage are the chief focus of the novel, sub-plots and the discourse of racial alterity work to subordinate 'love' to the business of governing the empire, and to position the reader's focus in relation to the question of the participation by Indians and Eurasians in ruling structures, both economic and governmental. Indeed, the narrative's attention to economic conditions and 'the Indian character', as well as its seemingly gratuitous instances of racist discourse, and its exhaustive and detailed descriptions of domestic arrangements (including those needed for official 'circuits') is as important, and occupies as much or more space, as the details of the progress of the romances. Although the plot is rife with *amours*, and the protagonists march towards the predictable outcome of marriage, this outcome is predicated on the newcomers acquiring knowledge of both the 'nature' of India (and thus, by opposition, of England) and the 'nature' of women, a knowledge that they must have because it is necessary for the discharge of their duties as imperial citizens.

The ruling spirit of a good marriage is service to the higher ideals of British imperialism and British civilisation; at the same time, however, the novel suggests that British civilisation rests on this marriage of imperial citizens. For *Babes in the Wood* is primarily a novel of the education and testing of imperial citizens, whose reward for the successful mastery of the lessons is marriage, an institution the book represents as crucial to continued British rule. The book's title foreshadows this education, but in case the reader misses the implications of the title, it is spelled out in the narrative. The 'old India hand' Scruby explains to the newly-arrived Trafford that those who live in the station he is to join are referred to as 'babes in the wood', an appellation conferred in jest by the Anglo-Indians elsewhere to mark the innocence and naivete of its inhabitants.[34] The phrase 'babes in the wood', then, has dual resonance, applying both to the newly-arrived Philip and Milly and to the isolated station to which they move, and oddly enough, although the novel adheres to the notion of separate spheres for men and women, the lessons to be learned and the educational progress of the two are remarkably similar.

In *Babes in the Wood*, love and marriage are clearly subordinated to imperial service. Joan Hampton's stepfather, Mr Castellas, is a Eurasian whom her widowed English mother has married for love. Via this family, the book rejects both the idea of 'love above all' and love as frivolous social activity, expressed most dramatically in Mrs Castellas' inability to refuse her daughter Lily, the indolent, selfish, 'child of her love' anything (*Babes:* 154). This unreasoning loyalty to the product of her love, and by extension, to the idea of 'love above all', has helped to drive the family to economic ruin. On the other hand, an Englishwoman's dedication solely to her own well-being is equally condemned. Philip and Milly's mother, a widow back home in England, repeatedly shown up as hard and self-centred, marries solely to advance her own social and economic position. The home she creates in Mayfair after the death of her unloved husband has no room in it for Milly or Philip, and when Milly returns home from school to live with her mother she is resented for her youthful beauty and ejected – sent to India – when her mother takes a second husband.

Mrs Trafford's self-interest and frivolous life serve as a foil to the lessons being learned by her children in India, and, by extension, the reader, for they are taught in the grammar of familiar codes defining 'ladies' and 'gentlemen'. Philip repels the advances of the deceptive, unscrupulous, and sexually rapacious widow, Mrs Heron, whose depth of moral decay is signalled by her sexual overtures, and Milly remains unaffected by the round of social activities but is strangely affected by Eliot Scruby, the man of little means but much worth, which the novel locates in an individual's qualities. Gresham, an Anglo-Indian masterminding the poaching scheme Philip uncovers, is 'a man of good birth and education' (*Babes:* 325), while Philip, who suspects that his own condition – 'shabby and famished ... without a single rupee to his name' – may be the natural indicator of his worth is, in the novel's terms, the 'gentleman' (*Babes:* 75). A man or woman of honour and gentility is invariably one who subordinates individual desire to the service of imperial rule, not one who, like Gresham, is born to an aristocratic family. Milly does cause a stir in the station, but this *divertissement* is froth, and both Milly and the narrative soon reject it. In fact, the novel refutes quite firmly the charges of frivolousness levelled at Anglo-Indian women: 'the big matrimonial stake' in this novel takes place not in India but in England, and only in England under her mother's roof had Milly's life been 'one incessant whirling round that left her giddy' (*Babes:* 215). Milly, described as a 'born country girl, with country tastes', had in England been deflected from this 'natural' self, but life in an Anglo-Indian station allows her sensible character to reassert itself (*Babes:* 215). In India, she neither engages in a round of concerted husband-hunting nor abandons her brother in the hot weather to flee to the cooler hills. These are choices, necessary steps in proving oneself a good imperial citizen, for as the narrative tells us 'camp life is a sure and searching test of character' (*Babes:* 323).

Only after passing their citizenship tests do both Philip and Milly marry. Their partners are those who uphold the British imperial cause and represent its ideal agents, and who are, besides, the old India hands who have instructed Philip and Milly on Anglo-Indian life. Philip's bride, Joan Hampton, is frugal, 'plucky', and knows her way around India; it is she who tells the newly-arrived Assistant Conservator of Forests, lost in the forest he has been sent to administer, 'You see the forest looks so simple – but it really is a maze' (*Babes:* 115). Milly's spouse, Eliot Scruby, himself upright in the British mission of civilisation, at one point reels off to Milly the benefits of English rule: 'The villagers have their vernacular schools, dispensaries, post office and telegraph. Think of that!' (*Babes:* 289).

These representations of the ideal agent/subject are, however, ideological, masking, in both cases, the English economic mission. For despite a plot structure that deflects attention from economics onto the course of romance and marriage, this novel highlights for us the economic benefits of English rule (for the English) and the economic threat posed by Indian desires or schemes for economic gain. The Castellas family also serves as an example of how the book utilises the discourse of alterity to position the reader in relation to the employment of Indians.

Joan Hampton, for example, tells us that although her Eurasian stepfather always fails to carry out his hare-brained economic schemes – his current one is to manufacture and sell perfume to the Indians – other men, less weak, have taken them over and enriched themselves. In the book's hierarchy of races, that is, Joan's Eurasian stepfather is destined for failure. Despite the usual deployment of racial stereotyping, however, in this book race *per se* is less important than its effect on one's economic status: the reason the book offers for not marrying an Indian or Eurasian is not that an Indian or Eurasian man is of a different race, but that life will 'bear the hallmark of a pitiful economy' (*Babes:* 93). Although the book never explicitly ascribes Otto Castellas' failure to race, the complex of suggestion surrounding him makes clear that his failure stems from his racial make-up. For stepdaughter Joan, the 'slough of despond' is an economic rather than a moral one; at the point in the text when she warns Philip about the deceptively simple forest 'maze' that he must learn, he has come across her in a clearing in the forest he administers, and found her crying over money (*Babes:* 117). Through the trope of mixed marriage, then, India is made a threat to the economic well-being of England; mixed marriage is a narrative strategy that masks – even reverses – the economic oppression of India by England.

This narrative organisation indeed speaks to the point, for the forest's economic potential for the English is Philip's province and the source of his 'test': Trafford may have been since childhood 'profoundly interested in ... the lore of trees and fields', but his real job as forest conservator is to keep the Indians from living off the jungle. Knowing forest lore means having 'a good business sense', knowing, that is, 'the probable output of wood, the quantity of sal and teak, and the all-important matter of transport' (*Babes:* 10). The 'Freedom' of Philip's credo 'Woods, Forests, and Freedom' is economic freedom for him and for the rest of the British, and Trafford's 'test' is to find out who is poaching from the forest and put a stop to it (*Babes:* 10). 'Managing' the forest preserve means keeping it firmly under the control of the Government of India. In fact, the smuggling and poaching scheme Philip uncovers has been carried out – under the direction of a rogue Englishman – by a Eurasian, Mr Beaufort, a 'subordinate official' who has been the subject of conversations among the Anglo-Indians about the advisability of admitting Indians or Eurasians to the Service. 'The book of Nature' that, since childhood, Philip has been drawn to learn becomes, that is, a metaphor for Nature of a much larger kind, and in order to discover the poachers and apprehend them, and be rewarded with marriage to the economically-savvy Joan, Philip has to learn the 'nature' of many things, chiefly that British imperialism is the result of a 'natural' ordering. British rule is thus naturalised in a particularly literal way.

Woman's ability to order the domestic establishment is also represented as natural: women order and rule their homes so seamlessly because it is part of their nature. Joan Hampton, for example, sees immediately what Philip's bungalow requires to make it a fit dwelling for his sister:

> '... do let me look round', said Joan ...
> As they entered the sitting-room together, Trafford explained that he would get a piano, and armchairs, and bookcase.
> 'Yes, and a nice bright chintz, ... and colour the walls white, and hang pretty cheerful prints. You might put the piano across that corner ... and I *think* a sofa would just fit along that wall. Really, with some flowers and books and dogs ... the place would be quite gay.'
> (*Babes:* 131)

This naturalising is ideological, of course, as the circular logic makes clear: the house needs to be made civilised so that an Englishwoman, similar to the one who is engaged in creating this civilisation, can come and live in it. But woman's ability to order is a crucial one, because, as the novel demonstrates repeatedly, a well-ordered domestic establishment is both essential to the public business of government and to the private well-being of the individual. The home is, in fact, elsewhere in colonial discourse explicitly figured as a microcosm of the British empire. According to Grace Gardiner and Flora Annie Steel's manual for housekeeping in India, 'an Indian household can no more be governed peacefully, without dignity and prestige, than an Indian Empire'.[35] The statement is meant as more than an analogy, for the hierarchies of life are inscribed in that household:

> Finally, when all is said and done, the whole duty of an Indian mistress towards her servants is neither more or less than it is in England. Here, as there, a little reasonable human sympathy is the best oil for the household machine. Here, as there, the end and object is not merely personal comfort, but the formation of a home − that unit of civilisation where father and children, master and servant, employer and employed, can learn their several duties.[36]

The home's traditional function of succouring life takes on extra urgency in the face of such a hostile environment; it keeps 'India', repeatedly figured as the jungle, at bay.

In addition to these material functions, the domestic establishment also projects the image of British civilisation. For in Croker's representation, India is a jungle peopled by men who are animals at best – the fabled buffalo that haunts the jungle to pursue whatever man intrudes is clearly meant to represent Indian 'human' nature – or debased men, whose debasement is revealed by their willingness to poach animals, and whose own domestic establishments are both devoid of the niceties Joan envisions in Philip's bungalow, and revelatory of their devotion to superstition:

> There is not much to be seen in a Gond dwelling; a plastered mud floor, a charpoy reared against the wall, cooking pots, an axe, an iron spoon, a hasi, or sickle, and a broom. There was also on a shelf a multitude of little figures ... the family gods. (*Babes:* 291)

In contrast to the undifferentiated 'multitude' of 'family gods', the presiding spirit and ruling presence of British civilisation in the Anglo-Indian home is the wife of the highest ranking administrator. At her home Philip cannot tell if he has left England or not, a crucial feat given India's capacity, in this novel, to madden Englishmen. Indeed, Philip himself almost succumbed to the Indian jungle on his first night in his bungalow, and the transformation of Philip's home from dismal to inviting is her doing: she supplies a cook and kit, and her prominently visible initials on the tablecloth remind us all, Philip and reader alike, that it is she who enables Trafford to take up his duties. And in case we miss the significance of this detail, Scruby makes a point of commenting to Trafford on her excellence, characterising her as 'an angel without wings', more important even than her husband.

The trope of mixed marriage and miscegenation, a *sine qua non* of alterity if ever there was one, is the chief narrative strategy by which the novel rearticulates the principles on which a union should be based. By marrying an Indian or a Eurasian, succumbing to 'all for love' and to 'India', an Englishwoman reneges on her imperial obligations. The usual racism is present and operating in this novel, but there is little horror at 'race-mixing': Lily, the love-child, is painted as indolent and slightly stupid – inferior, but not sinister. But the real tragedy of the Castellas household, after all, is not the weak and silly Mrs Castellas, who by marrying a Eurasian has forsaken the principles of British rule; nor is it the caricature that is Lily, who is proof positive that there is nothing of Britain in Mrs Castellas to be passed on. It is poverty; it is the straitened circumstances that are the result of giving over all to love.

The journey to knowledge

In *Babes in the Wood*, there is no horror attached to a mixed marriage and miscegenation because neither is meant to serve as a moral example. They are, instead, an object of study – something to be observed. Milly and Philip, by observing this marriage and its product, 'learn', and come to knowledge. What the newcomers learn, of course, is that imperialism is naturally ordained. The trope of a 'journey to knowledge' enables a false inductivism: difference is naturalised – empirically observed – and then invoked to explain and justify the imperialist position. This methodology essentially replicates that of the positive science of the times: one takes a deductive stance towards the object of study, but describes the understanding one assembles by observing that object of study as though knowledge about it were reached inductively. That a novel ostensibly about marriages should evoke the scientific method is not as odd as it seems: it is entirely in keeping with Said's notion of a vast confluence of disciplines, all engaged in 'managing' the Orient.[37]

Let us turn for a moment to Radcliffe-Brown, the pre-eminent English social anthropologist, an imperialist, and one whose formulations about 'functionality' and 'institutional systems' (as opposed to 'culture') were turned admirably to the business of colonial administration.[38] Radcliffe-Brown advocated 'the investigation of social phenomena by methods essentially similar to those used in the physical and biological sciences',[39] which were, according to him, 'the systematic investigation of the structure of the universe as it is revealed to us through our senses'.[40] For social anthropology to qualify as a science, it would need a 'discrete reality' to study, which Radcliffe-Brown defined as 'persons', studied not as individuals, but as general types and in their institutional roles: 'social structure [is] an arrangement of persons in institutionally controlled or defined relationships, such as the relationship of king and subject, or that of husband and wife'.[41] 'Individuals' are to be distinguished from 'persons', and persons should be studied in the 'system of social positions':

> human beings as individuals are objects of study for physiologists and psychologists. The human being as a person is a complex of social relationships. He is a citizen of England, a husband and a father, a bricklayer, a member of a particular Methodist congregation ... and so on. ... we cannot study persons except in terms of social structure.[42]

Furthermore, for Radcliffe-Brown the 'social systems of which the component units are human beings' ought to be studied comparatively:

> the use of comparison is indispensable. The study of a single society may provide materials for comparative study ... which then need to be tested by reference to other societies ... If we are to have a real comparative morphology of societies, however, we must aim at building up some sort of classification of types of structural systems.[43]

This 'scientific' method explains why *Babes in the Wood* so emphatically eschews Love for Reason. Milly, observing the Castellas household, and Joan, confidently kitting out Trafford's bungalow, are engaged in a little 'scientific observation' of their own, with domestic arrangements Radcliffe-Brown's 'discrete reality' of study.

Miscegenation is in this text thus not a moral example but a social one, and the Castellas household is the ideal text for this study because in such a marriage the two 'systems' meet, and, in the product of the marriage, Lily, collide. Lily is never meant to be an individual, as her caricature of a characterisation makes clear: she speaks like neither parent, for example, but with an accent she could only have acquired from her genes. She is one of Radcliffe-Brown's institutional subjects, and a particularly instructive one, for she allows 'comparative' study in one person, to be observed for what she can reveal about institutional systems. What observation of her reveals to Milly, and to the reader, of course, is the truth of Radcliffe-Brown's insistence that it is impossible to combine 'king and subject' in one institutional role.

We might usefully think of this novel and others like it as engaged in the science of literary imperialism, a combination of ethnography and social anthropology, as Radcliffe-Brown would define them, for they both observe and theorise:

in anthropology ... the study of what are called the primitive or backward peoples, the term ethnography applies to what is specifically a
mode of ideographic enquiry, the aim of which is to give acceptable
accounts of such peoples and their social life. Ethnography differs from
history in that the ethnographer derives his knowledge, or some major
part of it, from direct observation of or contact with the people about
whom he writes, and not, like the historian, from written records.[44]

Radcliffe-Brown argues that 'the theoretical study of social institutions in general is usually referred to as sociology', while
historical explanations are distinguished by their exclusive concern with observable facts: thus history is history only when it
gives an account of what happened and does not attempt to
theorise why it did.[45] History, he says, 'should be confined to
telling us what happened and how it happened. Theoretical or
nomothetic enquiries should be left to sociology'.[46] These novels
are ethnography because they utilise 'observation' of 'primitive
peoples' to create a 'vision' or theory about why these people are
as they are. Their flat characters are not so much the product of
literary conventions, then, as they are representations of 'social
types'. 'Let us consider', writes Radcliffe-Brown, 'what are the
concrete, observable facts with which the social anthropologist
is concerned. ... We can observe the acts of behaviour ... we
do not observe a "culture", since that word denotes, not any
concrete reality, but an abstraction'.[47] It was widely argued,
especially by the Anglo-Indian community, that 'facts' about
India – including those about 'social types' – were indeed
required for understanding it, and these novels were considered
to provide 'facts'.

Thus the Anglo-Indian never sees a particular Indian, but a
'subject' who is part of a social institution. And in India, after
all, the British were all to some extent social scientists – to be
an administrator was to be a social anthropologist, and to be a
social anthropologist was crucial. Philip's predecessor Frost, for
example, is driven mad precisely because he has no object of
study: he is not interested in botany or ethnography. He is unable
to come to an 'objective' knowledge of India, unable to turn either
India or Indians into objects of study. India might be subject to
British rule, but as a subject in its own right it has the power to
affect Frost subjectively – to drive him mad and kill him. This
need to objectify applies equally to miscegenation: if threats are
eliminated by objectifying them, then turning such a concern into
the object of study in a romance nullifies its threat.[48]

The advancement of imperialism as inductively-reached knowledge is admirably served by the marriage plot, both because in a romance a girl has to move from innocence of the world to knowledge of the world, of herself, and of men in order to make the right choice, as, indeed, Milly does, and because mixed marriages are the perfect sites for comparative study. Our understanding of the way these texts are shaped by a prevailing social anthropology so suitable to the aims of imperialism also allows us to rearticulate and multiply Armstrong's notions of textual and bodily desire: mastering the 'text' or 'subjects' of India in historiographies and ethnographies enables pleasure and economic gain to be extracted from India's material body.

Conclusion

When we examine the intersection of the discourse of patriarchy and imperialism in the Anglo-Indian domestic novel, we find a reconstitution of both the imperial subject and the middle-class domestic subject into one subject position: a female imperial citizen. The novels seek to enfranchise middle-class English women, making them partners – even the central agents – in the enterprise of empire, even though their formal forebears – the sentimental novel, the domestic romance, and the gothic – uphold the separation between public and private spheres. The main concern of *Babes in the Wood*, after all, is not to chronicle the private relationship between men and women, but rather to centre women, via marriage and domesticity, in the task of extending and maintaining the empire. In advancing the notion that the crucial imperial citizen is a female one, the novels are also engaged in an ideological struggle over the national enterprise of imperialism, contesting the notion of empire-building as a masculine enterprise that requires a passive and private femininity. In Anglo-Indian fiction, and in colonial discourse in general, we find two contesting visions of imperial citizenship: will the nation be defined by 'doing a man's work in the world'[49] out on the frontier with the warlike tribes, or by women who are engaged in demonstrating and extending 'civilization'?

Anglo-Indian domestic novels thus offer a distinctly different construction of the colonial woman than that usually offered by the texts of male writers of British India. Even a cursory consideration of the two most famous – Kipling and Forster – is instructive on this point. Kipling's negative portraits of women are legendary, the gallery replete from his earliest work with frivolous, unfaithful wives whose indiscretions bring down the state, and whose very names divulge their characters: Cornelia Agrippina ('Army Headquarters'), Delilah ('Delilah'), Potiphar's wife ('Study of an Elevation, in India Ink'). In his short story 'William the Conquerer', a woman has a place in India if, and only if, she takes up the work of administration as a man would, as if she were a man, but a lesser version or younger brother. 'William' of the title is the antithesis of the usual Kipling portrait of women, although her marked departure from the type both defines and brings it to mind. When the story opens William is rolling cigarettes for her brother Martyn, tossing them over to him 'with a gesture as true as a school-boy's throwing a stone';[50] so skilfully does she throw that he need not interrupt the shop-talk she 'delighted in hearing'.[51] The opening teems with other indices of her worth as well: in the four years she has been house-keeping for her brother, she has refused to marry, stayed down in the plains during the hot weather instead of migrating to a hill station, 'had entirely fallen out of the habit of writing to her aunts in England', and never ever perused 'the pages of the English magazines'.[52]

A Passage to India, for its part, plays on the most conventional of stories told by Anglo-Indian domestic novels, a young girl journeying to India to acquire an imperial consciousness and a husband; in doing so, however, it exposes and overturns the assumptions that lie behind that plot. Unlike the heroines of countless Anglo-Indian domestic novels, its heroine, Adela, is emphatically not integrated into Anglo-Indian life; like her counterparts, she may acquire a new consciousness, but hers is one that demands she leave India – and without a husband. Although one might surmise that Adela has simply failed the test that would grant her citizenship in the empire, Adela and Ronnie's engagement is treated in ways that reveal and then contest the imperialist ideology advanced by the Anglo-Indian romance: the 'knowledge' of English superiority acquired by the principles and methods of an inductivist inquiry and achieved via a journey from innocence to experience of Indian character; women naturalised into icons of English civilisation and Indians into icons of superstitious degeneracy. Further, the engagement of Adela and Ronnie is shadowed by the friendship of Aziz and Fielding, and this relationship, although played out in the shadow of Adela and Ronnie's heterosexual romance, emerges none the less as the central relationship of the text. The centrality of marriage in the colonial context, Forster suggests, is to be deplored rather than celebrated, for it prevents friendship between Indian and English men.

A *Passage to India* contests and overturns the imperialist ideology developed by Anglo-Indian domestic novels. It retains the genre's positioning of women at the centre of imperialism, but does so in order to create a space for male friendship outside of history. Forster simultaneously exposes to view the falsity of the ideological construction of separate spheres while positing women as the real force of government: the primordial female sexuality of 'mother' India, represented by the caves, unsettles the sensible Adela, whose marriage to Ronnie contextualises the friendship of Aziz and Fielding. Racial alterity is thus displaced onto gender alterity, a displacement that absolves English men of the responsibility of their imperialism and frees them from obligations to it. In A *Passage to India* it is women and Woman – Indian and English alike – who create a universe hostile to friendship between Indian and English men.

In the Anglo-Indian domestic novel, however, woman is both the image and impetus of civilisation: the home and the rituals of home-making define 'Englishness', and woman's home-making skills – and the homes made with them – are necessary because in them the business of government takes place. Women help their husbands in their roles as hostesses and with administrative work, and they uphold 'the purity of the race' by resisting the seductive pull of India and Indians, who would trespass the borders dividing English and Indian. Under these circumstances, marriage is not merely an act that takes place between women and men who happen to be engaged in colonial administration. Marriage takes on a special character, derived from its place in the consolidation and extension of the British empire. The nature of English womanhood, as these novels construct it, is significant because properly recognised and appreciated, it provides the strength on which the British empire rests. Marriage takes centre stage, not as the desired goal or inevitable future of a young girl, but as the warp onto which the weft of the fabric of empire should be woven.

Notes

1 Other fairly prolific writers of the Anglo-Indian domestic novel include Alice Perrin, Edith Constance Turton-Jones (writing as Susan Gillespie), E. M. Bell (writing as John Travers), Fanny Emily Farr Penny, Hilda Caroline Gregg (writing as Sydney C. Grier), and Ethel M. Dell. But this is only a partial list: there were many writers, who produced many hundreds of novels.

2 Fanny Park, *Wanderings of a Pilgrim in Search of the Picturesque*, 2 vols. (1836; reprinted Karachi: Oxford University Press, 1975) and Philip Meadows Taylor, *Confessions of a Thug* (1839; London: Anthony Blond, 1967).

3 Jenny Sharpe, *Allegories of Empire: The Figure of Woman in the Colonial Text* (Minneapolis: University of Minnesota Press, 1993).

4 Critics offering these definitions are, respectively, Bhupal Singh, Benita Parry, and Margaret Stieg.

5 Bhupal Singh, *A Survey of Anglo-Indian Fiction* (London: Oxford University Press, 1934), p. 1.

6 *Ibid.*, p. 3.

7 Benita Parry, *Delusions and Discoveries: Studies on India in the British Imagination* (London: Allen Lane, 1972), p. 70.

8 'The Romance of India', cited by Parry, p. 53.

9 Margaret Stieg, 'Anglo-Indian Romances: Tracts for the Times', *Journal of Popular Culture* (Spring 1985), p. 2.

10 *Ibid.*, p. 2.

11 Rachel Anderson, *The Purple Heart Throbs: The Sub-Literature of Love* (London: Hodder Stoughton, 1971), p. 14, cited by Stieg, p. 2.

12 'Unselfconsciously' is Stieg's term, 'innocently' Parry's. See Stieg, 'Indian Romances', p. 3, and Parry, *Delusions and Discoveries*, p. 70.

13 Rosemary Hennessey and Rajeswari Mohan, 'The Construction of Woman in Three Popular Texts of Empire: Towards a Critique of Materialist Feminism', *Textual Practice*, 3 (1989), p. 327.

14 *Ibid.*, p. 345.

15 *Ibid.*, p. 323.

16 Sharpe, p. 7.

17 *Ibid.*, p. 2.

18 *Ibid.*, p. 3.

19 *Ibid.*, p. 8.

20 Program, Scottish Anti-Suffrage Demonstration, Curzon Collection; Letters and Papers on Women's Suffrage, India Office Library and Records.

21 *Ibid.*, p. 23.

22 All that remains of the NLOWS correspondence with Mrs Walton are her own letters to the League, c. 1910–13; the file containing the letter sent from the League to India and the Government of India's reply was destroyed by bombing in WW II.

23 Walton to NLOWS, no date, Curzon Collection, Letters and Papers on Women's Suffrage, India Office Library and Records.

24 Walton to NLOWS, July 1, 1913, Curzon Collection, Letters and Papers on Women's Suffrage, India Office Library and Records.

25 Articles on the subject of the manliness of empire can be found in J. Mangan and J. Walvin (eds.), *Manliness and Morality: Middle-class Masculinity in Britain and America, 1800–1940* (Manchester: Manchester University Press, 1987) and John M. MacKenzie (ed.), *Imperialism and Popular Culture* (London: Manchester University Press, 1986).

26 For a full discussion of the ways in which domesticity elided class difference, see Nancy Armstrong's analysis of conduct books in 'The Rise of the Domestic Woman', Ch. 2 in Nancy Armstrong, *Desire and Domestic Fiction: A Political History of the Novel* (Oxford: Oxford University Press, 1987).

27 *Ibid.*, pp. 3–4.

28 *Ibid.*, p. 5.

29 *Ibid.*

30 *Ibid.*, p. 6.

31 This idea is repeated throughout Foucault's works. See *Discipline and Punish: The Birth of the Prison*, trans. Alan Sheridan (New York: Vintage, 1979); *A History of Sexuality*, trans. Robert Hurley (New York: Vintage, 1988); *Power/Knowledge: Selected Interviews and Other Writings*, trans. Colin Gordon *et al.* (New York: Pantheon, 1980).

32 Parry, p. 71.

33 Singh, p. 173.

34 Bithia Mary Croker, *Babes in the Wood: A Romance of the Jungles* (Leipzig: B. Tauchnitz, 1910), p. 46. All further citations from the text referred to as *Babes*.

35 Flora Annie Steel and Grace Gardiner, *The Complete Indian Housekeeper and Cook* (4th rev. edn. London: Heinemann, 1902), p. 9.

36 *Ibid.*, p. 10.

37 Edward Said, *Orientalism* (New York: Vintage Books, 1979). In the 'Introduction' to *Orientalism*, Said defines orientalism as 'an enormously systematic discipline by which European culture was able to manage – and even produce – the Orient politically, sociologically, militarily, ideologically, scientifically, and imaginatively', p. 3.

38 It is not my intention to suggest that Croker knew Radcliffe-Brown's work, which although underway at this time was not published until later (e.g. *Andaman Islanders: A Study in Social Anthropology* (1922), *Social Organization of Australian Tribes* (1931)). In any case, it is unnecessary to draw such a direct link in order to suggest the intellectual context in which Croker and other writers of the Anglo-Indian domestic novel worked.

39 A. R. Radcliffe-Brown, *Structure and Function in Primitive Society* (1952; New York: The Free Press, 1965), p. 189.

40 *Ibid.*, p. 190. Although in his influential *History of British India* (1817) James Mill argues that his history is the most accurate precisely because he has not let India confuse his senses, we should understand that the philosophical tenet that one apprehends the universe through one's senses is not at issue; rather what is at issue for Mill is that India overwhelms one's senses. Anglo-Indians often claimed superior knowledge of India based on years of familiarity with it – observing it – and the Anglo-Indian insistence on 'knowing' the country is entirely consonant with Radcliffe-Brown's precept that any theory must concern itself with the concrete and observable.

41 *Ibid.*, p. 11.

42 *Ibid.*, pp. 11, 194.

43 *Ibid.*, pp. 190, 194–5.

44 *Ibid.*, p. 2.

45 *Ibid.*

46 *Ibid.*, pp. 2–3.

47 *Ibid.*, p.190.

48 A necessary transformation, apparently, since as B. Singh notes, such liaisons are 'inevitable', p.171.

49 The phrase is Emily Lorimer's, who in a letter home from India excoriates a correspondent for his 'disgraceful lie ... accusing us in Mesopotamia of the most dastardly murder of Arab women and children'. 'Punitive expeditions', Lorimer asserts, 'have to be undertaken', and she accuses the correspondent of being one of a breed of 'anemic stay at homes' and compares him, unfavourably, to 'men who are trying to make the world safe for the weak and the oppressed' – those men doing 'a man's work in the world'. Letter, June 13 1920, Lorimer Papers, India Office Library and Records.

50 Rudyard Kipling, 'William the Conquerer', in *The Day's Work*, Part 1, *The Works of Rudyard Kipling*, vol. XIII (New York: Scribners, 1899), p.229.

51 *Ibid.*, p.228.

52 *Ibid.*, p.227.

Bibliography

Unpublished sources

Curzon Collection, Letters and Papers on Women's Suffrage, Mss. Eur F 111 and 112 (India Office Library, London).

Lorimer Papers, Letters of Emily Overend Lorimer, Mss. Eur F 177/28 (India Office Library, London).

Published sources

Armstrong, Nancy, *Desire and Domestic Fiction: A Political History of the Novel* (Oxford: Oxford University Press, 1987).

Croker, Bithia Mary, *Babes in the Wood: A Romance of the Jungles* (Leipzig: B. Tauchnitz, 1910).

Foucault, Michel, *Discipline and Punish: The Birth of the Prison*, trans. Alan Sheridan (New York: Vintage, 1979).

—— *A History of Sexuality*, trans. Robert Hurley (New York: Vintage, 1988).

—— *Power/Knowledge: Selected Interviews and Other Writings*, trans. Colin Gordon *et al.* (New York: Pantheon, 1980).

Hennessey, Rosemary, and Rajeswari Mohan, 'The Construction of Woman in Three Popular Texts of Empire: Towards a Critique of Materialist Feminism', *Textual Practice*, 3 (1989), pp.323–59.

Kipling, Rudyard, 'William the Conquerer', in *The Day's Work*, Part 1, *The Works of Rudyard Kipling*, vol. XIII (New York: Scribners, 1899).

MacKenzie, John M. (ed.), *Imperialism and Popular Culture* (London: Manchester University Press, 1986).

Mangan, J. and J. Walvin (eds.), *Manliness and Morality: Middle-class Masculinity in Britain and America, 1800–1940* (Manchester: Manchester University Press, 1987).

Mill, James, *The History of British India* (1817; Chicago: University of Chicago Press, 1975).

Park, Fanny, *Wanderings of a Pilgrim in Search of the Picturesque*, 2 vols. (1836; reprinted Karachi: Oxford University Press, 1975).

Parry, Benita, *Delusions and Discoveries: Studies on India in the British Imagination* (London: Allen Lane, 1972).

Radcliffe-Brown, A. R., *Structure and Function in Primitive Society* (New York: The Free Press, 1965).

Said, Edward, *Orientalism* (New York: Vintage Books, 1979).

Sharpe, Jenny, *Allegories of Empire: The Figure of Woman in the Colonial Text* (Minneapolis: University of Minnesota Press, 1993).

Singh, Bhupal, *A Survey of Anglo-Indian Fiction* (London: Oxford University Press, 1934).

Steel, Flora Annie, and Grace Gardiner, *The Complete Indian Housekeeper and Cook* (4th rev. edn. London: Heinemann, 1902).

Stieg, Margaret, 'Anglo-Indian Romances: Tracts for the Times', *Journal of Popular Culture* (Spring 1985), pp. 2–15.

Taylor, Philip Meadows, *Confessions of a Thug* (1839; London: Anthony Blond, 1967).

7

Volatile desire: ambivalence and distress in Forster's colonial narratives

CHRISTOPHER LANE

Fantasy and the difficulty of difference

> Are the sexes really races, each with its own code of morality, and their mutual love a mere device of Nature to keep things going? Strip human intercourse of the proprieties, and is it reduced to this?[1]

> Physical love means reaction, being panic in essence.[2]

How can postcolonial theory engage with E. M. Forster's accounts of interracial desire? In this essay, I follow recent theorists in interpreting the difficult, often treacherous, terrain of interracial desire in colonial literature; my aim is to foreground the ambivalent sexual and unconscious fantasies that underpin relations between coloniser and colonised in Forster's work.

Forster's treatment of colonial and sexual relations is particularly complex because he professed a liberal-humanist commitment to interracial friendship that often falters in his fiction. The gap between his political maxim that we must 'only connect the prose and the passion' (*Howards End*: 174) and his private fantasies about the pain and price of this connection clarify the precarious quality of interracial desire in his fiction. To interpret this real and often antagonistic gap between Forster's politics and fiction, and again between his 'public' novels about friendship and his 'private' and posthumous stories about sex between men of different races, I want to compare *A Passage to India* (1924) with the short stories 'The Life to Come' (1922) and 'The Other Boat' (1915–16), arguing that Forster's accounts of racial difference often build on his assumptions of an intractable 'geographical' divide between men and women. Though Forster assumed this divide could be bridged to bring men of different races and nationalities into closer proximity, the result is often startling in its ambivalence: far from resolving political distance into personal connection, interracial sexuality usually compels Forster's characters to disavow or redefine the precise meaning of their national and sexual identities.

If same-sex racial integration was Forster's ideal, his fiction failed repeatedly to realise it. Though 'Live in fragments no longer' is the imperative governing *Howards End* (pp. 174–5), sexual indeterminacy and colonial ambivalence suffuse his short stories. The political and psychic constituents of this ambivalence surface when we examine Forster's accounts of homosexuality, homophilia, and homophobia. Forster's difficulty in representing homosexual and racial intimacy raises unconscious meanings that resonate beyond his writing. His stories' oscillation between racially 'similar' and 'different' objects yields a complex interpretive interest by its epistemological and sexual uncertainty.

Let us start by comparing the violence and ambivalence of Forster's sexual fantasies in his posthumous collection, *The Life to Come and Other Stories* (1972), with the following, relatively benign proposition in *A Passage to India*: 'Between people of distant climes there is always the possibility of romance ...' In the context of the repeated failure of this possibility in that novel and *The Life to Come*, we should note that Forster completed the sentence as follows: '... but the various branches of Indians know too much about each other to surmount the unknowable easily'.[3] If we attribute this difficulty in overcoming the 'unknowable' to Indians' generic differences from Europeans, as Forster seemed to intend, where does his statement place the European's apparently 'knowable' concerns and desires? Part of my purpose in asking this question is to determine the meaning of sexual desire for Forster's white characters, and the possibility of sustained homosexual intimacy for men of different races, classes, and nations; Forster's narratives consistently frustrate these encounters by wounding or destroying the protagonists that attempt to fulfill them.

In many accounts of British colonial relations, an intimate bond between coloniser and colonised seems to underpin economic mastery and subordination. Several theorists have claimed that this bond exceeded, and even displaced, the intimacy British men and women professed for one another. Ashis Nandy, for example, has argued that

> white women in India were generally more exclusive and racist because they unconsciously saw themselves as the sexual competitors

of Indian men, with whom their men had established an unconscious homo-eroticized bonding. It was this bonding which the 'passive resisters' and 'non-cooperators' exploited, not merely the liberal political institutions. They were helped in this by the split that had emerged in the Victorian culture between two ideals of masculinity... [T]he lower classes were expected to act out their manliness by demonstrating their sexual prowess; the upper classes were expected to affirm their masculinity through sexual distance, abstinence and self-control.[4]

Though Nandy does not elaborate on the significance of this unconscious competition and bonding, I suggest that both factors clarify a psychic difficulty about race that impedes Forster's imperative to 'connect'. Forster tends to repress this difficulty in his political essays, but it surfaces repeatedly in his fiction as a conflict between a representation of racially divided hetero-sexuality and an apparently racially integrated model of same-sex romance. To understand this difficulty in connection, we need to consider Forster's often troubled relation to his writing.

Writing homosexuality at home and abroad: censorship and the literary taboo

What the public really loathes in homosexuality is not the thing itself, but having to think about it.[5]

Many critics have noted that despite his continuing production of essays, criticism, and biography, Forster published no fiction after A Passage to India in 1924.[6] His decision to write nonfiction thereafter, and to foreclose the publication of Maurice after its completion in 1913–14, suggests that the difficulty of representing homosexual relations in such novels as The Longest Journey and Maurice contributed to the geopolitical issues that Forster recounted (and tried to resolve) in A Passage to India. Although Forster wrote The Longest Journey, A Room with a View, Howards End, and Where Angels Fear to Tread at close intervals between 1905 and 1914, and the public received them favourably, the choice of material for subsequent texts seemed to generate much experiential and literary anxiety.

Entries in Forster's diary and correspondence with friends confirm this difficulty. In 1911, Forster explained his 'weariness of the only subject that I both can and may treat – the love of men for women and vice-versa'.[7] The remark clarifies the effect of external and internal constraints on his writing; censorship impeded both. However, Forster's statement acquires more significance when we connect it to the short stories – the earliest of which he produced alongside the novels; it illustrates a creative conflict over whether to write about one subject under the pretext of representing another (in this instance heterosexuality for homosexuality) by suppressing the creative impulse, or whether to choose a subject from internal choice, and risk public humiliation, by ignoring legal definitions of obscenity. As his publication history testifies, Forster wavered between each option, first 'distorting' the initial material (the early novels), then establishing an 'authentic' and private relation to it without the public crisis publication would generate (Maurice). However, he returned to an ambiguous compromise (A Passage to India) before disbanding the fictional project altogether as an unworkable procedure. It is interesting that his decision not to publish Maurice seemed to exacerbate, rather than relieve, this conflict between impulse and representation; the completion of this novel unsettled Forster's production, leaving Arctic Summer and Nottingham Lace as unfinished and discarded fragments.[8]

This troubled relation between creativity and sexual representation suggests that Forster neither discarded nor directly addressed the issue of homosexuality; he allowed it to surface on another terrain. If we reconsider my earlier citation from A Passage to India – 'Between people of distant climes there is always the possibility of romance ...' (Passage: 264–5) – we might argue, following George Steiner, that A Passage to India partially fulfilled Maurice's idealistic closure by making Aziz and Fielding's interracial friendship displace the earlier novel's unresolved homosexual intimacy. Steiner observed: 'The encounters between white and native, between emancipated rulers and "advanced" Indians, in A Passage to India, are a brilliant projection of the confrontations between society and the homosexual in Maurice'.[9] This suggests that a shift in geographical setting was the condition for homosexuality to re-emerge tangentially in Forster's texts; he transposed the problem of homosexuality onto race and colonialism. This analogy pits travel as a liberating alternative to domestic life in Britain, representing exile as the condition through which an otherwise impossible homosexual drama fleetingly could emerge.[10]

Forster seemed to adopt this perspective about exile on several occasions; he wrote a series of fantasies that elaborate, manage, and compress an almost insoluble disjuncture in Britain between homosexuality's creative impulse and the public's representation of it. Forster's fantasies also mark the transition between his fictional and nonliterary writing, though their fictional terrain is quite significant because it describes a passage between Europe, Africa, India, and a mythical atopia. These fantasies rarely occur on British soil, and when they do, Forster represents their setting in either abstract or pastoral terms.[11]

What comes out of Forster's account of fantasy are the qualities that realism resists, cannot explore, and consigns to the responsibility of 'another world'.[12] The title of Forster's later collection of stories, *The Life to Come*, is interesting in this regard because it refers to a future uncoupled from any direct relation to the present. Forster defers homosexuality as a narrative code in this collection because its immediate realisation is unimaginable. In other words, the future is convenient for displacing the present difficulty of incorporating homosexuality in psychic and symbolic terms, and for demonstrating the conflict and alienation this incorporation would entail for Forster's narrative.

If we examine the closing scene of *A Passage to India* in these terms, it begins to clarify some of the tension surrounding its attempt at such an incorporation: the ending refuses to develop or curtail Aziz and Fielding's sexual intimacy; geography intervenes, bringing their contact to a provisional halt without irreparable damage. The novel's closing sentences foreground a drama about the men's sexual intimacy and the abstract forces that keep them apart:

> 'We shall drive every blasted Englishman into the sea, and then' – [Aziz] rode against him furiously – 'and then', he concluded, half kissing him, 'you and I shall be friends'.
> 'Why can't we be friends now?' said the other [Fielding], holding him affectionately. 'It's what I want. It's what you want'.
> But the horses didn't want it – they swerved apart; the earth didn't want it, sending up rocks through which riders must pass single file; the temples, the tank, the jail, the palace, the birds, the carrion, the Guest House, that came into view as they issued from the gap and saw Mau beneath: they didn't want it, they said in their hundred voices: 'No, not yet', and the sky said: 'No, not there'.
>
> (*Passage*: 316)[13]

Forster's anxiety about fantasy's acceptable and controllable limits often transformed his preoccupation with travel into a metaphor for psychic and symbolic exploration. His stress on the effort of the journey – and the mapping of points among what he anticipated, feared, and knew – clarifies a passage between external boundaries and internal constraints by using one set to elaborate the other. Yet the psychic and symbolic 'passage' that Forster underscored in this novel does not mitigate or resolve the external, political questions that accompany it. As Tony Davies remarks in an important collection of essays on this novel, 'the "not yet ... not there" that so tantalisingly defers the narrative closure ... seems inevitably to prompt the question "when, and where?" '14 As my brief account of *The Life to Come*'s title suggests, this second set of questions engages both homosexual desire and colonial relations; for Forster, the terms of the former repeatedly played out upon – and overdetermined – the literal and imaginary field of the latter.

I suggest that *A Passage to India*'s closing statement about deferring intimacy and harmony helped Forster to displace, and apparently resolve, pressing issues about interracial desire that he detailed explicitly in 'The Life to Come' (1922). If *A Passage to India* could end only by shunting its principal issues onto another terrain, this short story amplifies and anticipates what the novel strove to silence and shake off. In this respect, David Lean's recent film adaptation of *A Passage of India* (1984) reproduced and partially resolved many of the problems that beleaguered Forster's completion of the novel: Lean chose to excise much of Forster's emphasis on the men's interracial friendship by foregrounding Adela Quested's sexual confusion and apparent 'hysteria'. As he explained to a reporter from *The Guardian*:

> Forster was a bit anti-English, anti-Raj and so on. I suppose it's a tricky thing to say, but I'm not so much. I intend to keep the balance more. I don't believe all the English were a lot of idiots. Forster made them so. He came down hard against them. I've cut out that bit at the trial where they try to take over the court. ... One other thing: I've got rid of that 'Not yet, not yet' bit. You know, when the Quit India stuff comes up, and we have the passage about driving us into the sea? Forster experts have always said it was important, but the Fielding-Aziz friendship was not sustained by those sorts of things. At least I don't think so. The book came out at the time of the trial of General Dyer and had a tremendous success in America for that reason. But I thought that bit rather tacked on. Anyway, I see it as a personal not a political story.15

The irony of Lean's perspective lies in its partial fidelity to Forster's vision of politics. As Forster acknowledged in 'Three

Countries' (1959), '[*A Passage to India*] is not really about politics ... It's about something wider than politics, about the search of the human race for a more lasting home ... It is – or rather desires to be – philosophic and poetic' (*Hill of Devi*: 298). The novel's turbulent politics resonate most strongly in this final qualifier; the gap between Forster's liberal vision and his narrative's faltering practice underscores a caesura between what he represents as the novel's ideal (harmony, union) and what he demonstrates inadvertently is part of its colonial practice (acrimony, division). This gap is particularly significant for liberal-humanist accounts of sexual relations and interracial fantasy; Lean's excision of this sexual interest confirms not only his desire to foreclose on the difficulty of interracial intimacy between men, but also Forster's wish to curb those narrative elements that spiral out of control. Though Forster would have balked at such an analogy, the *tone* (not the content) of many of his stories' sexual fantasies may correlate with the egregious racism McBryde exemplifies in *A Passage to India*'s court scenes. McBryde's accusations of sexual treachery by Aziz upheld a powerful Anglo-Indian consensus about the horrors of mis-cegenation at the turn of the last century; as I will demonstrate in the next section of this essay, Paul and Lionel's accusations against Vithobai and Cocoanut in 'The Life to Come' and 'The Other Boat' respectively elicit a similar, paradoxical judgement from their author:

> Mr. McBryde paused. He wanted to keep the proceedings as clean as possible, but Oriental Pathology, his favourite theme, lay all around him, and he could not resist it. Taking off his spectacles, as was his habit before enunciating a general truth, he looked into them sadly, and remarked that the darker races are physically attracted by the fairer, but not vice versa – not a matter for bitterness this, nor a matter for abuse, but just a fact which any scientific observer will confirm.   (*Passage*: 222)

If my comparison of Forster and McBryde seems contentiously to place the former in a less than liberal light, consider such stereotypical comments by the narrator as 'The celebrated oriental confusion appeared at last to be at an end' (*Passage*: 143), or the following narrative claim when Aziz prepares to defend himself against charges of sexual impropriety and rape: 'Suspicion in the Oriental is a sort of malignant tumour, a mental malady, that makes him self-conscious and unfriendly suddenly; he trusts and mistrusts at the same time in a way the Westerner cannot comprehend. It is his demon, as the Westerner's is hypocrisy' (*Passage*: 276). This passing indictment of the European does not mitigate the narrator's preceding claims about oriental character, or his implicit 'accusations' against Aziz; because the novel is about racial judgement and interpretation, this passage alerts us to a furtive and unfortunate complicity between the novel's legal prosecutor and its author's assumptions about Indians' pre-existing *propensity* to treachery. Since 'The Life to Come' and 'The Other Boat' are fantasies, and thus perhaps freer with their convictions, they play out this narrative complicity in the assumption of the native subject's savage propensity in still more alarming ways.

To understand Forster's emotional dynamic between Aziz and Fielding, then, we need to consider what apparently is resolved – but more often only partially repressed – in the sexual encounters between Vithobai and Paul in 'The Life to Come', and between Cocoanut and Lionel in 'The Other Boat'. The following accounts of these short stories frame their dynamic through the lens of fantasy and physical intimacy; I want to underscore the terms permitting Forster's literal and conceptual relation between race and homosexuality, and the real and imaginary ground on which he was able and willing for it to occur.

Interracial desire: the violence of connection

> There is no such thing as ordinary democratic intimacy in India; the cooli and I both knew that we were specializing. We watched one another down architectural vistas.   (*Hill of Devi*: 312)
>
> Nothing is more obdurate to artistic treatment than the carnal.[16]

Forster wrote 'The Life to Come' in 1922, two years before he published *A Passage to India*. As I argued in the previous section, the short story anticipates and exceeds the ambiguous resolution of the interracial friendship in that novel by detailing sexual intimacy between an English missionary and an African prince. The shame that surrounds their intimacy, and the extent to which the Englishman denies its meaning, suggest a complex emotional and physical attachment. The story elaborates each man's relation to his desire: the missionary (Paul) is so troubled by guilt, he can recognise homosexual desire only by disavowal; the prince (Vithobai) is eager for contact without a need for explanatory vocabulary. The story represents one stereotype of sexual guilt (the white man consumed by it, the black man indifferent toward it) by reversing another: the myth, still current in many post-colonial cultures today, that homosexuality was a white man's export whose imposition produced a twofold emasculation of African culture.

Forster's association of African homosexuality with the clandestine affairs of a white missionary reiterated the brutal effects of Christian hypocrisy in Africa in the 1910s and 1920s by implicating the Church in a practice it repeatedly condemned. Forster's disdain for religious zeal underpinned his general antipathy toward the Church; he criticised the missionary's belief that he or she exports a system of ethics quite different from or superior to that of native Africans. Besides its imposition of colonial values, evangelism works by scourging sexual pleasure: the missionary Paul strenuously 'sublimates' his homosexuality to punish the native for failing to repress his own. Forster elaborates on the hypocrisy of this scenario by Vithobai's ironic confusion between religious and homosexual conversion: in 'The Life to Come' homosexuality is an act of sublime faith. Vithobai also scorns the missionary's demand for sexual ascesis to comply with God's 'Law'; both men find this injunction impossible to obey.

Once urged to 'embrace' Christianity, Vithobai confuses the religion with its proponent and reintroduces a banished sexual component to religious worship. Though Forster risks endorsing a stereotype of the intransigent native, Vithobai's naivety draws out the spurious and dishonest aims of the missionary's faith. Vithobai's insistence, 'God orders me to love you', finds no other response than Paul's confused retort, 'He orders me to refrain'.[17] In this tale, different ethical systems and notions of pleasure manipulate God's word; Vithobai's desire draws out the muddled precepts of a religion that encourages devotion to God while forbidding demonstrative love for another man. The missionary's hypocrisy transforms the words of St Paul, and the biblical commands of Romans and Leviticus, into an anxiety about physical intimacy and a horror of the body's drives. By redefining religious conflict as a drama about the interpretation of sexuality, Forster unravels the internal forms of control that religion imposes on each protagonist. Vithobai's indifference to any distinction between love for God and love for another man implies that he is a more successful Christian because phobia does not define or delimit his affection. While Paul suffers from a frantic demand for self-control, Vithobai – like the unconscious – recognises no difference between homo- and heterosexual objects.

This division between sexual and racial relations is a recurrent concern in Forster's writing. As June Perry Levine argued recently, his fiction tends to construct a division between 'tame' and 'savage' elements of personality.[18] These elements do not coexist in each partner but define one or the other's exclusive property; a relatively simple schema aligns each character with a specific set of traits. To this structural division of tame and savage qualities, Forster adds other elements and values: the 'tame' lover is conventionally moral, independently wealthy, well-educated, and white. (Maurice, Paul in 'The Life to Come', Fielding in *A Passage to India*, and Lionel in 'The Other Boat' are obvious examples.) Conversely, the 'savage' man generally represents Forster's idealised notion of the working-class hero as self-educated, poor, and enticingly amoral. Insofar as each savage partner represents 'otherness', his marginal properties signify a virile rebellion against orthodox behaviour. (This type includes Scudder in *Maurice*, Vithobai in 'The Life to Come', Cocoanut in 'The Other Boat', and Aziz in *A Passage to India*.) As Levine argues, if tame characters precariously retain 'civilised' power, their savage counterpart displays greater integrity because he is in tune with the environment's 'natural' authority.[19] This clarifies Forster's axiom that the savage lover is closer to nature and sexual freedom; civilised power emasculates the tame hero, leaving him vulnerable to the hostility of heterosexual culture.

Though Forster's 'savage' characters demonstrate less commitment to homosexuality than their 'tame' lovers, their relationship to homosexuality is less inhibited and reliable, due to their marginal relation to culture. Paradoxically, the savage man's relation to nature creates an assurance of masculinity, which his homosexuality does not compromise but enhance. Wrapped in tortuous self-interrogation and sexual guilt, the tame man's cerebral understanding of his desire defines him as both more and less homosexual than the man he chooses for a partner. While the anxiety of sexual self-definition emasculates the hero by robbing him of spontaneity and bisexual variance, the savage partner's physical confidence is defiantly independent of the social-symbolic order. Forster's well-known fantasy of an aggressive working-class lover is not unrelated to this scenario; it adds tension to that lover's sexual indeterminacy, as if the pleasure of a drifting heterosexual were more alluring and intriguing than sustainable intimacy with a committed homosexual.[20]

This idealisation of sexual fluidity inverts the power relation informing each tame and savage partnership. Though the 'savage' man is always at an economic and cultural disadvantage, the tame man's sexual and emotional dependence on his partner gives the latter enough power and responsibility to redeem the former's sexual guilt. The tame man never possesses an independent sexual identity; he valorises this element as the savage man's attractive – and threatening – quality. Since the tame man's projection onto his beloved disinhibits his sexual anxiety, this produces a binding, and often violent, transference: in 'The Life to Come' and 'The Other Boat', both Vithobai and Cocoanut pay for this sexual guilt with their lives. Since this 'tame' and 'savage' scenario resonates in racial and sexual terms in both of these stories, it is worth considering Forster's fantasies about masculine friendship (or homophilia) more closely.

In *Maurice*, a scene in the British Museum illustrates the inversion of this scenario: Alec Scudder interrupts Maurice's romantic allusion to Greek homophilia by threatening him with blackmail (*Maurice*: 192–9). The scene jars with the rest of the novel, in which the men fall in love and elope to the boathouse: an imperative governs the text that their romance succeed; they must overcome all disequivalences between civilised and savage power. The fantasy of otherness that Alex represents for the novel clearly is at odds with the narrative's insistence that romantic love between two men can endure both external and internal opposition; the power differential between Alec and Maurice that is first a prerequisite to their desire must also vanish to sustain their intimacy. Forster's solution was to leave Maurice socially insecure, since his sexual and emotional happiness is incompatible with a tame desire for economic comfort. Rather than 'emasculate' Alec by drawing him – and homosexual desire – into the frame of the social, Forster disparaged the attempt, leaving the lovers to banish themselves before their community forced them apart.

As an early reader of Forster's manuscript, however, Lytton Strachey disputed the permanence of Forster's characters' attachment and their ability to live in virtual isolation did not convince him.[21] While *Maurice* draws on a mythology of romantic love as socially exclusive and self-sufficient, there is clearly an underside to this fantasy that *Maurice* and *A Passage to India* cannot permit – a relation I would argue of profound dependency on, and ambivalence toward, the beloved. As Forster's literary and sexual ambivalence demonstrates, each novel elaborates this underside in a supplemental narrative. 'The Life to Come' arguably is to *A Passage to India* what 'The Other Boat' is to *Maurice*; Forster could achieve the literary success of *Maurice* and *A Passage to India* only by substituting one fantasy (of difference, violence, and ambivalence) for another (of friendship, intimacy, and solidarity).

This distinction between homophilia and homosexuality allows us to read sexual antagonism in Forster's texts as responsible for much of their narrative violence. According to the logic of homophilia, one man claims to find his 'other' unthreatening because he represents the other's difference as the basis of their attachment. However, homosexuality appears to shatter this idealism because it represents the 'other's' difference as violently at odds with the friendship that homophilia dictates. In the transition from novel to short story, Forster oscillates between these familiar and unfamiliar accounts of friendship and sexual relations, though this movement always hinges on the violent management, and final erasure, of racial difference.

In his political writing, Forster's anti-imperialism often attests to this difficulty of neutralising racial difference: the maxim 'only connect' derives from his belief that humanity can surmount the diverse formations of culture and language of which it consists. Whatever ideal this expresses, its failure manifests as an inattention to colonial subjection and exploitation. This suggests that liberalism is both inattentive to historical antagonisms, and that it displaces unconscious hostility, suspicion, and aversion toward the 'other'. Forster is significant in this respect because he projects this antagonism onto the colonised at the precise moment his coloniser denies responsibility for his cultural and economic advantage. Thus Forster's liberalism permits a conscious (and even conscientious) tolerance of diversity by repressing its accompanying structural ambivalence.[22] Since Forster requires certain ideas about class, race, and sexuality to stay at the margins of his novels, these ideas acquire immense significance in his literary fantasies. This may explain why he experienced such difficulty making his fantasies available to an audience wider than his friends, and why the decision to represent fantasy added tension to an already acute ontological crisis. Forster usefully confirmed this problem in 'What I Believe':

Psychology has split and shattered the idea of a 'Person', and has shown us that there is something incalculable in each of us, which may at any moment rise to the surface and destroy our normal balance. We don't know what we are like. We can't know what other people are like. *How, then, can we put any trust in personal relationships, or cling to them in the gathering political storm? In theory we cannot. But in practice we can and do* ... For the purpose of living one has to assume that the personality is solid, and the 'self' is an entity, and to ignore all contrary evidence.[23]

Insofar as they elaborate class and racial difference, *Maurice* and *A Passage to India* tell only one side of the story – the residue of ambivalence surfaces in their fictional supplements as an indication of Forster's limited tolerance. Here, benign difference transforms into a threatening antagonism in which the 'other' wields an imaginary potency – one that emerges from the discrepancy between the 'other's' physical presence and the tame man's perception of his power. This discrepancy represents the 'incalculable ... something' that emerges between the 'split and shattered ... idea of a "Person"' and the mistaken assumption that the 'personality is solid'. However, in Forster's terms, the 'other's' potency is wholly unaccountable: the lovers of Paul ('The Life to Come') and Lionel ('The Other Boat') are affectionate and 'supple' to a degree that would promote another fantasy of sexual malleability, were it not for the violence they finally enact. As the narrator of 'The Life to Come' explains by recounting Paul's troubled thoughts: 'He had scarcely recognised the sardonic chief in this gracious and bare-limbed boy' (*Life*: 96).

In 'The Life to Come', the narrative strives to understand the precise meaning of Paul and Vithobai's intimacy in order to recognise Paul's desire for Vithobai. Paul's mission splits between two incommensurate aims: to convert Vithobai to Christianity and to accept his own sexual desire. The narrative implies that Paul's primary intention is Vithobai's sexual – not religious – conversion. This puts his missionary zeal in disrepute by emptying it of religious meaning and by disclosing its sexual ambition. Forster's willingness to combine a reluctant homosexual (Paul) with an influential homophobe (St Paul) in his naming of the missionary is also astutely ironic: ' "Come to Christ!" he had cried, and Vithobai had said, "Is that your name?" He explained No, his name was not Christ, although he had the fortune to be called Paul after a great apostle, and of course he was no god but a sinful man, chosen to call other sinners to the Mercy seat'

(*Life*: 96). Paul cannot judge Vithobai's repentance, though as Forster makes clear, this inability derives not from his homosexual 'sin' (which is ethically relative) but rather because his self-deception projects all of his desire onto a cause:

> He confessed his defilement (the very name of which cannot be mentioned among Christians), he lamented that he had postponed, perhaps for a generation, the victory of the Church, and he condemned, with increasing severity, the arts of his seducer. On the last topic he became truly eloquent, he always found something more to say, and having begun by recommending the boy to mercy he ended by asking that he might be damned.   (*Life*: 97–8)

This shift from unmentionable 'vice' to accusing those who do not resist it is carefully sardonic. Vithobai succumbs to Christianity and renames himself 'Barnabas', though his faith in sexual salvation mimics his 'master's' failed religious ideals; Vithobai converts religious service into a sexual demand.[24] In despair, Paul forbids all reference to their desire, destroys the hut in which they first had sex, and tries to persuade himself and Vithobai to marry: Paul to counter fears for his respectability (the fear is entirely self-made); Vithobai to comply with his tribe's expectations. These constraints do not diminish homosexual desire; they give it an obsessional urgency that overcomes the impediment of marriage: Paul continues to 'watch him furtively' while urging Vithobai to atone and repent (*Life*: 107). Paul draws more heavily on projection (while Forster leans more critically on Christian hypocrisy) by reconverting Vithobai in psychic terms into an abject figure, investing him with the severity of his own self-hatred:

> Did God, in His mystery, demand from [Paul] that he should cleanse his brother's soul before his own could be accepted? The dark erotic perversion that the chief mistook for Christianity – who had implanted it? He had put this question from him in the press of his earlier dangers, but it intruded itself now that he was safe. Day after day he heard the cold voice of the somewhat scraggy and unattractive native inviting him to sin ...   (*Life*: 106)

Ironically, the rejection of homosexuality appears to *work* in Forster's narrative by 'cleansing' Paul of desire and recasting Vithobai as a sexual and rhetorical 'bad object'. In the process, Forster reactivates in Paul the mechanism he previously deplored;[25] the success of Paul's sexual redemption and projection leaves Vithobai vulnerable to racist accusation and violence.

This projection transforms Vithobai from a 'boy wild with passion' into something 'festering, equivocal, and perhaps acquiring some sinister power' (*Life*: 102, 108). Strangely, the narrative endorses this change in perspective by moving from mockery of Paul's self-deception and hypocrisy to a palpable horror of Vithobai. In other words, the narrative fails to differentiate Paul's spiralling projection from its own. Though this perspective foregrounds the deceit of Paul's marriage, it judges Vithobai more harshly by failing to quell his sexual interest in Paul. When Vithobai avows this desire in a cart on their way to the forest, for instance, Paul's revulsion mirrors the *narrator's* alarm at Vithobai's indiscretion. By offering no response to Paul's hypocrisy, the narrative begins to rationalise his physical and psychic dread:

> Without replying, Barnabas handed him the reins, and then jerked himself out of the cart. It was a most uncanny movement, which seemed to proceed direct from the will. He scarcely used his hands or rose to his feet before jumping. But his soul uncoiled like a spring, and thrust the cart violently away from it against the ground. Mr. Pinmay had heard of such contortions, but never witnessed them; they were startling, they were disgusting. And the descent was equally sinister. Barnabas lay helpless as if the evil uprush had suddenly failed.
> (*Life*: 105)

After Forster's previous indictment of Christian hypocrisy in 'The Life to Come', the term 'evil uprush' to represent homosexual desire is bizarre and inexplicable. Besides the manner of his exit from the cart, Vithobai's reckless expression – 'which seemed to proceed direct from the will' – fuels the narrator's disdain, as if Vithobai's lack of restraint transforms his desire into something 'startling ... disgusting ... sinister ... [and] evil ...'[26]

Thus Vithobai embodies a 'dark erotic perversion' whose passion is vulgar and unbearable because he cannot defer it until 'the life to come' (*Life*: 105). His demand for immediate gratification unleashes a 'monstrous' homosexual drive that stubbornly resists the voice of Law and its punitive ascesis. Ironically, 'The Lord's Prayer' represents this conflict in the expression 'Thy *will* be done'; 'will' defines each character's psychic confusion: either submit to a higher authority to ward off sexual distress, or act on one's own will and experience the terror and bliss of shattering each psychic and religious impediment. As Vithobai admits to Paul in the throes of death, and in response to a plea that he must finally surrender his will: 'It was a deed ... which now you call joy, now sin' (*Life*: 109).

With the scene of temptation briefly reversed, Paul offers religious salvation by kissing Vithobai on the forehead: 'Do not misunderstand me this time ... [it is] in perfect purity' (*Life*: 110). However, the act backfires because the narrator represents Vithobai as the cause of Paul's seduction and downfall: 'Mr. Pinmay feared to venture the kiss lest Satan took an advantage' (*Life*: 110). On the point of death, Vithobai corroborates this fear by recovering a feverish energy, grabbing hold of a knife, and stabbing Paul in the heart. The act is so gratuitous and bathetic that the text hovers on the brink of farce. However, Vithobai's murder of Paul actually seems consistent with the narrator's anxiety about managing colonial and sexual fantasy. As I suggested earlier in my account of *A Passage to India*, the closing frame of many Forster stories interrupts and disbands what would otherwise spiral out of control. Although racial difference precipitates Paul and Vithobai's sexual encounter, difference is finally a horrifying trap from which Paul is unable to escape.

Since the narrative defines race as a violent problem, Forster privileges restraint and discretion over the satisfaction of his characters' sexual desire. However, his caution (like Paul's anger) attributes each failure of sexual discretion to the colonised, whose lack of inhibition apparently represents psychic destruction and death. Thus the narrative aligns the colonised with the violent force of psychic drives by destroying the subjective cohesion of its European lovers and Forster's fictional closure. The closing image of Vithobai signifies this horror of desire run amok as he mounts Paul's corpse in delirious passion before leaping to his death. This image not only forges a comparison between sexual desire and colonial insubordination but also assumes, as its corollary, an analogy between the unconscious and a state of savagery. Vithobai's (always anticipated) regression into 'perversion', insanity, and barbarism confirms his inability to 'sublimate' his homosexual drives: 'Mounting on the corpse, he climbed higher, raised his arms over his head, sunlit, naked, victorious, leaving all disease and humiliation behind him, and he swooped like a falcon from the parapet in pursuit of the terrified shade' (*Life*: 111–12).

Judith Scherer Herz considers this ending 'not gratuitous, and not merely poetic [but rather] a final spending of all the energies that have built up through the story'.[27] June Perry Levine by contrast seems oblivious to the characters on whom these 'energies' are 'spen[t]', going further than Herz in her claim that Forster's 'art pays homage to the redemptive possibilities inherent in the love of the totally other, one who must be reached by stepping over the chasm of class or race'.[28] But what 'redemptive possibilities' inhere in the 'other' in these stories? Since Forster does not step over, but consciously retains, this 'chasm' of class or race, his claim of defending a friend over loyalty to one's country in 'What I Believe' is exposed as simply idealist; in fact, in these stories, Paul's and Lionel's loyalty to Britain prevails over their sexual transgressions.[29]

Conclusion: managing 'The White Man's Burden'

> There was a saying among young Indians that friendships made with white men seldom stood the strain of separation and never the acuter strain of reunion on the Indian's native soil.[30]

> The structure of a friendship is seldom submitted to analysis until it comes under pressure.[31]

Many of these tensions recur in 'The Other Boat' (1915–16), a short story written after *Maurice*, that Forster first abandoned and subsequently published in 1948 as a fragment. The text describes a relationship between an English officer (Lionel) and an Indian naval secretary (Cocoanut) on a ship bound for India. While the narrative elaborates their furtive intimacy in more detail than 'The Life to Come', it presents an equally violent collision of homophobia, sexual racism, and national prejudice. Forster's mythopoetic account of travel adds a metaphoric significance to the boat, which is – like the boat in Joseph Conrad's *Lord Jim* (1900) – representative of exile, expatriate community, and other colonial problems.

The direction of travel is significant here because proximity to England exacerbates the racial constraints operating between Lionel and Cocoanut. Their sexual intimacy begins when they enter the Mediterranean, and they consummate this intimacy when they reach the Red Sea. However, 'The Other Boat' cannot locate all racial and sexual prejudice outside the lovers. While Lionel expresses his homosexuality only below deck in a locked cabin, this desire connects defiantly to the rest of the ship. Unlike *Maurice*, there is no place to which Lionel and Cocoanut can happily retire and escape. The proximity of homosexuality to the wider community renews Forster's problem of integrating desire within his narrative; Lionel's confusion between desire for

Cocoanut and hatred of other Indians makes their relationship as fraught with antagonism inside the cabin as it is without.

Critics often overlook this point by simplifying and idealising their attachment. For instance, June Perry Levine describes the story as one of 'thwarted love',[32] while Norman Page argues:

> Their mutual infatuation overrides differences of race and social background, so that in the cabin they inhabit a world different from that of the deck and the dining-room; as the boat retraces in reverse the route of the earlier voyage, the two recapture the relationship of their boyhood, except that the tentative and half-realized sexuality of that time is now fully explicit.[33]

However, Lionel and Cocoanut are in fact unable to 'override' these differences. Although their intimacy largely derives from them, following 'The Life to Come', it subsequently founders on them. The cabin is not, as Page claims, 'a world different from that of the deck', as if culture and prejudice ended with a lock on the door; the fantasies that this locked door enable intensify the antagonism that surfaces behind it.

In the context of this story, the Forsterian maxim 'only connect' confirms intractable points of resistance between conscious knowledge and unconscious antagonism. Stuart Hampshire touched on this problem when he argued about *A Passage to India*: 'The connection that needs to be made is between the upper and literate reaches of the mind and the lower and unwashed, or proletarian, levels of consciousness, which can no longer be downtrodden and despised'.[34] J. R. Ackerley, novelist and Forster's friend, went further down this path by characterising the unconscious in palpably racist terms: 'However honestly we may wish to examine ourselves we can do no more than scratch the surface. The golliwog that lies within and bobs up to dishonour us in our unguarded moments is too clever to be caught when we want him'.[35]

For Ackerley, as perhaps for Forster, the ego is a white man as the unconscious is a black man. 'The Other Boat's' narrative is a palimpsest that positions Cocoanut within a cabin that is, in turn, inside the ship, as if to frame the potential insurrection of this racially 'unwashed' whenever it 'bobs up to dishonour us'.[36] Lionel publicly disparages the occupant of his cabin, then returns to him in ritualised shame. The narrator explains, 'his colour-prejudices were tribal rather than personal, and only worked when an observer was present' (*Life*: 211). Later, making what the narrator considers a 'shrewd move', Lionel 'brays': ' "I got a passage all right ... but at the cost of sharing my cabin with a wog" '. The narrator continues: 'All condoled, and Colonel Arbuthnot in the merriest of moods exclaimed, "Let's hope the blacks don't come off on the sheets ..." ' (*Life*: 212). What comes off on the sheets – and emerges in the text – is Lionel's sexual guilt, which erupts when he strangles Cocoanut. Arbuthnot's 'joke' symbolises a murder that is, according to its narrator, 'ecstasy hardened into agony' and a 'sweet act of vengeance' (*Life*: 233). Within this tale's perverse logic, Cocoanut precipitates Lionel's disgust, rendering his gratuitous violence an inevitable and justifiable response to Cocoanut's provocation.

While Lionel moves between cabin and deck, resuming an identity among 'The Ruling Race' that keeps his homosexuality under wraps, Cocoanut's desire is dangerously profuse. Since the narrator proclaims throughout that Cocoanut is part Indian, his indeterminate racial identity apparently explains his sexual manipulation of Lionel. Thus the narrator juxtaposes the 'decent and reliable' Lionel with a lover he describes as behaving 'like a monkey', 'almost like a vulture snatching', 'no better than a monkey' and 'the little snake' because Cocoanut forgets to lock their cabin door (*Life*: 210, 216, 218, and 228). (Perhaps we should note that the narrator of *A Passage to India* also claims, 'a crowd of dependents were swarming over the seats of the carriage like monkeys' [p. 141], when Aziz meets Adela and Mrs Moore at the station in Chandrapore.) Finally, Cocoanut's proper name is also curious – it derives apparently from his head's disfiguration – for the narrator shortens it repeatedly to 'Cocoa'; a name that renders him both an embodiment of race and, by its proximity to two homonyms, representative of both their sexual 'cocoon' (the cabin/closet) and the figurative 'ca-ca', or excrement, that apparently warrants his death.

Following Vithobai's example, Cocoanut's transformation occurs over a substantial period of time. At the tale's beginning, the narrator describes Cocoanut as a 'subtle supple boy' (*Life*: 210), his disfigurement a feature of charm, and his character considerably more honest than that of his lover. Points of ambivalence later distort this image: the narrator indicates more than once that '[Cocoanut] had no scruples at perverting Lionel's instincts in order to gratify his own, or at endangering his prospects of paternity' (*Life*: 219).

Like Vithobai, Cocoanut assumes the role of precipitating his lover's downfall by drawing him into a conspiracy that obviously will ruin him. The narrator condemns Cocoanut for his conscious abuse of sexual intimacy and the way he permits himself to be desired; this renders him a symptom of Lionel's ardent and impossible longing. While Cocoanut and Vithobai hold an ambiguous relation to colonial Law and Forster's ethics of sexual discretion, they are clearly at the mercy of an accompanying racial projection and its hate-ridden contents. By dwelling on what Lionel and Paul have to lose (colonial privilege) and, by implication, what Cocoanut and Vithobai have to gain (a vested interest in power), the narrator merges sexual and racial projection into a wider colonial schema, aligning himself with the white lover by proposing that the black man is responsible for Cocoanut and Lionel's social and psychic collapse.

At these moments of narrative ambivalence, various conflations between narrator and character make it almost impossible to distinguish Forster's account of Lionel's sudden hatred for Cocoanut from his own account of sexual and racial hostility in *Hill of Devi and Other Indian Writings*. In 'Kanaya' (1922), a fragment written in the same year as 'The Life to Come', Forster describes his sexual relationship with an Indian boy in similar ways to the ill-fated relationships between Paul and Vithobai, and Lionel and Cocoanut. He begins by stating his resistance to Kanaya's effeminacy and compliance, and ends in exasperation: 'What relation beyond carnality could one establish with such people?' (*Hill of Devi*: 323). Nevertheless, Forster chose to heighten rather than disband this ambivalence, and so

> resume ... sexual intercourse, but it was now mixed with the desire to inflict pain. It didn't hurt him to speak of, but it was bad for me, and new in me, my temperament not being that way. I've never had the desire with anyone else, before or after, and I wasn't trying to punish him – I knew his silly little soul was incurable. I just felt that he was a slave, without rights, and I a despot whom no one could call to account.   (*Hill of Devi*: 324)

The assumption that Indians experience no pain prevails throughout 'The Other Boat', where the 'sweet act of vengeance' of Cocoanut's murder is apparently 'sweeter than ever for both of them' (*Life*: 233), as if strangulation were the sublime culmination of his implacable Indian masochism. With little to lose, and no apparent ego to speak of, Kanaya and Cocoanut confirm their status, each as a 'silly ... slave'. By contrast, in murdering Cocoanut, the 'Half Ganymede, half Goth' figure of *Lionel* reinscribes the masculinity that homosexual desire and its disclosure seem to destabilise (*Life*: 215). As in Forster's piece on Kanaya, Cocoanut's murder intensifies and reaffirms what previously was in doubt: the white man's authority and right to inflict pain. Forster was conscious of this dubious right when he described the response of the Indian coolies to his affair with Kanaya: 'They weren't openly rude but there was an air of *rollicking equality*: "You're no better than we are, after all" and probably a little racial vengeance' (*Hill of Devi*: 321; my emphasis).

Rather than experience the shame of 'rollicking equality', Lionel leaps to his death without a 'racial' stain on his skin; however, he still bears traces of Cocoanut's sperm on his body. His corpse floats 'northwards – contrary to the prevailing current' before it is consumed by sharks (*Life*: 234). When the scandal breaks, other – human – sharks dis-seminate it, inducing such disgust in Lionel's mother than she resolves 'never [to] mention ... his name again' (*Life*: 234). The public (and narrative) give little further attention to Cocoanut's death beyond the presumption that he instigated it himself, as if this projection absolves Lionel of guilt and homosexual desire by upholding the public's refusal to accept their intimacy.

The text ends this homosexual fantasy by repeating 'The Life to Come's' erasure of interracial desire. In both stories, the narrator replaces *peripeteia*, the rhetorical trope that denotes abrupt and inexplicable change, by *preterition*, which silences the subject altogether. This substitution of hostility for desire again seems to resolve an otherwise insoluble drama. This point contradicts the claim that love between men was unrepresentable at this time beyond a furtive encounter or fleeting intimacy; as fantasies, Forster could have inscribed these relationships more optimistically had he so chosen. I suggest that his continuation of such fantasies was impossible, given the sexual and racial politics they uncover, because it would have meant examining the racial inequalities that determine their structure. In this respect, Forster's account of interracial friendship in *A Passage to India* is idealist and only one side of the (colonial) story; to grasp this novel's political concerns, we need to consider the sexual and racial ambivalence that Forster foregrounds in *The Life to Come*. Although these fantasies are politically and psychically reactionary, they are nonetheless useful to contemporary criticism in elaborating aspects of colonial subjection that otherwise would never be mentioned.

Notes

1 E. M. Forster, *Howards End* (1910; Harmondsworth: Penguin, 1954), p. 224. Subsequent references give pagination in main text.

2 Forster, *Maurice: A Romance* (1913–14; Harmondsworth: Penguin, 1987), p. 198. Subsequent references give pagination in main text.

3 Forster, *A Passage to India* (1924; Harmondsworth: Penguin, 1984), pp. 264–5. Subsequent references give pagination in main text.

4 Ashis Nandy, *The Intimate Enemy: Loss and Recovery of Self Under Colonialism* (Oxford: Oxford University Press, 1983), pp. 9–10. For other theorisations of this phenomenon, see Octave Mannoni, *Prospero and Caliban: The Psychology of Colonialization*, trans. Pamela Powesland (Ann Arbor: University of Michigan Press, 1990); Frantz Fanon, *Black Skin, White Masks*, trans. Charles Lam Markmann (New York: Grove, 1967).

5 Forster, 'Terminal Note' to *Maurice*, pp. 221–2.

6 See Annan, 'Love Story', p. 12; Samuel Hynes, 'A Chalice for Youth', *Times Literary Supplement* 3, 632 (8 October 1971), p. 1215; George Steiner, 'Under the Greenwood Tree', *The New Yorker*, 47 (9 October 1971), p. 164; Norman Page, *E. M. Forster's Posthumous Fiction* (Victoria, BC: University of Victoria Press, 1977), p. 12.

7 Forster, diary entry for June 16 1911, unpublished manuscript held at King's College, Cambridge.

8 See Forster, *Arctic Summer and Other Fiction* (London: Edward Arnold, 1980).

9 Steiner, 'Under the Greenwood Tree', p. 166.

10 See Forster, 'Kanaya', *Hill of Devi and Other Indian Writings*, ed. E. Heine (c. 1922; London: Edward Arnold, 1983) – subsequent references give pagination in main text; J. R. Ackerley, *Hindoo Holiday: An Indian Journal* (1932; Harmondsworth: Penguin Travel, 1988); André Gide, *Travels in the Congo*, trans. Dorothy Bussy (1927–28; Harmondsworth: Penguin Travel, 1986). For an interpretation of this phenomenon, see Jonathan Dollimore, 'Different Desires: Subjectivity and Transgression in Wilde and Gide', *Textual Practice*, 1, no. 1 (1987), pp. 48–67.

11 Examples of pastoral fantasies include 'The Story of a Panic', 'The Other Side of the Hedge', 'Other Kingdom', and 'Ansell'. Notable dystopic fantasies are 'The Celestial Omnibus', 'The Machine Stops', 'The Point of It', and 'The Torque', in Forster, *Collected Short Stories* (1947; Harmondsworth: Penguin, 1954).

12 Forster, 'Fantasy', *Aspects of the Novel* (1927; Harmondsworth: Penguin, 1990), p. 106.

13 Sara Suleri gives this passage – and its wider resonance – a brilliant reading in *The Rhetoric of English India* (Chicago: University of Chicago Press, 1992), pp. 132–48.

14 Tony Davies, 'Introduction', *A Passage to India: Theory in Practice*, ed. Davies and Nigel Wood (Buckingham: Open University Press, 1994), p. 4.

15 David Lean in conversation with Derek Malcolm, *The Guardian*, 23 January 1984, quoted in Salman Rushdie, 'Outside the Whale', *Granta*, 11 (1984), pp. 128–9.

16 Forster, letter to Siegfried Sassoon, 11 October 1920, *Selected Letters of E. M. Forster, vol. I: 1879–1920*, ed. Mary Lago and P. N. Furbank (London: Collins, 1983), p. 316.

17 Forster, *The Life to Come and Other Stories* (1972; Harmondsworth: Penguin, 1989), p. 101. Subsequent references give pagination in main text.

18 June Perry Levine, 'The Tame in Pursuit of the Savage: The Posthumous Fiction of E. M. Forster', *PMLA*, 99, 1 (1984), pp. 72–88.

19 Stephen Adams, *The Homosexual as Hero in Contemporary Fiction* (London: Vision, 1980), pp. 106–30.

20 *Ibid.*, p. 125; and John Sayre Martin, *E. M. Forster: The Endless Journey* (Cambridge: Cambridge University Press, 1976), p. 77.

21 Lytton Strachey, letter to Forster, 12 March 1915, *Forster: The Critical Heritage*, ed. Philip Gardner (London: Routledge and Kegan Paul, 1973), pp. 430–1.

22 Paul Scott usefully observed of the interracial friendship between his protagonists, Edwina Crane and Mr Chaudhuri: '... there had been between [them] right from the beginning what Miss Crane thought of as an almost classical reserve – classical in the sense that she felt they each suspected the other of hypocrisy, of unrevealed motives, *of hiding under the thinnest of liberal skins deeply conservative natures* ...' (Scott, *The Jewel in the Crown* [1966; New York: Avon, 1979], p. 42, my emphasis).

23 Forster, 'What I Believe', *Two Cheers for Democracy* (London: Edward Arnold, 1951), p. 68 (my emphasis).

24 Homi Bhabha, 'Of Mimicry and Man: The Ambivalence of Colonial Discourse', *October*, 28 (1984), pp. 125–33; Pascal Bruckner, 'The Ambivalence of Exotic Taste', *The Tears of the White Man: Compassion as Contempt*, trans. William R. Beer (New York: Free Press, 1986), pp. 167–9.

25 Forster, 'The Menace to Freedom' (1935), 'Jew-Consciousness' (1939), 'Racial Exercise' (1939), 'Tolerance' (1941), and 'A Letter to Madan Blanchard' (1931), *Two Cheers for Democracy*, pp. 9–14, 17–20, 43–6, and 305–14.

26 In *Aaron's Rod*, D. H. Lawrence argues that the Indian doctor represents to Aaron 'the same danger, the same menace' as women because his speech and intentions are '*maggoty with these secret lustful inclinations to destroy the man in a man*' (1922; Harmondsworth: Penguin, 1976, 34, my emphasis).

27 Judith Scherer Herz, *The Short Narratives of E. M. Forster* (New York: St Martin's Press, 1988), p. 46.

28 Levine, 'The Tame in Pursuit of the Savage', p. 87.

29 Forster, 'What I Believe', *Two Cheers for Democracy*, p. 66.

30 Scott, *The Jewel in the Crown*, p. 267.

31 *Ibid.*, p. 261.

32 Levine, 'The Tame in Pursuit of the Savage', p. 84. Levine concludes that 'Lionel's revulsion is not homophobic but against the bigotry of his class. When he finally does throw himself into the sea, it is not because he is disgusted with what has happened between Cocoa and himself but because "if he forfeited [his caste's] companionship he would become nobody and nothing" ' (p. 86). This explains only his suicide, not his prior recoil from Cocoa. Thus Levine ignores both homo- and negrophobia in this story by acknowledging only Lionel's *conscious* 'pursuit' of the other.

33 Page, *E. M. Forster's Posthumous Fiction*, p. 57. Jeffrey Meyers claims also that 'these men overcome racial, social and sexual prejudices, and achieve temporary liberation by sodomizing ... before lapsing back into their "apparatus of decay" or plunging to a violent death' (*Homosexuality and Literature, 1890–1930* [London: Athlone Press, 1977], p. 108). This statement assumes that their sexuality can be detached from both the prejudice that surrounds them and their internal drive toward death.

34 Stuart Hampshire, '*The Cave and the Mountain: A Study of E. M. Forster* by W. Stone', *New York Review of Books*, 12 May 1966, pp. 14–16.

35 Ackerley, *My Father and Myself* (1968), quoted in Donald Salter, 'That Is My Ticket: The Homosexual Writings of E. M. Forster', *London Magazine* 14, 6 (1975), p. 31.

36 For detailed examination of this point, see Sander Gilman and J. Edward Chamberlain (eds.), *Degeneration: The Dark Side of Progress* (New York: Columbia University Press, 1985); Joel Kovel, *White Racism: A Psychohistory* (New York: Columbia University Press, 1984), pp. 51–92.

Bibliography

Ackerley, J. R., *Hindoo Holiday: An Indian Journal* (1932; Harmondsworth: Penguin, 1988).

Adams, Stephen, *The Homosexual as Hero in Contemporary Fiction* (London: Vision, 1980).

Annan, Noël, 'Love Story', *New York Review of Books*, 17, 6 (21 October 1971), pp. 12–19.

Bhabha, Homi, 'Of Mimicry and Man: The Ambivalence of Colonial Discourse', *October*, 28 (1984), pp. 125–33.

Bruckner, Pascal, *The Tears of the White Man: Compassion as Contempt*, trans. William R. Beer (New York: Free Press, 1986).

Davies, Tony, and Nigel Wood (eds.), *A Passage to India: Theory in Practice* (Buckingham: Open University Press, 1994).

Dollimore, Jonathan, 'Different Desires: Subjectivity and Transgression in Wilde and Gide', *Textual Practice*, 1, 1 (1987), pp. 48–67.

Fanon, Frantz, *Black Skin, White Masks*, trans. Charles Lam Markmann (New York: Grove, 1967).

Forster, E. M., *The Longest Journey* (1907; Harmondsworth: Penguin, 1988).

—— *Howards End* (1910; Harmondsworth: Penguin, 1954).

—— *Maurice: A Romance* (1913–14; Harmondsworth: Penguin, 1987).

—— *A Passage to India* (1924; Harmondsworth: Penguin, 1984).

—— *Aspects of the Novel* (1927; Harmondsworth: Penguin, 1990).

—— *Collected Short Stories* (1947; Harmondsworth: Penguin, 1954).

—— *Two Cheers for Democracy* (London: Edward Arnold, 1951).

—— *The Life to Come and Other Stories* (1972; Harmondsworth: Penguin, 1989).

—— *Arctic Summer and Other Fiction* (London: Edward Arnold, 1980).

—— *Hill of Devi and Other Indian Writings*, ed. Elizabeth Heine (London: Edward Arnold, 1983).

—— *Selected Letters of E. M. Forster, Vol. I: 1879–1920*, ed. Mary Lago and P. N. Furbank (London: Collins, 1983).

—— *Diary*, unpublished manuscript, Cambridge: King's College Library.

Gardner, Philip (ed.), *Forster: The Critical Heritage* (London: Routledge and Kegan Paul, 1973).

Gide, André, *Travels in the Congo*, trans. Dorothy Bussy (1927–28; Harmondsworth: Penguin, 1986).

Gilman, Sander L., and J. Edward Chamberlain (eds.), *Degeneration: The Dark Side of Progress* (New York: Columbia University Press, 1985).

Hampshire, Stuart, '*The Cave and the Mountain: A Study of E. M. Forster* by W. Stone', *New York Review of Books*, 12 May 1966, pp. 14–16.

Herz, Judith Scherer, *The Short Narratives of E. M. Forster* (New York: St Martin's Press, 1988).

Hynes, Samuel, 'A Chalice for Youth', *Times Literary Supplement*, 3, 632, 8 October 1971, pp. 1215–16.

Kovel, Joel, *White Racism: A Psychohistory* (New York: Columbia University Press, 1984).

Lawrence, D. H., *Aaron's Rod* (1922; Harmondsworth: Penguin, 1976).

Levine, June Perry, 'The Tame in Pursuit of the Savage: The Posthumous Fiction of E. M. Forster', *PMLA*, 99, 1 (1984), pp. 72–88.

Mannoni, Octave, *Prospero and Caliban: The Psychology of Colonialization*, trans. Pamela Powesland (Ann Arbor: University of Michigan Press, 1990).

Martin, John Sayre, *E. M. Forster: The Endless Journey* (Cambridge: Cambridge University Press, 1976).

Meyers, Jeffrey, *Homosexuality and Literature, 1890–1930* (London: Athlone Press, 1977).

Nandy, Ashis, *The Intimate Enemy: Loss and Recovery of Self Under Colonialism* (Oxford: Oxford University Press, 1983).

Page, Norman, *E. M. Forster's Posthumous Fiction* (Victoria, BC: University of Victoria Press, 1977).

Rushdie, Salman, 'Outside the Whale', *Granta*, 11 (1984), pp. 125–38.

Salter, Donald, 'That Is My Ticket: The Homosexual Writings of E. M. Forster', *London Magazine*, 14, 6 (1975), pp. 5–53.

Scott, Paul, *The Jewel in the Crown* (1966; New York: Avon, 1979).

Steiner, George, 'Under the Greenwood Tree', *The New Yorker*, 47, 9 October 1971, pp. 158–69.

Suleri, Sara, *The Rhetoric of English India* (Chicago: University of Chicago Press, 1992).

8

'I am your Mother and your Father': Paul Scott's *Raj Quartet* and the dissolution of imperial identity

DANNY COLWELL

The Raj Quartet and colonial binarism

It is tempting for those wishing to place Scott within the 'Orientalist' tradition of English writing on India to see his work as perpetuating the dominant tropes of colonial discourse. As evidence they might point to his treatment of that recurrent dramatic event, the physical threat to a white woman from the native male, which runs from post-mutiny narratives, through *A Passage to India*, to reappear in the first volume of *The Raj Quartet*. In criticising *The Raj Quartet*, Salman Rushdie admonishes Scott: 'if a rape must be used as the metaphor of the Indo-British connection, then surely, in the interests of accuracy, it should be the rape of an Indian woman by one or more Englishmen of whatever class'.[1] Through this reading it is assumed that it is the figure of the Englishwoman who is made to represent both the colonial culture's sense of its 'civilisation', which must be protected and kept intact, and its insecurity about maintaining the integrity of that civilisation in the colonial setting. In this regard, the sense of threat to the integrity of the white woman is the projection of a perceived threat to the white man himself, and the power he holds over the native.

Rushdie, of course, uses Scott's work as part of his larger, Saidian critique of the persistence in western writing, after the end of empire, of representations of the East through forms that privilege the European's position, and thus continue to 'produce' India for western knowledge. In other words, the charge is made that Scott's vast work is, in effect, part of the discourse of writing on an Orient which remains passive, 'written about'. A view such as this, however, ignores the ambiguity of Scott's position. Writing in the 1960s, a decade which saw the demand for social liberation in Europe and the final moments of decolonisation in Africa, he looks back to the Second World War and the events leading up to the loss of India, Britain's most important colonial possession. It is in India that Scott locates the most significant and wide-ranging example of the disintegration of English imperial identity. He situates *The Raj Quartet* within the dominant paradigms of the representations of empire, and yet, this essay will argue, the novels challenge the tropes upon which the discourse of the Raj had been structured since the eighteenth century. Thus *The Raj Quartet* inhabits an ambiguous space between the colonial text, which established the dominant modes of representing India, and the postcolonial, which challenges them. It in fact reflects the decolonising mentality of the 1960s, rather than simply nostalgia for the imperial grandeur of the past. The tetralogy may begin with an image from Forster, but two thousand pages later, the narrative has mapped out the contours of a literary world that will be taken up by Salman Rushdie himself, in *Midnight's Children*.

If Scott's work deploys the established tropes of colonial discourse for unexpected ends, this would suggest that it also complicates the binarism of the influential theoretical model of colonial discourse which was established in Edward Said's *Orientalism*, and which pervades more recent postcolonial critiques such as Rushdie's essay and Abdul JanMohamed's *Manichean Aesthetics*. This theory argues that one important ideological strategy of colonial discourse is to establish a paradigmatic relationship between coloniser and colonised, structured around the masculine/feminine division. Moreover, it suggests colonial discourse naturalises the separation of mind and body along this binary divide, and provides a powerful and pervasive trope which fixes the role of the masculine/imperialist as giver of meaning, order, seed to the awaiting feminine/oriental body. For Edward Said, this typifies the structures of power underlying western representation in the colonial context. Focusing on Flaubert's encounter with an Egyptian courtesan, Said suggests that:

> He spoke for and represented her. He was foreign, comparatively wealthy, male, and these were historical facts of domination that allowed him not only to possess Kuchuk Hanem physically but to speak for her and tell his readers in what way she was 'typically Oriental'.... Flaubert's situation of strength in relation to Kuchuk Hanem was not an isolated instance. It fairly stands for the pattern of relative strength between East and West, and the discourse about the Orient that it enabled.[2]

However, Said's focus on the masculine West's possession of the feminine East's 'voice' relies upon the idea that such a division was the typical, incontrovertible condition of the colonial encounter. In this sense, it inadvertently replicates the colonial structures it seeks to criticise. For clearly, it attaches enormous importance to the role of the masculine on the colonial side of the binary division, and makes assumptions about the fixed nature of that masculine colonial identity without interrogating its role as an historical construct.

This essay will propose, then, that Scott's work is at its most destabilising of colonial discourse when it examines the construction of colonial masculine identity and the ambiguities which exist in its encounter not with the native female but the colonised male subject. Joseph Bristow has argued that the construction of masculine identity in the popular fiction of the nineteenth century was specifically linked to the development of Empire. He seeks to identify 'why imperialism staked such a high claim on a specific kind of masculinity to perpetuate its aims', and concludes that 'British culture invested so much energy in glamorizing male heroes because they represented ... a tremendous lack: they were not to be found in the empire [but] in the pages of story books ... It was within the compulsions of these boys' own narratives that all the problematic elements of male identity could, momentarily, cohere'.[3] Scott corroborates Bristow's argument that colonial masculine identity is a discursive construct, rather than a fixed, essential quality 'out there' in the empire. It is subjected to an exhaustive deconstruction throughout *The Raj Quartet*, which reveals it as something far from unitary or 'natural'. Indeed, the tetralogy is sceptical that such a unified identity could ever have been successfully established as part of a discursive structuring of imperial 'Self' and 'Other', of masculine colonisers and feminine colonised. *The Raj Quartet* thus challenges the historical foundation of an 'Englishness' formulated around secure models of both masculine and feminine colonial identity.

Black holes, rape, riot: *The Raj Quartet* and the tropes of empire

The dominant colonial tropes of British India mark out the Raj's defining historical moments. The 'black hole' in which the British were incarcerated following the defeat at Calcutta in 1756, recurred as a powerful image in colonial discourse thereafter. The 1857 Mutiny became a focal point for anxieties about the threat of general uprising and, in particular, paranoia about the potential rape of English women. So potent was the memory of the Mutiny that the events surrounding the Amritsar massacre of 1919, which haunt many of the characters in the quartet, seem prefigured in their minds by the events of 1857. The tropes that cluster around these events are all gathered into the first two volumes of *The Raj Quartet*.

As Rushdie points out, at the heart of the tetralogy lies an act of brutality. The dominant trope of the work is not the rape of an Englishwoman, however, important though the assault of Dorothy Manners is, but the 'rape' of an Indian man, of the enacting of an imperial desire for power and knowledge upon his naked body. Bent over a trestle, vulnerable to the gaze and the touch of an English police officer, Hari Kumar embodies a deeply ironic reversal of the paradigmatic colonial representation of the native's barbarism and his unrepressed sexuality.[4] This argues against established interpretations of what has been seen to be the novel sequence's central event. Bill Schwarz, for example, suggests that 'the core of the novel ... lies in the figure of Daphne Manners who, in the midst of the August 1942 Quit India campaign, first falls in love with a young Indian man, and subsequently is raped in the ominously named Bibighar Gardens'.[5] By identifying the novel's core concern in Daphne Manners' rape, Schwarz fails to recognise the more radical elements with which the narrative builds its interrogation of the Anglo-Indian relationship, ironically figured throughout as the 'imperial embrace'. Scott's focus on rape in the colonial encounter is vital; the attack on the Englishwoman sets the story in motion. But this will turn out to signify something more challenging than even Forster's exploration of colonial violence. In this context, the rape of a woman is no longer available as a metaphor for colonial anxieties about the potential of the colonised male to penetrate colonial power. Indeed, it serves rather to throw attention, in one direction, upon the existence of interracial love (between Kumar and Daphne Manners), and in the other, upon the problematic violation of an Indian man by an English officer. The novel sequence increasingly concentrates its critical attention on the sexual identity of the Englishman in India, and the role this plays in an unfolding crisis of imperial identity.

The key moment, in this respect, is the encounter between Ronald Merrick and Hari Kumar in the torture cell, which we might read as a modern, ironic version of the 'black hole'. Merrick's analysis of his relationship to Hari Kumar and by extension, England's to India, is given as he tortures his victim, and resonates throughout the four novels. Kumar, speaking some time afterwards, recalls that:

> he said for the moment we were mere symbols. He said we'd never understand each other if we were going to be content with that. It wasn't enough to say he was English and I was Indian, that he was ruler and I was one of the ruled. We had to find out what that meant. [For what would happen] if both of us recognized each other's claims to equal rights as human beings? Nothing would happen. Neither of us would learn a thing about our true selves.[6]

Even as Merrick proceeds on the path of discovery, though, its 'meaning' slips away from him. He sets out a critique of the Raj and its ruling elite that seeks to deconstruct its sentimental notions of sympathy and admiration for Indians into an absolute binarism expressed in 'the contempt on [Merrick's] side and the fear on [Kumar's] that was basic' (*Scorpion*: 307). Merrick believes that a person's 'true self' is based on the knowledge of where he stands in relation to this binary division. For Merrick, the assumption of equality between British and Indian is a liberal corruption and is ultimately only a pretence:

> The [Indian] man exercising bravery and loyalty was an inferior being and even when you congratulated him you had contempt for him. And at the other end of the scale when you thought about the kind of Englishmen who pretended to admire Indian intellectuals, pretended to sympathize with their national aspirations, if you were honest you had to admit that all they were admiring or sympathizing with was the black reflection of their own white ideals. Underneath the admiration and sympathy there was the contempt a people feel for a people who have learned things from them. The liberal intellectual Englishman was just as contemptuous of the Westernized educated Indian as the arrogant upper-class reactionary Englishman was of the fellow who blacks his boots and earns his praise. (*Scorpion*: 308)

Merrick's claim to a truer perception of the reality of the colonial relationship derives from his own socially ambiguous position within the Raj. His critique of the old Anglo-Indian elite centres on one of the key ideas in *The Raj Quartet*, the concept of *man-bap*. This is epitomised by Colonel Layton and Teddie Bingham, both of whom are officers of elite Indian regiments:

'*Man-bap*. I am your father and your mother. ... That act had been an inseparable part of [Layton's] life as a commander of Indian troops' (*Scorpion*: 344–5).[7] Merrick, of course, despises Layton for his acceptance of the 'maternal' side of this idea, for being a 'white man gone soft'. The values which it expresses call for some measure of complicity from the colonised subjects, that they acknowledge their position as 'children' within the loving, but firm embrace of the colonial parent. And yet Merrick, in seeking to break Kumar's individual personality, also seeks to reconfirm the dependence of the weaker 'partner' in the imperial relationship. Kumar, at least, is forced partially to fulfil this role:

> After I drank he told me I must say thank you, because he knew that if I were honest I'd admit I was grateful for the water. ... He would give me another drink of water. He would give it to me on the understanding that I was grateful for it, and would admit it. He pulled my head back again and put the cup close to my lips. Even while I was telling myself I'd never drink it and never say thank you I felt the water in my mouth. I heard myself swallow. He put the cup down and used both hands to turn my head to face him. He put his own head very close. We stared at each other. ... After a bit I heard myself say it.
>
> (*Scorpion*: 310)

The encounter between Kumar and Merrick, at its most radical level, confronts us with the fallacy of liberal paternalism, and the failure of the Raj to 'connect' with its colonial subjects. It is in this context that Scott situates such key elements of colonial anxiety as rape and riot. Kumar's experience in the cell is the direct result of Emergency laws, and the British giving up on their own rule of law. The riot that precedes it is not presented as simply an arbitrary upsurge of native violence and explicable in terms of anarchy, a colonial trope that goes back to the Mutiny. It is a signal that Britain's moral authority, and thus its time in India, had come to an end. During the riot, however destructive the Indians' actions are, they are never disconnected from the political events of British India in its last phase, and they reflect what we see in intense close-up in the enclosed space of the interrogation cell between Merrick and Kumar – the failure of British pretensions to liberalism in its overseas venture. The Anglo-Indian ruling class calls unavailingly on its now-bankrupt historic relationship with India to support its wavering faith in its own authority. At such moments, Scott draws attention to the absolute inability of the Raj to achieve a full 'imperial embrace'. In the intimate space of the prison cell, rendered in such detail, moreover, Scott identifies the crisis of imperialism with a crisis in the notion of an imperial, masculine 'Englishness' itself, and it is to this that we shall now turn.

Masculinity and homo-eroticism in *The Raj Quartet*

The Raj Quartet to a large extent confirms Sara Suleri's suggestion that it is 'evident that the colonial gaze is not directed to the inscrutability of an Eastern bride but to the greater sexual ambivalence of the effeminate groom'.[8] Merrick ridicules Bingham's belief in the idea of *man-bap* as sentimental weakness, and yet paradoxically he himself embodies its homo-erotic character. His identification with the Raj's imperial authority, and extreme wish to protect it is, ironically, at its closest to the Raj's psychological mainspring when he gives in to his own transgressive desires. Thus he covets the Indian's body both as carer and chastiser. As Kumar recalls:

> At one point he smeared his hands over my buttocks and showed me the blood on his palm. ... Then he smeared his hand on my genitals. ... Afterwards he came in alone with a bowl of water and a towel. My wrists and ankles were manacled to the legs of the charpoy. ... I was still naked. He bathed the lacerations.   (*Scorpion*: 310)

Merrick is both beater and bather of Kumar's naked buttocks, a quintessential representation of the homo-erotic nature of *man-bap*. This may appear to reaffirm that Merrick's freedom to act on his homo-erotic desire expresses the absolute nature of imperial power, its ability to dominate its supine colony. However, such a political relationship is no longer possible. The politically masterful aspect of imperial power is revealed throughout the novels to be under threat, both internally from the Indian people, and externally from the Japanese army. It is the vestiges of imperial power that allow Merrick, in the last moments of the Raj, to act out the fantasy of absolute mastery and the roles of ruler and ruled. But it is also his homo-erotic desire that undermines the very notions of masculine Englishness upon which the Raj was constructed. The complex nature of that desire is apparent. This is not the desire for domination of an India which is gendered as feminine, but of a male India that is weak and vulnerable. At the moment when the homo-erotic nature of the 'imperial embrace' might seem to reinforce notions of imperial power, then, its dissolution of a psychologically coherent, distinctively separate notion of imperial masculinity rebounds against the colonial Englishman.

This has two main implications in the quartet. Firstly, that the imperial relationship was not binarily separated into fixed positions of the masculine, civilised, intellectual in opposition to the feminine, disordered, emotional; and secondly, as a consequence, that the Indians were not so simply passively trapped in, or complicit with any such binarism. Suleri has pointed to the 'highly unsettling economy of complicity and guilt ... in operation between each actor on the colonial stage'.[9] However, we should bear in mind that, in the instance quoted, as Kumar is still chained and naked and has just been beaten, the complicity of the colonised subject and his admission of dependence is considerably undermined. The offer of protection and care from the colonial officer comes after the enactment of arbitrary power on the body of the Indian. Kumar, after a night in which he has some form of revelation about the ultimate inability of imperial authority to enforce his consent, chooses the only strategy available to him:

> He could ask his questions but there was no power on earth that said I had to answer them. He could try and probably succeed in making me answer them by using force, but it would be my weakness and not his strength that made me speak. So I came to a decision to go on saying nothing. I wouldn't answer his or anyone's questions except as it pleased me. I would never thank him again for a cup of water.
> (Scorpion: 312–13)

The coloniser's structure of desire manifests itself above all in Merrick's encounter with Aziz, a young Indian man, at the end of the Quartet. Here, at last, Merrick has a full sexual experience with another person. An old servant sees the youth leave Merrick's bedroom and comments: 'Colonel Sahib was with him, dressed in [his] Pathan clothes. ... He is at heart a Pathan, and Aziz is a fine sturdy boy. If I were not a dried-up old man I would be tempted myself'.[10] Count Bronowsky believes it to be Merrick's first homosexual experience, one which 'gave him a moment of profound peace' (Division: 571). As with his treatment of Kumar, however, the Englishman's encounter with the Indian male is deeply ambiguous. Merrick both makes love to, and violently beats Aziz. Despite the release of the Englishman's sexual desire and the additional orientalist element of his being dressed in Pathan costume while this occurs, the encounter is clearly not a simple fulfilment of western fantasies of the Orient, of sexual mythologies that can be casually played out in the empire but are prohibited at home. For, just as Merrick manipulates the homosexual contact between the English soldier Pinky and an Indian man in order to blackmail him, in his encounter with Aziz Merrick's sexuality is itself being controlled by others. In this case, by Indian nationalists: 'I think it is clear [Aziz] had been so instructed. Instructed to present himself, to stand there at the gate until Merrick had seen him. Also instructed to submit, without complaint, to whatever Merrick did' (*Division*: 568).

An interpretation derived from Said's theoretical position, for example, might locate this within a longstanding tradition of the repressed Englishman discovering his sexual identity in the East. However, Aziz takes part in the sexual encounter with Merrick, and suffers the beating from him, not because Indian men are there to be dominated and sexually possessed by Englishmen, but because of wider, political motives born out of the Emergency, the disintegration of the Raj, and the resistance of militant Indian opposition. Scott specifically draws attention to the absence of that reciprocating, consenting response from Indian men, both in terms of the sexual and the political demands made on them by the colonial rulers. Of the concluding image in *A Passage to India*, Richard Cronin has commented that whereas a heterosexual embrace is founded on a perception of difference, Fielding and Aziz 'join hands in recognition that they are both alike'.[11] We can see that *The Raj Quartet* has none of Forster's hope that recognition can mean a connection between Englishman and Indian. A homo-eroticised East is one that exists in the Englishman's own psychology, not an essential or intrinsic quality of an East he has discovered.

Merrick's brief recognition of sameness in the 'Other', paradoxically achieved through his sexual 'Otherness', has more to do with his own desire, than with any mutually recognised connection between the two. Far from being the perverted, 'bent' copper, though, Merrick embodies a vital ambiguity in the Englishness he so wants to protect. It would be easy, of course, to pass off Merrick's homo-erotic desires as the figurative mark of the outsider, and consequently, suggest that much of the horror of empire is projected onto him, leaving intact the honourable intentions and distinctive identity of the old elite, even as its failures are recognised.[12] But within the novel sequence, the members of that same elite are shown to be riven by the homo-erotic ambiguity which Merrick's interrogation of Kumar revealed at the heart of the concept of *man-bap*. It is in this sense that Merrick can be acknowledged by them as 'yes, our dark side, the arcane side' (*Scorpion*: 409).

The ideological construction of a masculine, imperial 'Englishness', of course, demands fixed psychological and sexual, as well as political, positions on both sides of the binary divide, and this is what *The Raj Quartet* seeks to deconstruct. The novel sequence confronts us with the sexual fragmentation of an English imperial identity which sought to represent itself as unified and fixed, while striving to repress the homo-erotic energies which lie at the root of the 'imperial embrace'. Merrick, in this sense, is the atavistic representative of those impulses that lead Bingham to his death, Colonel Layton to psychological collapse and the detached, liberal historian Guy Perron to a highly ambiguous encounter with Suleiman, Merrick's sidekick. Suleiman appears to be a stereotypical representative of the sexually corrupting Orient: 'the face clean-shaven but pock-marked. The eyes looked as though they were rimmed with kohl. A bazaar Pathan: handsome, predatory' (*Division*: 200). However, even with this apparently obvious orientalist representation of the decadent Eastern male by Scott, Suleiman is in fact playing the part that he thinks the European wants him to fulfil, rather than it being a reflection of what the Indian essentially is. He offers Perron 'whatever Sahib desires', but what Perron desires is far more complex than Suleiman is aware of.

Perron's reaction to Suleiman is extremely important for those who, like Schwarz, see him as Scott's liberal mouthpiece.[13] Perron continually needs to distinguish himself and the liberal values he represents, from Merrick. Yet his attitude to the native Suleiman is strikingly similar to Merrick's response to Kumar and Aziz. Perron, too, plays out on the body of an Indian male all the frustration, physical and sexual, of the Englishman in his empire. He wants to discover a legitimate reason to 'boot him in the arse. ... The arses of the Suleimans of India exist to be booted by British sergeants. It's traditional' (*Division*: 205). When the chance comes to put this into action the homo-erotic ambiguity resurfaces. Perron describes the fulfilment of his desire in some detail:

> As we approached the edge of the verandah my flat-palmed pushes became closed fist prods – not punches; but they brought his arms and hands from the appealing to the protective position. We established

a rhythm of prod and jerk and presently I grabbed his shoulders ...
steadied him ... and swung him round to face the way he was about
to go, which he did, borrowing rather than receiving thrust from the
sole of my bare foot, and adding some thrust of his own ... He fell,
rather heavily, spreadeagled, his lower body on the gravel and his
upper on the grass on the other side of the path. And lay there; winded
or pretending to be.   (*Division*: 245)

During this parodic version of sexual congress, Suleiman is like
Kumar and Aziz, not only passively open to the Englishman's
desire for power, but also the focus of his ambivalent sexual
feelings for the Indian male. If in the meeting with the colonial
male subject the Englishman desires an affirmation of his own
masculinity and his own stable identity as Englishman, what he
in fact discovers in himself is its antithesis.

In *The Raj Quartet* this is revealed in the Chillingborough
liberal intellectual, the Raj officer, and the grammar school
upstart alike. That is, they find their masculine English identity
represents not a given order of authority and mastery over the
colonised, but, in Joseph Bristow's phrase, a 'tremendous lack'.
It isn't there, the 'taxonomy of values enunciated by imperialist
discourse – virility, mastery, exploitation, action, leadership,
technology, progress',[14] has been emptied of meaning. Again,
the complex, 'postcolonial' identity of *The Raj Quartet* is seen
in its challenge to this taxonomy, which it reveals as being riddled
with ambiguity and contradiction.

**'Coming to the end of themselves': colonial disintegration
in *The Raj Quartet***

The previous section has emphasised the contradictions inherent
in the historical narrativisation of an imperial masculine identity.
In this section, I shall relate these to larger, objective historical
processes and the wider psychological responses which these
processes engendered in British India. The external pressures
for decolonisation, brought to a head by the Second World War,
bring out those contradictions which, Scott suggests, were all
along implicit in the psychology of empire. We must, though,
also examine the wider crisis within English imperial society,
which grew out of new metropolitan thinking about empire,
and the historical failure of imperialism to establish social and
political integration in England in the twentieth century.

The novel sequence opens with a series of events set in 1942, a momentous year for the history of the British empire. In January 1942, the 130,000 strong garrison in Singapore surrendered to a much smaller Japanese army. One of the most important pillars of power in the empire had been the maintenance of prestige, which underpinned the coloniser's assumption of his innate superiority over his subjects. As the historian Robert Blake has commented, 'that crushing blow by an Asiatic power was never forgotten. Britain's departure from India, Burma and Ceylon [five] years later was foreshadowed in this defeat'.[15] These events reverberate through the tetralogy. Teddie Bingham fails to re-integrate two Indian soldiers into the 'Muzzy Guides' after they defect to the Indian National Army, formed by the Japanese from Indian prisoners-of-war in Singapore. He refuses to believe that they could have a greater emotional attachment to something other than the regiment. He is, however, killed in his attempt to find them after their escape. Colonel Layton retreats into silence in the face of Britain's failure to protect India from Japanese attack, and the capture of large numbers of Indian and British troops.

Bingham and Layton, characters who represent the traditional values of the Raj, fail to understand the changed position of India, and Indians, after 1942. The Raj, refusing to share power with Indians, and following the loss of Singapore and Burma, the Quit India campaign, and the establishment of virtual martial law, is shown to be increasingly unable to present itself as an essentially benevolent and protective regime. The exercise of imperial power has become arbitrary, 'anything that offended was an offence. A man could be imprisoned without trial'. But there is no compensating security: 'what sort of Imperial power was it that could be chased out of Malaya and up through Burma by an army of yellow men? It was a question the Indians asked openly'.[16]

It is in this moment that we might see Scott as providing another version of Britain's 'finest hour'. At the time of metro-politan Britain's war, and eventual victory, against German tyranny, there was a simultaneous anxiety about the nature of empire and the identity of the nation. Churchill declared in November 1942 that 'we mean to hold our own. I have not become the King's First Minister in order to preside over the liquidation of the British Empire'.[17] But it was apparent that, as the war progressed, power was passing from the traditional imperial powers into the hands of new, anti-imperialist concerns.

The Second World War saw the role of dominant world power move to the Americans, who were committed to universal self-government and, by extension, the end of empire. Significantly, Britain's survival was increasingly dependent upon American military and industrial power. In Scott's novels, we see this subtle shift taking place. We learn, almost in passing, that one of the symbols of Raj authority, the Governor's summer residence in Pankot, was to be reopened not 'as a convalescent home for wounded British and Indian officers of all three services, but as a leave centre for American troops of non-commissioned rank'.[18]

Coupled with this was the development of new thinking on the nature of British society and empire from within the metropolitan centre itself. The Beveridge Report, published in December 1942, laid the basis of the welfare state and the National Health Service, and marked the shifting ideological climate. It provided the ideological underpinning of the Labour government's electoral success in 1945, and the election of that government rather than the war victor, Churchill, signalled a profound move away from Britain's role as an imperial power, and towards social democracy. Alongside the desire for a more democratic distribution of the spoils of victory the Attlee government believed that India must gain independence, a partial recognition of the incompatibility between aspirations towards social democracy and the role of imperial ruler.

Politically and psychologically, then, the events of 1942, and the years immediately after, led to a profound questioning of ideas about nation and class, in which empire had played a defining role over the previous century. In response to the perceived threats of social and political unrest, nationalism and imperialism had offered to many political thinkers a means of generating social integration and national renewal through consensus across class.[19] But what the empire seemed to promise had failed to be established. Thus, insofar as Merrick functions as an 'Other' within the Raj's elite society, he draws attention to the lack of social integration within the British themselves. There is no easily identifiable, all-embracing 'Englishness' that can be appealed to as a guarantor of identity, when it is in crisis. In this sense, Scott suggests, imperial English identity was always more fractured than it seemed to be, because the metropolitan society which it sprang from was itself fragmented.

Merrick is highly attuned to the nuances of class and race in the imperial setting, as much as the ruling elite are keenly aware that 'he's not quite our class' (*Division*: 365). It is the impossibility of his escaping his background, of course, which first makes him sensitive to Kumar's public school accent and air of English upper-class culture.[20] Perron's liberal sensibility sees them both as equally trapped in their different ways within the larger problem of being marginalised by the cultural centre. Kumar's privileged English background counts for nothing in India, whereas Merrick has been denied those privileges by the social hierarchy of his own country. To some extent, at least for Perron, this explains Merrick's brutality, for he has been denied that liberality of spirit that came with a Chillingborough education. As a consequence:

> Place Merrick at home, in England, and Harry Coomer abroad, in England, and it is Coomer on whom the historian's eye lovingly falls; he is our symbol of virtue. In England it is Merrick who is invisible. Place them there, in India, and the historian cannot see either of them. They have wandered off the guideline, into the jungle. But throw a spotlight on them and it is Merrick on whom it falls.
>
> (*Division*: 302)

Perron provides a critique of the failure of the ruling elite within England and the Raj to integrate its own socially marginalised elements. But it is one that intellectually distances the elite from its own role in creating this social division. One manifestation of this is when Perron says of Merrick, 'can't the fool see that nobody of the class he aspires to belong to has ever cared a damn about the empire' (*Division*: 208). The lower middle classes had subscribed to imperialism as a code of values that revolved around upper-class imperial notions of duty and sacrifice. The desire to belong to this code, and thus to the construction of 'Englishness' that it represented, was undermined by the very class that had originally established it. Perron, himself representative of the English ruling elite, absconds from India when things get too difficult, and refuses to accept the responsibility for the state in which India finds itself after 1947.[21]

Scott's characters are not permitted a comfortable withdrawal from empire. Ultimately, the various contradictory tensions within the construction of 'Englishness', and the weight of external, historical pressures upon it, are dramatised in the dissolution of a psychological coherence that occurs throughout the Raj. As a consequence, we see several of the main characters of *The Raj Quartet*, female as well as male, become psychologically fragmented by the experience of imperial power put to the test.

The death of Mabel Layton, for example, reflects an almost Conradian vision of the horror which permeates her experience of the Raj. Her tranquil last years, seemingly the fitting end to a life spent as a typical *burra memsahib* in the service of Empire, a true member of 'the ruling class in India' (*Towers*: 20), collapse into a moment of death that reveals something profoundly disturbing beneath the Raj's civilised surface. Her companion, Barbie Batchelor, tricks her way into the morgue and witnesses the death mask of the old ruling class: 'The eyes were open and looking directly at the doorway. The mouth was open too and from it a wail of pain and terror was emitting' (*Towers*: 238).

Batchelor's understanding of what this reveals is incomplete. It may be her 'first authentic vision of what hell was like' (*Towers*: 239), but what Mabel Layton's last terrible expression suggests is not so much a general metaphysical or religious comment on the world, as a specific commentary on the state of the Raj. Batchelor constantly muses over, while never finding out the meaning of, Mabel Layton's mumbled mentions in her sleep of 'Gillian Waller'. We are aware, though, that this name invokes Jallianwallah Bagh, the site of the Amritsar massacre of 1919. Whereas the man responsible, General Dyer, was widely applauded among the British for his actions, and a fund set up for him after he had been retired on half-pay, Mabel Layton sends money in support of the Indians who were killed. Clearly, beneath her distracted exterior, the memory of Amritsar continues to work on her. The horror inscribed on her face at the moment of death, then, has a specific political origin and connects the experience of the individual to those moments of colonial violence which provide an alternative narrative of empire to that which the Raj officially sought to establish for itself.

As *The Raj Quartet* progresses, the 'masculine public sphere' is increasingly disturbed not only by its own homo-erotic desires, but also by the 'irruption of the feminine/private'.[22] As Barbie Batchelor washes her hands, she is riveted by an image of 'the captains and the kings queuing to wash their own hands in Mr Maybrick's bowl after relieving themselves in Mr Maybrick's mahogany commode' (*Towers*: 219). The reduction in her mind of the pomp of empire to the mundane, coexists with a powerful vision of the hollowness of imperial rule. She was struck by 'this ordinariness, this shabbiness, this evidence of detritus behind the screens of imperial power and magnificence. The feeling she had was not of glory departing or departed but of its original and continuing irrelevance to the business of being in India' (*Towers*: 218). Following her vision of the death mask of Mabel Layton, Barbie Batchelor herself declines into speechless madness, which is traced in considerable detail in the significantly titled volume, *The Towers of Silence*.

In passing, we also hear the tale of Poppy Browning's daughter, whose husband had been killed in an earthquake with his Indian lover: 'a situation which [she] had celebrated by smothering her baby two days after it was born' (*Towers*: 256). Susan Layton, like Batchelor, retreats into a private world, after Bingham, her husband, is killed. Her role, as wife of an officer of the Raj, had conformed to the expectations of her family and peers, but she, like Poppy Browning's daughter, tries to kill her own child, and is committed to a psychiatric hospital. Her experience of life in the Raj leads her to posit an overwhelming question as to the nature of identity: 'But what am I? What am I? Why – there's nothing to me at all. Nothing. Nothing at all' (*Scorpion*: 342). In a strange echo of her comment on Merrick, Sarah Layton also sees in her sister a reflection of the larger disintegration of the Raj: 'we sense from the darkness in you the darkness in ourselves, a darkness and a death wish' (*Scorpion*: 491).

This extreme psychological distress can be seen both to pervade, and to be spurred on by, the political events leading to the end of empire. *The Raj Quartet* employs a set of images of disintegration, disorder and irrationality, which were traditionally used to represent the native societies encountered in the construction of empire. The novel sequence, however, turns such a tropology against the Raj itself. Ultimately, the rationality and psychological coherence underpinning the political and social order on which the empire was thought to be based, and which were meant to distinguish it from the colonised peoples and legitimise its right to rule, are the very qualities which, in crisis, are found to be lacking. That same English identity which had been constructed around the concept of a cohesive imperial nation, and which generated the corresponding tropes of its uncivilised and anarchic colonised 'Other', is all along at the point of fragmenting through its own internal sexual, psychological and cultural contradictions. Clearly, this claim for Scott's work as a reversal of colonial tropology, suggests he inhabits, at least in part, the aesthetic and discursive sphere of a postcolonial perspective. I shall conclude, then, by examining how this ambiguous position is inscribed at the level of form.

Conclusion: narrative form and *The Raj Quartet*

The Raj Quartet, in size and scope, seems to offer an epic vision of the end of empire. This has led some critics to make the comparison with Tolstoy.[23] It would be more useful, perhaps, to consider Scott's novel sequence as a challenge to the concept of the epic, that form most identified with the establishment of the nation's historical identity, for it questions the very idea of the nation in its imperial venture, and focuses instead on its unravelling.

It has been suggested that it is 'only the impudence of the trespasser, and the trespasser's master language which attempts to give an overall form to India'.[24] The four volumes of *The Raj Quartet*, however, are evidence that the story cannot be resolved or fitted together by a single voice. In this work, the undermining of a unified imperial identity is bound up with the disintegration of a univocal narrative perspective and, ultimately, the dismemberment of India itself. Despite its habitual inclusion in the 'Realist', or Tolstoyan tradition of the novel, *The Raj Quartet* is pluralistic in form, recounted through a polyphony of memoirs, letters, diaries, newspaper articles, political cartoons. Competing Indian 'voices', Hindu and Muslim, formulate a considerable amount of the narrative. Events, conversations, characters who have died, appear and reappear throughout the four volumes, viewed through different perspectives: for example, Teddie Bingham, whose memorial service takes place in *Scorpion* (pp. 337–43), takes an active part in the next volume, *Towers*, particularly in giving a detailed perspective on Merrick (see pp. 121–67).

The experience of India, then, is not imposed from an authoritative narrative centre; indeed, the unfixed and shadowy narrator, located in the post-imperial world of the 1960s, lacks all authority to fully understand the history he attempts to piece together. The narrative power which, Said suggests, enables western writers to represent 'what is beyond metropolitan borders',[25] is itself deconstructed in the decentred narrative authority of *The Raj Quartet*. This is due to the contrapuntally disruptive presence of those 'other' voices, which resist the binary structures of an active, masculine West that dominates a passive, feminine East. But it is also a result of the quartet's refusal to present a disintegrating imperial society within a traditional, linear narrative framework. The novel sequence does not seek to recuperate the

Raj into a world of privileged knowledge and meaning via the epistemological implications of the 'Realist' novel form; rather, the novel sequence's fragmentations are intimately linked with the themes of political and psychological dissolution.

Although it is narrated from a present time of 1964, *The Raj Quartet* tumbles dramatically and inexorably towards midnight of 14–15 August 1947, and thus anticipates another dialogic 'epic' of the subcontinent, *Midnight's Children*, for which that date is the catalyst. *The Raj Quartet* turns its vast energies upon analysing why, historically, the British were politically and psychologically unable to live up to the role they had designated for themselves (and which, we have suggested, is explored in microscopic close-up in the relationship of Merrick, Bingham, Perron and Layton to their Indian subordinates). By the end of the tetralogy, it is the fragmentation of the subcontinent into inter-religious massacres, and two separate nation states, that is seen as the most disastrous outcome of the Raj's misconception of its role in India. The retreating members of the old Raj interpret the violence of India at independence as a confirmation of its innate propensity to anarchy: ' "Savages", a woman was saying. And a man, "What do you expect? It's only the beginning. Once we've gone they'll all cut each other's bloody throats" ' (*Division*: 586). But we have already had an opposing Indian view, from Mohammed Ali Kasim, a senior Muslim politician: ' "communalism has been written into our political structure by the raj" ' (*Division*: 444). The terrible destruction during independence cannot be blamed on innate Indian cultural failings, but on the specific political agenda undertaken by the British.

The ultimate act of violence perpetrated by the Raj is the dismemberment of India, achieved in bloodshed and mayhem. As with Merrick's racial and sexual attitudes towards Kumar, we can see this at its most powerfully resonant when it is acted out on the body of an Indian man. At the end of the *Quartet*, Ahmed Kasim, travelling in a first-class compartment full of the departing English, calmly steps out of the train, to be dismembered by a crowd of Hindu extremists. It is a violent pre-enactment of Saleem Sinai's physical disintegration in *Midnight's Children*, both characters' fragmented bodies functioning as paradigms of India's entrance into the postcolonial world. In Scott's novel sequence, though, the British are not only the cause of such terrible violence, but have also, typically, absolved themselves of responsibility for it. At the end, it is Kasim who acts out the

image of the old phlegmatic Raj, just as the absconding represen-
tatives of the Raj want nothing more to do with such matters:

> I'm sure he smiled just before he went, and I'm sure he said, 'It seems
> to be me they want.' Major Peabody said he thought he said, 'Make
> sure you lock it after me.' Perhaps we all heard only what we wanted
> to hear. Perhaps there was nothing to hear because he said nothing,
> but just smiled and went ...   (*Division*: 593)

The Raj Quartet, then, provides a final ironic reversal of an
essential moment of twentieth-century imperial mythology, as
Ahmed Kasim responds to adversity in the manner of Captain
Oates at the South Pole, leaving the tent for certain death in
order to help the chances of the remaining members of Robert
Scott's expedition. He 'died a very gallant gentleman', Robert
Scott recorded in his diary, and Oates became one of the defining
figures of English heroism. Kasim's selfless act, of course, is a
gesture that seems to facilitate the safe passage of the departing
Raj, as the English move into a time where imperial mythologies,
which had once offered fictions of clearly definable moral and
political action, are no longer available. At the same time, however, such gestures are themselves ironic, futile repetitions of
roles which no longer have relevance, but are difficult to escape.
As Sarah Layton reflects, while filling up pots of water in the
aftermath of the massacre on the train:

> it was driven home to me that what I was doing was just as useless
> as what he'd just done ... And I hated Ahmed for not keeping the door
> locked and telling us he damned well wasn't going to die unless they
> smashed right through the windows and slaughtered the lot of us ...
> But when it came to it he didn't let any of it even begin to happen to
> us ... there wasn't any alternative, because everyone in the carriage
> automatically knew what he had to do. It was part of the bloody code.
>   (*Division*: 592–3)

It is the way the British left India, then, that most diminishes
them, and as a result, from Scott's perspective in 1964, they
are left rootless in history. The most problematic issue in the
empire was one they never addressed; the extent to which the
English were created, racially and nationally, by their involvement in India and in empire more generally. Hovering behind
Merrick's and Bingham's actions is the question of what it was
to be English, and how far 'Englishness' was in fact defined by
the relationship with its colonial 'Other'. What follows from
this, of course, is the problematic issue of in what form an English

identity can be reconstructed to meet the new conditions of the postcolonial era.

In his final novel, *Staying On*, which can, perhaps, best be read as a conclusion to *The Raj Quartet*, the focus on the English in India, twenty-five years after the end of the Raj, has narrowed to two minor characters from *The Raj Quartet*, Lucy and Tusker Smalley. The narrative tone is relentlessly and appropriately ironic. A new Indian elite has replaced the Raj. The Smalleys, who had desperately sought acceptance from the upper-class elite, such as Mildred Layton, and willingly ingested their narrowest views about India, and the non-pukka English, are now living on a small pension, harried by their Indian landlady, and deprived of status and authority. Rose Cottage, an embodiment in *The Raj Quartet* of the Laytons' elite position in the Raj, is now owned by a Mrs Menaktara, and 'crammed with priceless carvings and statuettes that make it look as if they've raided a Hindu temple'.[26] In the Smalleys' grim attempt to hold onto lost certainties, we are witness to a final interrogation of what decolonisation means for the British, for these leftovers of the Raj enjoy little security or superiority through their English identity now. They still feel they have to conform to a stereotypical imperial image of the 'white man' abroad, although it is beyond their means, and in an India that has moved on. Indeed, as Lucy Smalley perceives, the very notion of the role of 'white man' is pervaded by insecurity and ambivalence:

> [I sometimes feel] that my whole life has been a lie, a mere play-acting ... I need [a catalyst] to bring me back into my own white skin which day by day, week by week, month by month, year after year, I have felt to be increasingly incapable of containing me, let alone of acting as defensive armour.[27]

It was in the overseas venture above all that the attempt to construct a specific English identity took place, based on an imperial role, and forged in the encounter with a racial and cultural 'other'. And, of course, it was in India that this long historical enterprise was most symbolically potent, and most signally collapsed. Scott's novels, at a radical psychological, political and narrative level, examine what that involved for a model of Englishness that was formed over centuries of English imperial control. Ultimately, the notion that starts the whole novel sequence, that Britain and India were 'locked in an imperial embrace of such long standing and subtlety it was no longer possible to know ... what it was that held them together' (*Jewel*: 9), flatters Britain's centrality and historical importance to India as it approaches independence at the end of the war. As the Raj comes to an end, what many of the characters reluctantly perceive is its – and their own – irrelevance, their own marginality, which their temporary rule in India had concealed: 'the dispiriting fact had not escaped them [of] the terrible bleakness – thinness – that settled upon and somehow defined anyone whose connexion had been severed' (*Towers*: 320). That severance, which the 'imperial embrace' seemed to promise would not occur, was about to affect all of them, and finally revealed the British as what they always were, 'people from the small and distant island' (*Scorpion*: 10).

Notes

1 Salman Rushdie, 'Outside the Whale', in *Granta*, 11 (1984), p. 127.

2 Edward W. Said, *Orientalism* (London: Routledge and Kegan Paul, 1978), p. 6.

3 Joseph Bristow, *Empire Boys: Adventures in a Man's World* (London: Harper Collins, 1991), pp. 225–6.

4 It is worth noting how Kumar's experience both parallels and reverses that of Lawrence of Arabia, who suffers a similar assault by the Turkish Governor at Deraa. Lawrence dresses up in native garb, and can successfully convince the Turkish enemy that he is a native (thus taking his place in the tradition of Englishmen who can inhabit the native's identity, from Richard Burton to Kipling's 'Kim'). In Deraa, however, his imperial identity disintegrates: 'that night the citadel of my integrity had been irrevocably lost', *Seven Pillars of Wisdom* (Harmondsworth: Penguin, 1973), pp. 450–6. Just as Lawrence inhabits and undermines the role of imperial hero, Merrick and Kumar draw out the ironic nature of an imperial heroic venture in India. Merrick, too, makes trips to the bazaar in native dress in order to spy on subversives, and yet these are held up finally to be no more than self-delusion, 'mere bits of play-acting', as Count Bronowsky believes. Merrick, then, is an ironically conflated version of Lawrence as imperial hero with that of the sadistic Turkish Governor who assaulted him; while Kumar is an ironic reversal of the figure of Lawrence, assaulted by the sexually corrupt 'Oriental'.

5 Bill Schwarz, 'An Englishman Abroad ... And At Home: The Case of Paul Scott', in *New Formations*, 17 (Summer 1992), p. 97. The gardens are 'ominously named', of course, because it echoes the Bibighar massacre of women and children at Cawnpore in 1857.

6 *The Day of the Scorpion*, pp. 307, 309–10. Hereafter referred to as *Scorpion*, with page references given in the text.

7 See K. Bhaskara Rao's comment that '*man-bap* reaffirmed the superiority of the English-man, gave him renewed faith in his infallibility. *Man-bap*, with its condescending paternalism, was an important aspect of British racism in India', *Paul Scott* (Boston: Twayne Publishers, 1980), p. 113.

8 Sara Suleri, *The Rhetoric of English India* (Chicago: Chicago University Press, 1992), p. 16.

9 Suleri, p. 3.

10 Paul Scott, *A Division of the Spoils* (London: Granada, 1977), p. 567. Hereafter referred to as *Division*, with page references given in the text.

11 Richard Cronin, *Imagining India* (London: Macmillan, 1989), p. 153.

12 See Cronin, p. 154, for example, as well as Salman Rushdie's deprecation of Scott: 'Like [M.M.] Kaye, he has an instinct for the cliche. Sadistic, bottom-flogging police-man Merrick turns out to be (surprise!) a closet homosexual. His grammar-school origins give him (what else?) a chip on his shoulder', Rushdie, p. 127.

13 Bill Schwarz's comment that 'there is little doubt ... that Scott's own embattled liberal sentiments find fullest expression in the ... gentle, skeptical historian Guy Perron', (p. 101), seems to take the narrative persona at face value. In a novel of such complexity of narrative voice, and of such severe interrogation of English liberal values, this conflating of author and one of his narrators may seem dangerously naive.

14 Benita Parry, 'Problems in Current Theories of Colonial Discourse', in *Oxford Literary Review*, 9 (1987), p. 55.

15 Robert Blake, *The Decline of Power: 1915–1964* (London: Paladin, 1986), p. 259.

16 Paul Scott, *The Jewel in the Crown* (London: Granada, 1973), pp. 134, 168. Hereafter referred to as *Jewel*, with page references given in the text.

17 Clive Ponting, *Churchill* (London: Sinclair and Stevenson, 1994), pp. 689–90.

18 Paul Scott, *The Towers of Silence* (London: Granada, 1973), p. 348. Hereafter referred to as *Towers*, with page references given in the text. See also Scott's earlier novel, *The Alien Sky*, set in June 1947: 'the British are going and now it's [America's] turn. Whether you like it or not, all they're doing here is exchanging the Union Jack for the dollar sign' (London: Pan, 1953), pp. 31–2.

19 It may be seen that the growing concern with the empire, and its expansion in the latter part of the nineteenth century, may be in large part explained by the concern for the integrity of Britain itself. The imperial ideal of Cecil Rhodes, for example, was that the empire provided a 'solution for the social problem, i.e., in order to save the 40,000,000 inhabitants of the United Kingdom from a bloody civil war, we colonial statesmen must acquire new lands to settle the surplus population to provide new markets for the goods produced in the factories and the mines'. Quoted in Bernard Porter, *Critics of Empire* (London: Macmillan, 1968), pp. 46–7.

20 See *Jewel*, pp. 143–59.

21 As the events of the novel bear out, Ronald Merrick will prove to be an extreme defender of the Raj, and willing to take whatever action he thinks necessary in order to protect it. In this sense, he is a later version of General Dyer, the British officer responsible for the Amritsar massacre. As an Indian character says of Dyer, 'Why do you call that man a monster? He believed God had charged him with a duty to save the empire' (*Scorpion*: p. 70). The irony of Merrick's actions, of course, is that, like Dyer, he is, historically speaking, too late.

22 Schwarz, p. 103.

23 See Francine S. Weinbaum, *Paul Scott: A Critical Study* (Texas: University of Texas Press, 1992), p. 191, for example. Scott was deeply upset by a review of the *Quartet* by Anthony Thwaite in the *Observer*, who criticised its 'overall lack of essential spark, so that what I suppose aims to be ... something with Tolstoyan impact gives off a Galsworthian smell of over-furnished blandness'. Quoted in Hilary Spurling, *Paul Scott: A Life* (London: Hutchinson, 1990), p. 370.

24 Cronin, p. 25.

25 Edward W. Said, *Culture and Imperialism* (New York: Knopf, 1993), p. 66.

26 Paul Scott, *Staying On* (London: Granada, 1978), p. 111.

27 *Ibid*.

Bibliography

Blake, Robert, *The Decline of Power: 1915–1964* (London: Paladin, 1986).

Bristow, Joseph, *Empire Boys: Adventures in a Man's World* (London: Harper Collins, 1991).

Cronin, Richard, *Imagining India* (London: Macmillan, 1989).

JanMohamed, Abdul, *Manichean Aesthetics: The Politics of Literature in Colonial Africa* (Amherst: University of Massachusetts Press, 1983).

Lawrence, T. E., *Seven Pillars of Wisdom* (Harmondsworth: Penguin, 1973).

Parry, Benita, 'Problems in Current Theories of Colonial Discourse', in *Oxford Literary Review*, 9 (1987).

Ponting, Clive, *Churchill* (London: Sinclair and Stevenson, 1994).

Porter, Bernard, *Critics of Empire* (London: Macmillan, 1968).

Rao, K. Bhaskara, *Paul Scott* (Boston: Twayne Publishers, 1980).

Rushdie, Salman, 'Outside the Whale', in *Granta*, 11 (1984).

Said, Edward W., *Culture and Imperialism* (New York: Knopf, 1993).

—— *Orientalism* (London: Routledge and Kegan Paul, 1978).

Schwarz, Bill, 'An Englishman Abroad ... And At Home: The Case of Paul Scott', in *New Formations*, 17 (Summer 1992).

Scott, Paul, *A Division of the Spoils* (London: Granada, 1977).

—— *Staying On* (London: Granada, 1978).

—— *The Alien Sky* (London: Pan, 1953).

—— *The Day of the Scorpion* (London: Granada, 1973).

—— *The Jewel in the Crown* (London: Granada, 1973).

—— *The Towers of Silence* (London: Granada, 1973).

Spurling, Hilary, *Paul Scott: A Life* (London: Hutchinson, 1990).

Suleri, Sara, *The Rhetoric of English India* (Chicago: Chicago University Press, 1992).

Weinbaum, Francine S., *Paul Scott: A Critical Study* (Texas: University of Texas Press, 1992).

9

Salman Rushdie: from colonial politics to postmodern poetics

TIM PARNELL

> [W]hat is being disputed is nothing less than *what is the case*, what is truth and what untruth.[1]
>
> Doubt ... is the central condition of a human being in the 20th century.[2]

In spite of the range of commentary on Rushdie's growing corpus, critics have returned regularly to the problem of what Kumkum Sangari has called the 'double coding'[3] of the novels. For many commentators, *Midnight's Children, Shame* and *The Satanic Verses* exhibit a schizophrenia which results from Rushdie's efforts to address both a western and a subcontinental readership. Unsurprisingly, the dilemma is one Rushdie appears to be keenly aware of. In an oft-quoted passage, in the second chapter of *Shame*, Rushdie has his narrator articulate some of the tensions endemic in his position by anticipating, with some prescience, the kind of response which has characterised many readings of the novels:

> *Outsider! Trespasser! You have no right to this subject!* ... I know: nobody ever arrested me. Nor are they ever likely to. *Poacher! Pirate! We reject your authority. We know you with your foreign language wrapped around you like a flag: speaking about us in your forked tongue, what can you tell but lies!*[4]

Such a pre-emptive strike may bespeak confidence as much as anxiety, yet the issues involved go beyond the Indian writer's ambivalent relationship with the language of the erstwhile coloniser. Rushdie writes with a 'forked tongue' not only because of his 'translated'[5] status as a Bombay-born Muslim who has lived most of his adult life in England, but because the novels self-consciously partake of Euro-American as well as Indian literary traditions. Such traditions do not simply offer the author a set of neutral narrative techniques, but are saturated by the value-systems of the cultures from which they spring. Because the 'flag' which envelops the novels is inscribed not only with the English language but also with the conventions of western literature, it inevitably evokes some of the baggage of colonialism and hints at a potential complicity in an insidious, ongoing, cultural imperialism. Dangerous as it is to generalise about such vast groupings as 'western' and 'subcontinental' audiences, the perceived tensions in the novels between different ways of seeing are, in part, explicable in terms of the culturally specific responses of distinct readerships. Yet it remains difficult to dismiss the problem in terms of Eurocentric misreadings of the 'trilogy'.[6]

While Rushdie himself has argued for the liberating possibilities afforded by the 'literary migrant['s]' (*Imaginary Homelands*: 21) freedom to mix traditions, others have seen the resulting *mélange* as fractured by the collision between *incompatible* 'structures of feeling'. In re-presenting the subcontinent in the familiar idioms of postmodernist fiction, Rushdie not only brings into focus the temporal simultaneity of postmodernity and the postcolonial, but raises important questions about the relationship between the two discourses.[7] It is clearly reductive to seek to 'explain' the novels in terms of a polarised debate, particularly when neither 'postmodernism' nor 'postcolonialism' can be reduced to a neat monolith. But the terms can usefully describe constellations of politically charged ideas and discourses which impinge upon an understanding of many of the peculiar features of the trilogy. Thus, before turning to the novels themselves it is important to outline some of the theoretical issues at stake in a bit more detail.

Postmodernist theory and postcolonial politics

To some extent, Rushdie's simultaneous engagement with postmodernist poetics and postcolonial politics can encourage important discriminations between varieties of postmodernism. But because the extreme scepticism of much postmodernist thought has arisen in the West alongside a massively diminished faith in the real possibility of political action, radical textual strategies have often been seen as bespeaking little more than a gestural politics of despair. While for some this makes it impossible for postmodernism and politics to cohabit, others have argued that the nexus should bring about a reassessment of the effects and strategies of postmodernist fiction. Linda Hutcheon, for example, argues that the negative view fails to take account of the fact that postmodernism is best able to reveal the contingent and constructed nature of oppressive discourses, which have hitherto masqueraded as 'common sense' or timeless human truths. For Hutcheon, part of the problem is that the 'postmodern' is often ill-defined and so she advocates a more precise definition in which the term describes 'art which is paradoxically self-reflexive ... and yet grounded in historical actuality'.[8] I will return to Hutcheon's reading of the politics of postmodernism in due course, but for the time being it is worth stressing the inadequacy of most general accounts of postmodern poetics when it comes to the specifics of particular texts. While even to talk of 'Euro-American' postmodernism is to generalise reductively, to subsume Carter's feminist fictions or Marquez's and Rushdie's novels into a universal 'crisis of representation'[9] is to elide the specificity of their cultural location and political engagement. As Sangari points out in her illuminating discussion of Marquez and Rushdie, their narrative strategies 'inhabit a social and conceptual space in which the problems of ascertaining meaning assume a political dimension qualitatively different from the current postmodern scepticism about meaning in Europe and America'.[10]

To describe Rushdie as a postcolonial writer can be a neutral description of fact or can create another pigeonhole within which to contain the disparate energies of the texts.[11] This caveat accepted, the term does encompass what are surely the central concerns of Rushdie's novels. Indeed, Rushdie has described his own project in terms of a 'determination to create a literary language and literary forms in which the experience of formerly colonized, still-disadvantaged peoples might find full expression' (Imaginary Homelands: 394). But whether 'postcolonial' is employed in its relatively neutral sense to describe the condition of the former colonies, or to denote, in Stephen Slemon's words, 'a specifically anti- or post-colonial discursive purchase in culture',[12] the category calls forth issues of identity, of political agency and of value, in a manner which appears to bring it into direct conflict with the centreless scepticism of much postmodernist theory and practice. For some critics, it is not just that Rushdie adopts relativising discursive strategies which threaten to dismantle the very critique which he articulates, but that such strategies are implicated within a peculiarly western way of seeing.[13] Tim Brennan, for example, has argued that the discourse of postmodernity can be read 'allegorically' as a means by which 'the decline in Western dominance [is described] as a crisis in European art'.[14] The issue here is the degree to which the techniques of postmodernist fiction can be said to carry with them the culturally specific ideologies which grow out of the late-capitalist West. In this reading, Rushdie's affiliations with the poetics and philosophical underpinnings of postmodernity make him vulnerable to accusations of inappropriately applying the world-view of a moribund post-colonising culture to the post-colonised cultures of India and Pakistan.

Even if we set aside this ideological conflict between 'First-' and 'Third-' world ways of seeing, problems remain at a more abstract theoretical level. In an important essay – 'Postmodernism or Post-Colonialism Today'[15] – Simon During clearly outlines the ambivalence of the relationship between the two discourses. For During, the most positive aspect of 'postmodern thought' in terms of postcoloniality is that it 'refuses to turn the Other into the Same'. In deconstructing the opposition between centre and margin the various discourses of postmodernism are able to provide 'a theoretical space for what postmodernity denies: otherness'. Yet, at the same time such thinking suggests that 'the Other can never speak for itself *as* the Other'.[16] Paradoxically, then, the deconstructive drive of postmodernist theory is at once enabling and disabling in terms of postcolonial identity.

While this impasse may appear to be unresolvable, it has been possible for some to adopt the kind of pragmatic position recommended by Slemon in his own discussion of the relationship between the two discourses. Such a compromise would enable postcolonial criticism to 'draw on post-structuralism's suspension of the referent in order to read the social "text" of colonialist power and at the same time would reinstall the referent in the service of colonized and post-colonial societies'.[17] That Slemon is negotiating the different terms on which postcolonial texts need to be *read* within the rubrics of postmodern reading strategies is suggestive. Because both postcolonial texts and criticism often draw upon the same idioms as their 'disinterested' postmodernist counterparts, a radical – if uneasy – rethinking of the ramifications of postmodernist scepticism becomes necessary. Rather than rejecting a scepticism which is potentially so all-encompassing as to preclude the very possibility of postcolonial identity and agency, Slemon attempts, instead, to set significant limits on the free play of the signifier.

Once postmodernism is seen not as a world-view, but as offering a set of literary and theoretical *strategies* which can assault the certainties of oppressive discourses, the positive aspects of postmodern thought for a rethinking of postcolonised subjectivities becomes clearer. In recent years much postcolonial theory has moved towards a conception of a hybrid cultural identity which stands outside the oppressive binarism of self and other that helped validate both the imperial project and the post-colonial project in its early stages.[18] Thus, Edward Said locates the 'potential for an emergent non-coercive culture'[19] in the alternative discourses of Woolf's *A Room of One's Own, Midnight's Children* and Toni Morrison's *Tar Baby* and *Beloved*. In a passage which finds many parallels in Rushdie's own comments on the political implications of his chosen narrative strategies, Said describes the distinction between these texts and the discourses of patriarchy, imperialism and racism which they seek to subvert:

> These are not new master discourses, strong new narratives, but ... another way of telling. When photographs or texts are used merely to establish identity and presence – to give us merely representative images of *the* Woman, or *the* Indian – they enter what Berger calls a control system. With their innately ambiguous, hence negative and anti-narrativist waywardness *not* denied, however, they permit unregimented subjectivity to have a social function.[20]

It is in this light that we can begin to understand why Rushdie is able, on the one hand, to condemn the kind of narcissistic postmodernism of a novel like Eco's *Foucault's Pendulum*, and on the other to embrace the postmodern fragmentation of truth.[21] For Homi Bhabha, like Rushdie and Said, the end of the Enlightenment metanarratives need not lead to quietist despair but can open up 'the enunciative boundaries of a range of other dissonant, even dissident histories and voices – women, the colonized, minority groups, the bearers of policed sexualities'.[22] On such ground the concerns of postmodernism and postcolonial criticism interpenetrate rather than collide.

In a real sense the debate that I have outlined must remain just that – a dialogue between productively conflicting voices. To attempt a resolution of the issues themselves through a neatly closed reading of the novels is neither possible nor desirable. But the inevitable generalisations of a debate treating complex abstractions are best tested and qualified by the texts which they seek to describe. Reading Rushdie as a postmodernist or a post-colonial writer is, in part, a matter of stressing one set of concerns over another. However, in their very cross-cultural hybridity, the novels enact a dialogue between discourses which raises important questions about Rushdie's relationship with both Indian and western traditions. It is, therefore, productive to address the question of the discursive location of the novels, before looking more closely at particular problems which result from Rushdie's intertextual strategies and his deployment of the conventions of what Hutcheon has called 'historiographic metafiction'.[23]

Hybridity and eclecticism: the problem of mixed traditions

> Eclecticism, the ability to take from the world what seems fitting and to leave the rest, has always been the hallmark of the Indian tradition. (*Imaginary Homelands*: 67)

In an interview given in Denmark just after the publication of *Shame*, Rushdie takes some pains to counter what he perceives to be misreadings of his work. Keen to resist dominant western readings of the novels, he stresses the importance of Indian traditions for a full understanding of *Midnight's Children* and *Shame*. Rushdie explains how Indian oral storytelling influenced his own narrative modes, how the Hindu god Ganesh 'stands behind Saleem',[24] and how the forms of the novels might be meaningfully compared to the architectural principles of the Hindu temple.

While it is no doubt true that many western readers can read the novels and remain blithely unaware of the importance of Indian traditions and the extent of Rushdie's engagement with real events, the degree to which the texts encourage partial readings cannot be ignored. Dangerous as it is to underestimate the capacities of readers to respond to genuinely new forms, it is also true that generic conventions and the recognition of family resemblances between texts significantly inform – either tacitly or consciously – reader responses. Because, at a formal level, the novels are characterised by an eclectic blending of genres, modes and motifs drawn from Indian, English and international 'traditions', the reader is, in part, licensed to emphasise any one element in his or her reading without feeling that they have failed to grasp the whole. Clearly, as Saleem Sinai comments of Padma, no 'audience is without its idiosyncrasies of belief',[25] but this situation is exacerbated in the trilogy by Rushdie's simultaneous address to English, Indian, Pakistani and diverse international readers. I will consider how the novels' intertextual strategies open them to an easy assimilation into western postmodernist traditions in due course. For the time being it is instructive to glance at some aspects of the critical debate around the novels in order to understand why what might, in other contexts, be celebrated as a laudable cultural pluralism or be put down to the ambiguities endemic to literary discourse, becomes peculiarly problematic in Rushdie's case.

In his discussion of the reception of *Midnight's Children* and *Shame*, Aleid Fokkema divides critical responses into readings which tend to stress one of the following features: the 'literariness of the text ... the identity, or nationality, of the writer, and ... the political and satirical strategies employed in [the] texts'.[26] As well as identifying the way in which a particular emphasis produces quite different readings, Fokkema highlights the political nature of almost any response to Rushdie. Rushdie's identity and his thematic concerns – including not only a critique of British imperialism (past *and* present), but also a damning indictment of the failures of India's and Pakistan's post-Independence leaders – mean that there is no such thing as a purely 'innocent' literary-critical reading of the novels. The western critic who stresses the 'Indianness' of Rushdie's novels is in danger of subscribing to an orientalist notion of otherness, and of ignoring the fact that the Indian novel in English has a colonial past. And yet, the focus on his transnational or 'cosmopolitan' location has led to criticisms of Rushdie for commenting on the postcolonial subcontinent 'from the comfort of the observation tower'.[27] Short of naively claiming that novels have nothing to do with the world, there is no meaningful context for the trilogy which is not also a site of conflict.

Because of his direct engagement with the postcolonial subcontinent Rushdie has come to occupy a central position within what Aijaz Ahmad has called the 'counter-canon' of 'Third-World' literature. Unsurprisingly, as a consequence the novels have been subject to kinds of scrutiny seldom afforded to texts within the more 'comfortable' canon of 'English Literature'. In this respect, Ahmad's questioning of the sometimes limited agenda imposed by the formation of the 'Third World' canon is apropos. What troubles Ahmad is that the 'range of questions that may be asked of the texts ... within this categorical counter-canon must predominantly refer ... in one way or another to representations of colonialism, nationhood, post-coloniality, the typology of rulers, their powers, corruptions, and so forth'. The issue, for Ahmad, is not that these questions are irrelevant but that because the agenda comes prior to analysis of the object of inquiry it can preclude 'other kinds of questionings'.[28] Notwithstanding that Ahmad's critique of Rushdie is as trenchant as any, his warnings about reading the novels simply within the terms of questions which have their own inexorable and interested logic are salutary. Because of their location within the discourse of postcolonialism the texts are, perhaps, often made to bear more political weight than they can actually sustain. The expectation that the novels *will* register – explicitly or implicitly – the full complexities of the condition of postcoloniality can, as we shall see, lead to some strained readings.

Since Rushdie is apparently self-evidently a postcolonial writer, writing in English *about* India and Pakistan, he is inevitably sometimes read in the context of the traditions – colonial and postcolonial – of English India. Such a contextualisation is clearly valid, but Sara Suleri's recent reading of *Shame* and *The Satanic Verses* points to some of the pitfalls of subsuming the novels within the terms of a particular conception of postcolonial discourse. Having set up a complex, if surprisingly homogeneous, narrative of how the 'rhetoric of English India' consistently 'bears testimony to the dynamic of powerlessness underlying the telling of colonial stories',[29] Suleri is able to find plenty of supporting evidence in her interpretation of *Shame*. However, the very fact that this 'rhetoric' is so vast as to encompass both British and Indian texts, from the eighteenth to the twentieth century, might alone give us pause for thought. Yet because Suleri appears to view the 'rhetoric of English India' as a Foucauldian 'discourse' in which the 'delimitation of a field of objects, the definition of a legitimate perspective for the agent of knowledge, and the fixing of norms for the elaboration of concepts and theories'[30] is already predetermined by the complex interweavings of colonial *power*, it is impossible for her to imagine a situation in which Rushdie might think, or write, outside such a discourse. Consequently, narrative strategies which Rushdie quite deliberately 'borrows' and appropriates from writers such as Grass, Kundera and Marquez are not read as such, but are seen rather as 'paradigmatic of the casualties frequently accrued by contemporary postcolonial writing'.[31] The perceived power of the 'rhetoric of English India' is such that Suleri is able not only to account for 'Rushdie's complications of tone' simply in terms of postcolonial history, but to posit an insidious anxiety of influence in which *Shame* bespeaks 'the great embarrassment of what it must mean to be fathered by *Kim*'.[32] In this model, the discourse of which the English 'Novel of Empire' partakes *determines* Indian post-colonial writing in English to the degree that Rushdie's texts can only be read as seismographs which passively register a despairing rhetoric of anxiety. Thus, while Suleri's reading of the novels is frequently insightful, the theoretical underpinnings of her approach deny the rather more obvious possibility that Rushdie's *chosen* textual practices sit uneasily with his political agenda. Likewise, the fact that Rushdie *consciously* alludes to Kipling and other novelists of Empire is ignored. This is not to argue that postcolonial politics do not complicate the tone of the novels, but to suggest that a symptomatic reading of this kind can obscure instead of clarifying an understanding of Rushdie's quite deliberate adoption of hybrid forms. To accept with Suleri that Rushdie's novels are implicated within the complicated network of colonial and postcolonial Anglo-Indian texts is not to agree that their peculiar *rhetoric* can be best understood in these terms.

The real sense in which the ambivalence of the trilogy is deter-mined less by the discursive formation of English India and more by the postmodernist rhetoric which Rushdie deploys is suggested clearly in the instance of the novels' self-conscious intertextual play. Like most aspects of Rushdie's practice, this one is open to at least a double reading: the one positive and tied to postcolonial politics, and the other negative and viewed in terms of common readings of western postmodernism as politically disengaged. But, because the very characteristics which appear to link the novels with a postcolonial oppositional discourse – parodic citation, a hotch-potch of cultural 'traditions', the problematisa-tion of the single-vision of the oppressors through a privileging of fragmentary vision – are also the hallmarks of many contem-porary Euro-American novels, a reading which stresses the post-colonial politics of the texts has to reassess, quite radically, the political implications of particular postmodernist strategies. I will return to this issue shortly, but for now it is important to look at some aspects of the 'positive' reading of the novels as part of a specifically postcolonial discourse.

Slemon has argued that a key feature of postcolonial writing is 'the figuration of a reiterative quotation, or intertextual citation, in relation to colonialist "textuality" '.[33] This politicised use of intertextual citation marks, for many critics, a crucial distinction between the postcolonial and the postmodernist text. Where the latter merely 'quotes' arbitrarily from a vast archive, the former cites colonial texts in a gesture of defiance comparable, perhaps, to the insistence in *The Satanic Verses* on the need to reclaim the language of racism in order to nullify it. By interweaving the techniques of Indian oral narrative with allusions to colonial and contemporary western texts, Rushdie is able both to indicate the real sense in which postcolonial India and Pakistan cannot simply efface the colonial legacy, and to construct an alternative discourse which does not merely replicate the dogmatic discourses of cultural nationalism. The novels also attempt to absorb their colonial precursors in order to indicate that the representational boot is now on the other foot. Hence, as Brennan has shown, the allusions to Forster and Scott in *Midnight's Children* signal 'an ironic awareness on Rushdie's part of the same English "Novel of Empire" that he is trying to overcome'.[34] The echoes of Kipling in *Midnight's Children* and *Shame* might be seen to serve a comparable function.[35] Alongside this satiric impulse the novels allude, without apparent irony, to a plurality of international texts. The sheer range of allusions suggests both a confident willingness to 'borrow' whatever can be used from world literature, and Rushdie's desire to affiliate his own project with that of other 'international' and politically engaged novelists, like Grass, Kundera and Marquez.[36]

Rushdie has explained the rationale behind his mongrel forms more broadly in terms of his own characterisation of an Indian ethos. In his discussion of 'Commonwealth Literature' as a category, he counters arguments that writers like himself are obliged to write from within a 'pure' Indian tradition by suggesting that 'as far as India is concerned ... it is completely fallacious to suppose that there is such a thing as a pure, unalloyed tradition from which to draw' (*Imaginary Homelands*: 67). In an important sense, then, the novels' eclectic narrative modes are informed by Rushdie's view of what is most admirable in Indian culture. Over against the dogmatic ideologies of the communalists, which he sees as threatening to tear India apart, Rushdie sets hybridity. Thus, in *The Satanic Verses*, Zeeny Vakil's book, written in opposition to the 'confining myth of authenticity', argues for 'an ethic of historically validated eclecticism' drawing its inspiration from an Indian 'national culture based on the principle of borrowing what-ever clothes seemed to fit, Aryan, Mughal, British, take-the-best-and-leave-the-rest'.[37] For Rushdie, at least, the hybrid forms of his novels do not partake of either a glib postmodern project of arbitrary citation of the world's texts, or an unconscious rhetoric of anxiety, but rather grow out of an empowering conception of Indian culture, which attempts, at the same time, to avoid reifying a monolithic sense of the 'Indian'. That said, the fact that such eclecticism succeeds in a political sense only at the level of form, while at the thematic level the novels continue to document real factional strife in India and Pakistan, is one of the more disturbing ironies which the texts generate.

It is not possible to do justice here to all the complex critical readings which have illuminated the ways in which the novels can be seen to engage with postcolonial politics. However, even an overview can suggest the very precise grasp of the politics of *style* which is required to uncover the nuances of Rushdie's treatment of the discourses of colonialism and nationalism. Clearly, Rushdie sets great store by the possibility that a dialogised and plural novelistic discourse can genuinely disturb dominant ideologies. Yet, to distinguish, as Brennan and Slemon are able to do, between the effects of postmodernist and postcolonial textual practices requires an understanding of theoretically sophisticated paradigms which have very little currency outside the academy. As Steven Connor has argued '[p]ostmodernist literature obediently falls into step with the ... preoccupations of institutionalized post-structuralist theory',[38] but it is hard to imagine what is a significant general readership for texts such as *Midnight's Children* or the *Name of the Rose* troubling themselves over-much about whether they are in the presence of 'blind' pastiche[39] or 'reiterative citation'. This is not to denigrate the capacities of 'general' readers, nor to install them as mythical final arbiters of a text's meaning, but rather to suggest that the very complexity of the novels militates against the possibility that Rushdie's 'ideal' readers could be anything but a rare breed.[40] Read by an audience so vast that he could not possibly have imagined the variety of their responses, Rushdie's novels appear to posit an extraordinarily informed and erudite 'ideal' reader. Such a reader requires, at the least, familiarity with the histories and cultures of the colonial and postcolonial subcontinent, with

English colonial writings, with the range of modernist and postmodernist theory and practice and with the developing conventions of magic realism. Of course, in important ways Rushdie caters for an uninformed western reader whose familiarity with the history of the subcontinent may be minimal. But this kind of consciousness-raising, which appears so crucial a part of Rushdie's address to a western readership, is surely most effective when it is actually supported and informed by the complex rhetorical strategies of the novels.

Intertextuality: the problem of audience

Writing in English, Rushdie can be fairly confident that the *majority* of his initial audience will be English or American. Consequently, his complaint that his western readers miss the specifically Indian aspects of the novels is hard to reconcile with the very construction of texts which evoke the conventions of western literary traditions at almost every turn. How, readers might legitimately ask, is it possible, in *Midnight's Children*, to distinguish between Rushdie's written 'oral' narration and the narrative strategies of Sterne, Grass, and Marquez? Similarly, the question of where Tristram Shandy's nose ends and Ganesh's trunk begins in the ancestry of Saleem Sinai's own fantastic nose is impossible to untangle.[41] While this seems to be part of Rushdie's design, the resulting tonal ambiguities threaten to engulf the novels' more serious concerns. Sensing this problem, critics often make considerable efforts to imbue the 'double coding' of the novels with a clear political thrust. In her discussion of 'parodic postmodern historiographic metafiction',[42] Hutcheon addresses the question of the relationship between *Midnight's Children* and *Tristram Shandy* in these terms:

> In Rushdie's text ... the intertextual presence of *Tristram Shandy* does more than simply work to undercut Saleem's megalomaniac attempts at ordering and systematizing by reminding us of the inevitability of contingency; it also points to the Empire, the imperialist British past, that is literally a part of India's self-representation as much as of Saleem's. The structure of the parody enables that past to be admitted as inscribed, but also subverted at the same time.[43]

What is interesting about this reading is that it offers a very clear example of the kind of interpretation which is needed in order to circumvent the possibility that Rushdie's intertextual strategies might not differ in kind and effect from those typically found in western postmodernist fiction. To be sure, Hutcheon is concerned to rehabilitate all forms of postmodernist practice, but it is no coincidence that this particular 'parody' is politicised only within the context of Rushdie's broader critique of an imperial past. It is, once again, Rushdie's thematic preoccupations with the postcolonial subcontinent which inform the critical need to re-read his deployment of devices, which are more often associated with apolitical postmodernist self-reflexivity.

If we presuppose, for the time being, a reader of *Midnight's Children* who is also familiar with *Tristram Shandy*, are we also to suppose that such a reader will immediately associate the novel with 'the Empire'? Given that Sterne's novel did not achieve anything like canonical status until the 1950s, and was considered immoral and frivolous during most of the nineteenth century, it can hardly be bracketed with Macaulay's conception of British literature as one 'before the light of which impious and cruel superstitions are fast taking flight on the banks of the Ganges'.[44] *If* we accept with Hutcheon that Rushdie is parodying Sterne in order to subvert the imperial past, then we can only conclude that he has made a huge error in his choice of text to represent that past. That this is not Rushdie's aim is borne out by his play with *Tristram* in the novel, and by his own listing of Sterne as one of the novelists who offered him a 'passport' into writing (*Imaginary Homelands*: 276). Hutcheon's reading also begs questions as to why *Midnight's Children* should foreground its relationship with a text which is most often seen to prefigure modernism and postmodernism, while alluding to the 'Novel of Empire' in such a coded way as to virtually bury the political significance of the references. But, a reading which starts with the given of Rushdie's postcolonial concerns and consequently finds them in all of his narrative strategies can only be blind to the more troubling consequences of the novelist's intertextual play. Even at a seemingly trivial level, Rushdie's very erudition threatens to undermine his more serious political concerns. Since the reader is regularly encouraged to indulge in the kind of learned allusion-spotting, more readily associated with the texts of Joyce, Beckett or Borges, there is a real danger that the self-conscious literariness of the novels can relegate the historical events, which they seek to represent, to little more than a side show. While the intertextual play which characterises the discursive texture of the novels can, with some effort, be read as parodic and political in intent, it can equally be seen as a retreat into game in the face of the stubbornly intractable and unpleasant reality of colonial and postcolonial history.

The reader who does pick up on the numerous allusions to *Tristram Shandy* in *Midnight's Children* must remain in some doubt as to their significance. In the first of Saleem's meta-fictional references to the moment of writing 'in a pool of Anglepoised light' Rushdie has his narrator articulate the central Shandean dilemma: 'most of what matters in our lives takes place in our absence: but I seem to have found from somewhere the trick of filling in the gaps in my knowledge' (*Midnight's Children*: 19). Thus, Rushdie sets up, even for the reader un-familiar with Sterne, the issue of reliable/unreliable narration which will consistently problematise Saleem's urgent efforts to re-member his own and his country's history. The reader familiar with *Tristram* but not with the strategies of audience entrapment deployed by Indian oral storytellers, can hardly be expected to 'place' the novel within broader Indian traditions. Likewise, Saleem's foregrounded use of a kind of prolepsis – 'years later, when ... he came to sacrifice himself at the shrine of the black stone god' (*Midnight's Children*: 11) – *may* be recognised as having its origins in oral narrative, but is just as likely to be seen as equivalent to the use of this stylistic trope in Sterne or Marquez. Worse still, perhaps, such narrative self-consciousness, by evoking a metafictional tradition which begins with Sterne but continues most prominently in postmodernist fiction, may sug-gest simply a 'universal' modern scepticism.

Although it might be argued that such quibbles are irrelevant to many readers, they do suggest some of the difficulties conse-quent upon Rushdie's eclecticism. This is not to point the finger at Rushdie and accuse him of failing to write from within the pale of 'native' Indian traditions, but rather to suggest why message and medium so often get crossed. To be sure, 'in' jokes for different readers are not solely directed at those steeped in Euro-American traditions. Thus, the significance of the Muslim Saleem's gaff, when Rushdie has him confound Vyasa, the author of the *Mahabharata*, with Valmiki, the author of the *Ramayana*, might escape many non-Indian readers.[45] And yet, at the same time Rushdie is employing one of Sterne's most characteristic devices for undermining Tristram's authority. Clearly, the joke can work for Rushdie's 'ideal' reader but other readers might only register a piece of 'exotic' and arcane information. While Slemon's description of these intertextual strategies as a way in which an 'excessive typology infuses the text and thus puts the question of cultural coding itself into play'[46] accords well with what I suggested above were Rushdie's intentions, an awareness that the codes are *mixed* depends upon relatively specialised knowledge. It remains all too easy for western readers to read the texts within the familiar code of contemporary Euro-American culture, in which a depoliticised cultural pluralism has become commonplace.

The problem is perhaps best demonstrated in the instance of what Brennan has called Rushdie's 'written orality'.[47] For many, the ties between Rushdie's narrative discourse and Indian oral storytelling are particularly important because in playing this tradition off against that of postmodernist metafictions, the novelist is able to reinscribe a specifically Indian 'cultural coding'.[48] Indeed, Slemon argues that this reinscription takes place in *Midnight's Children* through:

> the Vedantic thematization of its 'creator' as listener or reader: that is, as Padma (or Laksmi), the lotus goddess, who embodies the creative power of maya and who even at the text's moment of seemingly total cultural dissolution may be 'writing' the text of a post-colonial future not through the indeterminacies of interpretive slippage and 'freedom' but from solid grounding in pre-colonized cultural and religious agency.[49]

However, as Brennan has shown, rather than representing some kind of idealised embodiment of a 'pre-colonized cultural and religious agency', Padma is at best an ambivalent figure within the novel.[50] As Saleem's audience within the text she enables Rushdie to represent the narrative as an oral tale, but it surely goes without saying that *written* orality can only nostalgically mimic the communal experience of the real thing. Indeed, inscribing an illiterate Hindu auditor within the novel might be seen as an anxious gesture towards the mass Indian audience to whom Rushdie, unlike the storyteller of Baroda, can never speak.[51]

Perhaps Padma does 'create' the story she listens to, but it is a strange kind of creator whose every suggestion is ignored. Physically formidable as she is, like most of Rushdie's women she is not a shaper of events but an adjunct to the male.[52] Whatever the 'postcolonial future' might be that she prefigures, it seems unlikely that it can have much to do with her role as wife and carer to the impotent Saleem. In his desire to demonstrate the point where postmodernist textual play ends and postcolonial reinscription begins, Slemon not only has to idealise Padma's role in a manner never licensed by the text, but also to ignore Saleem's conclusion, which is more in keeping with the novel's 'vision': 'the nearly-thirty-one-year-old myth of freedom is no longer what it was. New myths are needed; but that's none of my business' (*Midnight's Children*: 457). If Saleem's pessimism is to be tempered for the reader by Padma's promise of a postcolonial future, it is surely highly significant that such a future can only be imagined *outside* the text and consequently outside the modern 'India' which the novel seeks to represent.

That the device of the reader in the text can be read simply as a generic marker of postmodernist fiction is borne out not only by the fact that Grass's Oskar narrates *his* life story to his jailor, but in more graphic fashion by Calvino's *If on a winter's night a traveller*, published in the same year as Rushdie's novel. In this respect Rushdie may mix his traditions so thoroughly that the western reader will take the line of least resistance and rest secure in the recognition of family resemblances. This does not mean, of course, that Rushdie's novels partake of a monolithic 'cultural logic of late capitalism'. But it does suggest that efforts to clearly discriminate between Rushdie's novels and contemporary post-modernist fiction, in terms of a postcolonial poetics which is able to reassert the possibility of effective critique and political agency for the oppressed, is hard to sustain. At the end of his discussion of *Shame*, Brennan attempts to show how Rushdie's novels represent a 'different type of ... postmodern writing'.[53] To this end he offers a list of distinctions in which, for example, post-modernist pastiche finds its counterpart in the digressions of oral storytellers, and postmodernist nostalgia finds its antithesis in tradition and 'popular roots'.[54] Quite how these poles can be so easily separated within the *textual* universe is not clear. Although popular Indian traditions are integrated into Rushdie's novels, their entanglements with Euro-American traditions mean that a western readership is likely to read them as exotic embellishments to familiarly sceptical and self-referential nar-ratives. Furthermore, while he is right to exculpate Rushdie from the 'postmodernist' sins which he enumerates, it is far from clear that most readers familiar with, say, Eco, Kundera, Marquez and Pynchon would be inclined to read the texts with either model in mind.

It has frequently been noted that the radical textual experiments of modernist writing regularly cohabit paradoxically with conservative and reactionary world-views. But the lesson that radical textuality and radical action outside the text are not synonymous is often forgotten in discussions of the politics of *post*modernism. Ahmad has commented damningly that 'Rushdie's kind of imagination' must be very attractive to readers 'brought up on the peculiar "universalism" of *The Waste Land*',[55] but one need not agree with his general critique of Rushdie to see the implications of the parallel. It suggests at once that the mixing of cultural codes is ambivalent in effect, and that the defamiliarisation often associated with hybridity may not function upon an audience long familiar with texts which transgress often mythical literary norms. The point is not that Rushdie is in any way comparable to Eliot or that his novels are informed by a conservative ideology, but that his textual pyrotechnics can only be tied to a political agenda within the terms of a relatively abstruse, and largely academic, set of reading strategies. Outside of such strategies, the novels can very easily be consumed and enjoyed alongside Sterne, Calvino and Barth without the political message hitting home. One has only to read the early reviews of the novels to see the ease with which Rushdie is 'placed' so as to universalise, and so emasculate, his postcolonial politics. Furthermore, a key problem with a sceptical and relativising narrative discourse is that although it can act as a foil to the dogmatism of opponents, its effects are so consistently ambiguous that all 'truths' appear to be undermined. While this matters little in terms of a hermetically-sealed aesthetic realm, its implications for Rushdie's efforts to give 'full expression' to 'the experience of formerly colonized, still-disadvantaged peoples' are more profound.

Rushdie as postcolonial historian?

[R]eal sewer systems with imaginary crocodiles in them.[56]

Towards the end of the Danish interview mentioned above, Rushdie issues the following caveat to his audience:

> it will be very easy when reading *Shame*, as it was for many people when reading *Midnight's Children* to forget that it's about a real place. Many people, especially in the West, who read *Midnight's Children*

talked about it as a fantasy novel. By and large, nobody in India talks about it as a fantasy novel; they talk about it as a novel of history and politics.[57]

Once again the problem of readerships is to the fore, but the misreadings in this instance are more fundamental and potentially more damaging. Indeed, the polar opposites of wrong and right readings – fantasy versus history and politics – describe the point where Rushdie's most characteristic formal techniques meet his central thematic concerns. If the political dimensions of Rushdie's intertextual strategies are too easily missed, it becomes doubly important that the more explicit presentation of key aspects of the post-Independence history of India and Pakistan is not obscured. However, in adopting the conventions of what Fredric Jameson has called 'fantastic historiography',[58] Rushdie is from the outset on precarious ground. To be sure, 'magic realism' as a mode has clear ties with what has been perceived as a specifically postcolonial discourse,[59] and Rushdie's problematisation of 'History', relates, in many instances, to an oppositional re-writing of falsifications of the historical record by the colonial and postcolonial rulers of India and Pakistan. Nevertheless, Rushdie's blending of 'fantasy and naturalism' (*Imaginary Homelands*: 19) brings with it many unwelcome ghosts. Thus, for Suleri, because English colonial discourse 'perpetually figured [India] as an arena of romance',[60] Rushdie's brand of 'magic realism' can be seen as being unwittingly complicit in a continuing orientalist exoticisation of the 'East'. Beyond the possibility that the allure of 'romance' will fuel a reading of the novels as 'fantasy', the view of the grand narrative of 'History' which informs Rushdie's presentation of 'events' and 'facts', particularly in *Midnight's Children* and *Shame*, resembles a radical Nietzschean scepticism to the degree that the history described may appear to have no ontological status at all. Once again, Rushdie's strategy asks the reader to make some fine distinctions so that the defamiliarisation of both 'history' and the postcolonial 'cultures' of India and Pakistan is not mistaken for a similar play with exotic imaginative geographies in writers such as Borges or Calvino.

Rushdie's 'debt' to Marquez's *el realismo magical* has been well documented, and is, perhaps, most clearly manifest in shared narrative techniques which seek to reflect cultures in which 'the impossibly old struggles with the appallingly new' and where 'truth has become controlled to the point at which it has ceased to be possible to find out what it is' (*Imaginary Homelands*: 301). Nevertheless, Rushdie's treatment of 'history' is quite different from the Colombian novelist's. Marquez's novels do engage with and re-present historical events – the 1928 strike against the United Fruit Company which figures in *One Hundred Years of Solitude*, for example[61] – and they are also directly concerned with Latin America's colonised past, but the foregrounded presence of the kind of historical events represented in the first two novels of Rushdie's trilogy does not feature in Marquez's fiction. Consequently, it is more useful to contextualise Rushdie's treatment of history in terms of the novels of, for example, Grass or Kundera and a host of other western novelists from Woolf through Fowles to Ackroyd, who have disputed the boundaries between the fictional and the historical. Without wishing to suggest that the interrogation of historical discourse undertaken by these writers is monolithic, it is worth stressing that the novels partake of a wide-ranging debate – which has preoccupied western historians as much as novelists in this century – about how the narrative of History has traditionally validated itself.

That Rushdie places himself within this revisionist mode of interrogating history is made clear in the novels themselves and in a number of articles and reviews. The discussion of the scepticism which underpins Saleem Sinai's unreliable narration is fairly typical in this respect: 'History is always ambiguous. Facts are hard to establish, and capable of being given many meanings. Reality is built on our prejudices, misconceptions and ignorance as well as our perceptiveness and knowledge' (*Imaginary Homelands*: 25). Hand in hand with this acceptance of the constructed, partial and subjective nature of historical narratives goes a didactic impulse born of a desire to tell his readers 'nothing less than *what is the case*, what is truth and what untruth'. Thus, the alternative history presented in *Midnight's Children* seeks to counter not only the lies of colonial narratives, but also the kind of nationalist propaganda which attempts to suppress knowledge of what really happened during the Indo-Pakistani war of 1965 or Indira Gandhi's Emergency of 1975. Similarly *Shame*'s sceptical form sets itself in opposition to 'an ... infinite number of falsenesses, unrealities and lies'[62] and *The Satanic Verses* offers a mordant critique of British racism under 'Mrs Torture'. That Rushdie's is a mitigated scepticism is evident even from these examples, but the tension in the novels between an almost absolute scepticism on the one hand and a commitment to unequivocal political truths on the other is far less easily resolved than my outline may suggest.

The investment of Rushdie's novels in exuberant invention and stylistic play often appears to be in inverse proportion to the bleakness of the world documented.[63] Thus, the sometimes self-indulgent near-allegory of *Shame* in many ways takes the 'fantastic' devices found in *Midnight's Children* one stage further, so that the text's purchase on the real can easily be missed by the reader unfamiliar with the recent history of Pakistan. While Saleem's narrative of modern India is hardly an unqualified celebration, *Shame* appears to accept, in the same gesture in which it attempts to resist, the view expressed by the narrator that 'History is natural selection' and that only 'the mutations of the strong survive' (*Shame*: 124). Such pessimism is by and large absent from *The Satanic Verses*, a novel in which, significantly, Rushdie is considerably more selective in his deployment of the fantastic. Indeed, even in the Ayesha sections where 'magic realism' figures most prominently, the reader is rarely allowed to forget an image's metaphorical relation to 'reality'. In spite of the fabulation of the early 'history' of Islam in two of the nine sections of the novel, the diminished use of the fantastic is such that 'comic realism' might be considered its most characteristic mode. There is a neatness to this account which requires some qualification, but it does suggest the sense in which Rushdie's play 'with historical shapes' (*Imaginary Homelands*: 25) can be understood in terms of what Jameson describes as 'the making up of unreal history' as 'a substitute for the making of the real kind'.[64]

For Jameson, 'fantastic historiography' is one symptom of a broader and debilitating postmodern loss of a sense of history. What troubles him most is that in the representation of 'real sewer systems with imaginary crocodiles in them – the wildest Pynchonesque fantasies are somehow felt to be thought experiments of all the epistemological power ... of Einstein's fables, and ... to convey the feel of the past better than any of the "facts" themselves'.[65] Jameson sums up here, albeit in pejorative terms, the often stated rationale behind the profusion of historiographic metafictions produced in the West since the 1960s.[66] For all that Rushdie, in his assertive and affirmative modes, clearly does not accept that agency has 'step[ped] out of the historical record',[67] his investment in *Shame*, and to a lesser extent in *Midnight's*

Children, in the rhetoric of 'the wildest Pynchonesque fantasies' actually does appear to deny the peoples of India and Pakistan the possibility of escaping from a labyrinth cunningly constructed by an imperial past and further developed by their post-Independence leaders. The multiple and fabricated narratives of history do tend to evoke a kind of 'conspiracy' from the clutches of which no one can finally be free. Thus, it is surely no coincidence that in *The Satanic Verses*, the most 'optimistic' of the three novels, the escape is figured in terms of an idealised conception of 'migrant' identity, what Ahmad calls a 'myth of excess of belongings'.[68] Part of the problem is clearly peculiar to Rushdie's attempts to come to terms with his own hybrid identity and thus cannot be put down to an all-encompassing condition of postcoloniality. Nevertheless, Rushdie's efforts to re-present the history of the subcontinent do, perhaps, reveal the limitations of particular kinds of postmodernist practice when they attempt to describe postcolonial cultures for whom a legitimation crisis is anything but empowering.

When Hutcheon attempts to read 'historiographic metafiction' in terms of a political agenda she is forced to repeat a set of claims about the political complicity and critique which is simultaneously characteristic of such fictions. Similarly, for all the range of texts which she comments upon, her reading of the politics of the fictional play with history can only circle around the notion of the power *implicit* in the problematising of dominant discourses. 'Problematisation' becomes an end in itself, and consequently Hutcheon is unable to suggest how such sceptical probing might be transformed into political action. What she ignores is that this problem-raising in relation to the metanarrative of history has been so often repeated in the West over the last thirty years that it has become banal. Furthermore, for all the 'denaturalizing [of] the natural'[69] since the 1960s the established structures of power have remained largely undisturbed. This is not to suggest that genuinely political representation is an impossibility, but rather to argue that much postmodernist practice works against it. Rushdie's seemingly endless foregrounding in the first two parts of the trilogy of the fact that 'what's real and what's true aren't necessarily the same' (*Midnight's Children*: 79), loses much of its power in its very excess. It appears gestural not only because of the hope which it denies, but because it seems only able to replay the same tune – 'if history is composed of fictions, then fiction can be composed of history'.[70]

Aware of the positive and negative potential of 'fantastic historiography', Jameson argues that although such fiction can be seen to suggest 'historical impotence', its imaginative exuberance can also become 'the figure of a larger possibility of praxis'.[71] It is, perhaps, too much to ask of a novel that it move beyond what Bhabha calls the 'enunciative boundaries' into what might only be a glib resolution to the enormously complex problems of postcolonial India and Pakistan. In Jameson's terms, at least, Rushdie is able to 'figure a larger possibility of praxis'; yet because he does so principally at the level of form the novels bespeak a desire for compensation as much as the hope of progress. In this light, the waning of Saleem's magic powers – as the dreams of August 15 1947 appear increasingly utopian – might be read as a metaphor for the political limitations of Rushdie's attempts to harness postmodernist poetics to a postcolonial political agenda. Having spent much of his energy, as convenor of the Midnight's Children Conference, trying to persuade his fellow children of independence that a genuinely alternative principle is needed to imagine the new India, Saleem's optimism is finally blunted in the face of the petty squabbles of the moment and the brute realities of a colonial past which permeates the postcolonial present. As the midnight's children fragment Saleem is left to conclude: 'If there is a third principle, its name is childhood. But it dies; or rather, it is murdered' (*Midnight's Children*: 256). In the trilogy, the principle is not 'murdered', but Rushdie, significantly, can only locate it in an exuberant postmodernist *textual* universe – a universe whose very logic threatens to deny the postcolonial subject a purchase on the past or the present from which genuine liberation might spring.

Notes

1 Salman Rushdie, 'Outside the Whale' in *Imaginary Homelands* (Harmondsworth: Granta Books, 1992), p. 100. Future references to the essays collected in this volume will be cited in the chapter by page numbers taken from this edition.

2 Rushdie, 'Bonfire of the Certainties', interview for Bandung File in L. Appiganesi and S. Maitland (eds.), *The Rushdie File* (London: Fourth Estate Ltd, 1989), p. 30.

3 Kumkum Sangari, 'The Politics of the Possible', *Cultural Critique*, 7 (1987), 176.

4 Rushdie, *Shame* (London: Pan Books Ltd, 1984), p. 28. Page numbers given in the chapter hereafter are taken from this edition.

5 Rushdie's narrator describes himself as a 'translated man' in *Shame*, p. 29.

6 For the problem of Eurocentric readings of Rushdie see Aleid Fokkema, 'English Ideas
   of Indianness: The Reception of Salman Rushdie' in Geoffrey Davis and Hena Maes-
   Jelinek (eds.), *Crisis and Creativity in the New Literatures in English* (Amsterdam:
   Rodopi, 1990), pp. 355–68. Rushdie described the three novels as a 'trilogy' in an interview with Madhu Jain, 'My theme is fanaticism' in L. Appignanesi and S. Maitland
   (eds.), *The Rushdie File*, p. 38.

7 For a collection of essays which focus on the postmodern/postcolonial nexus see Ian
   Adam and Helen Tiffin (eds.), *Past the Last Post: Theorizing Post-Colonialism and Post-
   Modernism* (Hemel Hempstead: Harvester Wheatsheaf, 1993). Books on postmodernism
   are now too numerous to list exhaustively, but the following texts are particularly
   useful for locating Rushdie's novels within contemporary constructions of postmodernist
   fiction. Steven Connor, *Postmodernist Culture: An Introduction to Theories of the
   Contemporary* (Oxford: Basil Blackwell, 1989); Linda Hutcheon, *The Politics of Post-
   modernism* (London and New York: Routledge, 1989) and *A Poetics of Postmodernism:
   History, Theory, Fiction* (London and New York: Routledge, 1990); Fredric Jameson,
   Postmodernism, Or, The Cultural Logic of Late Capitalism (London and New York:
   Verso, 1992); Jean-François Lyotard, *The Postmodern Condition: A Report on Knowledge*,
   translated from the French by Geoff Bennington and Brian Massumi (Manchester:
   Manchester University Press, 1984); Brian McHale, *Postmodernist Fiction* (London and
   New York: Methuen, 1987).

8 Hutcheon, ' "Circling the Downspout of Empire" ', in *Past the Last Post*, p. 168.

9 For a brief discussion of 'the so-called crisis of representation' see Jameson's foreword
   to *The Postmodern Condition*, pp. viii–ix.

10 Sangari, 'The Politics of the Possible', p. 157.

11 See Aijaz Ahmad, *In Theory: Classes, Nations, Literatures* (London and New York:
    Verso, 1992), p. 124.

12 Stephen Slemon, 'Modernism's Last Post', in *Past the Last Post*, p. 3.

13 See, for example, Sangari, 'The Politics of the Possible' and Helen Tiffin's introduction
    to *Past the Last Post*. For a wide range of views on how Rushdie's postmodernist location
    impinges upon *The Satanic Verses* 'Affair' see the essays collected in 'Beyond the
    Rushdie Affair', *Third Text* (Special Issue), 1990.

14 Tim Brennan, *Salman Rushdie and the Third World: Myths of the Nation* (Basingstoke:
    Macmillan Press, 1989), p. 139.

15 Simon During, 'Postmodernism or Post-Colonialism Today', *Textual Practice*, 1, 1
    (1987), 32–47.

16 *Ibid.*, p. 33.

17 Slemon, 'Modernism's Last Post', p. 5.

18 For a concerted theoretical effort to think outside such binaries see Homi Bhabha,
    The Location of Culture (London and New York: Routledge, 1994).

19 Edward Said, *Culture and Imperialism* (London: Vintage, 1994), p. 405.

20 *Ibid.*

21 For Rushdie's review of *Foucault's Pendulum* see 'Umberto Eco' in *Imaginary Home-
    lands*, pp. 269–72.

22 Bhabha, *The Location of Culture*, p. 5.

23 Hutcheon, *A Poetics of Postmodernism*.

24 Rushdie, '*Midnight's Children* and *Shame*', *Kunapipi*, 7, 1 (1985), 1–19.

25 Rushdie, *Midnight's Children* (London: Pan Books Ltd, 1982), p. 55. Page numbers
    given in the chapter hereafter are taken from this edition.

26 Aleid Fokkema, 'English Ideas of Indianness: The Reception of Salman Rushdie', p. 364.

27 Brennan, *Salman Rushdie and the Third World*, pp. viii, ix.

28 Ahmad, *In Theory*, p. 124.

29 Sara Suleri, *The Rhetoric of English India* (Chicago: Chicago University Press, 1992), p. 1.

30 Michel Foucault, *Language, Counter-Memory, Practice*, ed. and trans. Donald F. Bouchard and Sherry Simon (Ithaca: Cornell University Press, 1977), p. 199.

31 Suleri, *The Rhetoric of English India*, p. 174.

32 *Ibid.*, p. 178.

33 Slemon, 'Modernism's Last Post', p. 3.

34 Brennan, *Salman Rushdie and the Third World*, p. 82.

35 For echoes of Kipling in *Midnight's Children* and *Shame* see Colin Smith, 'The Unbearable Lightness of Salman Rushdie' in *Critical Approaches to the New Literatures in English*, I (Essen: Blaue Eule, 1989), p. 114. For a very different reading of the relationship betwen Rushdie and Kipling see Richard Cronin, 'The Indian English Novel: *Kim* and *Midnight's Children*', *Commonwealth Essays and Studies*, 8, 1 (1985), pp. 57–73.

36 For a discussion of a key intertextual relationship and its possible significance see Patricia Merivale, 'Saleem Fathered by Oskar: Intertextual Strategies in *Midnight's Children* and *The Tin Drum*', *Ariel*, 21, 3 (1990), pp. 5–21.

37 Rushdie, *The Satanic Verses* (London and New York: Viking Penguin Inc., 1988), p. 52.

38 Connor, *Postmodernist Culture*, p. 128.

39 Jameson, *Postmodernism*, pp. 16–19.

40 For a discussion of the relationship which *Midnight's Children* sets up with its readers, the kind of reader it presumes and why the text might allude to *Tristram Shandy* see Keith Wilson, '*Midnight's Children* and Reader Responsibility', *Critical Quarterly*, 26, 3 (1984), pp. 23–37.

41 For the view that an oral narrator and a modernist narrator 'send each other up' see Sangari, 'The Politics of the Possible', p. 179.

42 Hutcheon, *The Politics of Postmodernism*, p. 103.

43 *Ibid.*, p. 106.

44 Thomas Babington Macaulay, 'The Literature of Britain' in *Speeches on Politics and Literature* (1909), cited in Chris Baldick, *The Social Mission of English Criticism 1848–1932* (Oxford: Oxford University Press, 1983), p. 71.

45 Rushdie, *Midnight's Children*, p. 149. Rushdie discusses the significance of this passage in ' "Errata": Or, Unreliable Narration in *Midnight's Children*', in *Imaginary Homelands*, pp. 22–5.

46 Slemon, 'Modernism's Last Post', p. 8.

47 Brennan, *Salman Rushdie and the Third World*, p. 139.

48 Slemon, 'Modernism's Last Post', p. 8.

49 *Ibid.*

50 Brennan, *Salman Rushdie and the Third World*, pp. 102–07.

51 For an account of the storyteller of Baroda see Rushdie, '*Midnight's Children* and *Shame*', p. 7. For an alternative reading of the role of oral narrative in *Midnight's Children* see Aruna Srivastava, ' "The Empire Writes Back": Language and History in *Shame* and *Midnight's Children*' in *Past the Last Post*, pp. 74–5.

52 On Rushdie's representation of women see Ahmad, *In Theory*, pp. 123–58, and Gayatri Spivak, 'Reading *The Satanic Verses*' in *Outside in the Teaching Machine* (New York and London: Routledge, 1993), p. 223.

53 Brennan, *Salman Rushdie and the Third World*, p. 141.

54 *Ibid.*, p. 142.

55 Ahmad, *In Theory*, p. 128.

56 Jameson, *Postmodernism*, p. 368.

57 Rushdie, *'Midnight's Children* and *Shame'*, p. 15.

58 Jameson, *Postmodernism*, p. 367.

59 See Slemon, 'Magic Realism as Post-Colonial Discourse', *Canadian Literature*, 116 (1988), 9–23.

60 Suleri, *The Rhetoric of English India*, p. 181.

61 See Stephen Minta, *Gabriel Garcia Marquez: Writer of Colombia* (London: Jonathan Cape, 1987), pp. 162–79.

62 The phrase comes from Saleem's characterisation of Pakistan in *Midnight's Children*, p. 326.

63 For Rushdie's comments on this feature of *Midnight's Children* see 'Imaginary Homelands' in *Imaginary Homelands*, p. 16.

64 Jameson, *Postmodernism*, p. 369.

65 *Ibid.*, p. 368.

66 See Hutcheon, *The Politics of Postmodernism*, especially chapters 2 and 3.

67 Jameson, *Postmodernism*, p. 369.

68 Ahmad, *In Theory*, p. 127. Ahmad's essay is particularly insightful in its analysis of Rushdie's conception of migrant identity and in pinpointing the political problems raised by Rushdie's privileging of certain postmodernist positions.

69 This is the title of the first section of Hutcheon's second chapter, *The Politics of Postmodernism*, pp. 31–42.

70 Nancy E. Batty, 'The Art of Suspense: Rushdie's 1001 (Mid-)Nights', *Ariel*, 18, 3 (1987), 64.

71 Jameson, *Postmodernism*, p. 369.

Bibliography

Adam, Ian and Helen Tiffin (eds.), *Past the Last Post: Theorizing Post-Colonialism and Post-Modernism* (Hemel Hempstead: Harvester Wheatsheaf, 1993).

Ahmad, Aijaz, *In Theory: Classes, Nations, Literatures* (London and New York: Verso, 1992).

Appiganesi, L. and S. Maitland (eds.), *The Rushdie File* (London: Fourth Estate Ltd, 1989).

Baldick, Chris, *The Social Mission of English Criticism 1848–1932* (Oxford: Oxford University Press, 1983).

Batty, Nancy E., 'The Art of Suspense: Rushdie's 1001 (Mid-)Nights', *Ariel*, 18, 3 (1987), pp. 49–65.

'Beyond the Rushdie Affair', *Third Text* (Special Issue), 1990.

Bhabha, Homi, *The Location of Culture* (London and New York: Routledge, 1994).

Brennan, Tim, *Salman Rushdie and the Third World: Myths of the Nation* (Basingstoke: Macmillan Press, 1989).

Connor, Steven, *Postmodernist Culture: An Introduction to Theories of the Contemporary* (Oxford: Basil Blackwell, 1989).

Cronin, Richard, 'The Indian English Novel: *Kim* and *Midnight's Children'*, *Commonwealth Essays and Studies*, 8, 1 (1985), pp. 57–73.

During, Simon, 'Postmodernism or Post-Colonialism Today', *Textual Practice*, 1, 1 (1987), pp. 32–47.

Fokkema Aleid, 'English Ideas of Indianness: The Reception of Salman Rushdie', in Geoffrey Davis and Hena Maes-Jelinek (eds.), *Crisis and Creativity in the New Literatures in English* (Amsterdam: Rodopi, 1990), pp. 355–68.

Foucault, Michel, *Language, Counter-Memory, Practice*, ed. and trans. Donald F. Bouchard and Sherry Simon (Ithaca: Cornell University Press, 1977).

Hutcheon, Linda, *The Politics of Postmodernism* (London and New York: Routledge, 1989).

—— *A Poetics of Postmodernism: History, Theory, Fiction* (London and New York: Routledge, 1990).

—— ' "Circling the Downspout of Empire" ', in *Past the Last Post*, pp. 167–83.

Jameson, Fredric, *Postmodernism, Or, The Cultural Logic of Late Capitalism* (London and New York: Verso, 1992).

Lyotard, Jean-François, *The Postmodern Condition: A Report on Knowledge*, translated from the French by Geoff Bennington and Brian Massumi (Manchester: Manchester University Press, 1984).

Macaulay, Thomas Babington, 'The Literature of Britain' in *Speeches on Politics and Literature* (1909), cited in Baldick, *The Social Mission of English Criticism 1848–1932*, p. 71.

McHale, Brian, *Postmodernist Fiction* (London and New York: Methuen, 1987).

Merivale, Patricia, 'Saleem Fathered by Oskar: Intertextual Strategies in "Midnight's Children" and "The Tin Drum" ', *Ariel*, 21, 3 (1990), pp. 5–21.

Minta, Stephen, *Gabriel Garcia Marquez: Writer of Colombia* (London: Jonathan Cape, 1987).

Rushdie, Salman, *Midnight's Children* (London: Pan Books Ltd, 1982).

—— *Shame* (London: Pan Books Ltd, 1984).

—— *The Satanic Verses* (London and New York: Viking Penguin Inc., 1988).

—— *Imaginary Homelands: Essays and Criticism 1981–1991* (Harmondsworth: Granta Books, 1992).

—— 'Outside the Whale', *ibid.*, pp. 87–101.

—— 'Umberto Eco', *ibid.*, pp. 269–72.

—— 'Imaginary Homelands', *ibid.*, pp. 9–21.

—— 'In Good Faith', *ibid.*, pp. 393–414.

—— ' "Commonwealth Literature" Does Not Exist', *ibid.*, pp. 61–70.

—— 'Gunter Grass – Essays', *ibid.*, pp. 273–81.

—— 'Gabriel Garcia Marquez', *ibid.*, pp. 299–307.

—— ' "Errata": Or, Unreliable Narration in *Midnight's Children'*, *ibid.*, pp. 22–5.

—— 'Bonfire of the Certainties', interview for Bandung File in *The Rushdie File*, pp. 27–31.

—— 'My theme is fanaticism', interview with Madhu Jain, in *ibid.*, pp. 38–41.

—— '*Midnight's Children* and *Shame'*, *Kunapipi*, 7, 1 (1985), pp. 1–19.

Said, Edward, *Culture and Imperialism* (London: Vintage, 1994).

Sangari, Kumkum, 'The Politics of the Possible', *Cultural Critique*, 7 (1987), pp. 157–86.

Slemon, Stephen, 'Modernism's Last Post', in *Past the Last Post*, pp. 1–11.

—— 'Magic Realism as Post-Colonial Discourse', *Canadian Literature*, 116 (1988), pp. 9–23.

Smith, Colin, 'The Unbearable Lightness of Salman Rushdie' in *Critical Approaches to the New Literatures in English*, I (Essen: Blaue Eule, 1989), pp. 104–05.

Spivak, Gayatri, 'Reading *The Satanic Verses*' in *Outside in the Teaching Machine* (New York and London: Routledge, 1993), pp. 217–41.

Srivastava, Aruna, ' "The Empire Writes Back": Language and History in *Shame* and *Midnight's Children*' in *Past the Last Post*, pp. 74–5.

Suleri, Sara, *The Rhetoric of English India* (Chicago: Chicago University Press, 1992).

Wilson, Keith, '*Midnight's Children* and Reader Responsibility', *Critical Quarterly*, 26, 3 (1984), pp. 23–37.

Index